BETTER THAN WELFARE?

WORK AND LIVELIHOODS FOR INDIGENOUS AUSTRALIANS AFTER CDEP

BETTER THAN WELFARE?

WORK AND LIVELIHOODS FOR INDIGENOUS AUSTRALIANS AFTER CDEP

Edited by
KIRRILY JORDAN

Australian
National
University

PRESS

Centre for Aboriginal Economic Policy Research
College of Arts and Social Sciences
The Australian National University, Canberra

RESEARCH MONOGRAPH NO. 36
2016

ANU PRESS

Published by ANU Press
The Australian National University
Acton ACT 2601, Australia
Email: anupress@anu.edu.au
This title is also available online at press.anu.edu.au

National Library of Australia Cataloguing-in-Publication entry

Title:	Better than welfare : work and livelihoods for Indigenous Australians after CDEP / editor Kirrily Jordan.
ISBN:	9781760460273 (paperback) 9781760460280 (ebook)
Series:	Research monograph (Australian National University. Centre for Aboriginal Economic Policy Research) ; no. 36.
Subjects:	Community Development Employment Projects (Australia) Indigenous peoples--Employment--Australia. Indigenous peoples--Australia--Social conditions. Indigenous peoples--Government policy--Australia. Indigenous peoples--Australia--Government relations.
Other Creators/Contributors:	Jordan, Kirrily, editor.
Dewey Number:	331.639915

Cover design and layout by ANU Press.

Cover photograph: The Pmara Jutunta CDEP Office was formerly a community office. It was reconditioned by CDEP participants in 2007 to become the administrative and organisational centre for the community's CDEP activities. While CDEP was delivered in a variety of ways across different locations, there were many offices like this across the country. Photo: Will Sanders, 2008.

Contents

List of figures

List of tables

Contributors

Jon Altman is an economist/anthropologist who first engaged with the Community Development Employment Projects scheme in 1977 when it was established. Since then he has maintained an abiding interest in this highly innovative scheme in his research and policy advocacy for appropriate and sustainable forms of Indigenous economic development from the local to the national. Jon was an academic researcher at The Australian National University (ANU) from 1982 to 2014 and foundation director of the Centre for Aboriginal Economic Policy Research 1990 to 2010. He is currently a research professor at the Alfred Deakin Institute for Citizenship and Globalisation at Deakin University; ANU Emeritus Professor at RegNet: School of Regulation and Global Governance; and Adjunct Professorial Fellow at the Research Institute for Environment and Livelihoods at Charles Darwin University.

Bree Blakeman is an Australia-based anthropologist and writer. She completed her PhD, 'An ethnography of emotion and morality: Toward a local Indigenous theory of value and exchange on the remote Yolŋu Homelands in Arnhem Land, Australia', in 2015. Her research interests include economic anthropology, anthropology of emotions, value theory, psychological anthropology, kinship, sociality of being, feminism and anthropological linguistics. Other interests include property relations and land tenure, poetry and anarchist political philosophy. Bree is currently a sessional tutor and lecturer of anthropology in the School of Archaeology and Anthropology at The Australian National University. She blogs about anthropology and related topics at: fieldnotesandfootnotes.wordpress.com.

Boyd Hunter is IZA Research Fellow and Senior Fellow at the Centre for Aboriginal Economic Policy Research, Research School of Social Sciences at The Australian National University (ANU), where he has worked for 20 years. He is currently editor-in-chief of the *Australian Journal of Social Issues,* the official publication of the Australian Social Policy Association (and the only social policy journal in Australia). In addition to his work in labour economics, he has considerable expertise in a range of social sciences fields: criminology, econometrics, economic history, geography, poverty analysis, survey design and analysis and Indigenous economic policy. He was recently awarded, along with John Carmody, the 2015 Sir Timothy Coghlan Prize for the best article in *Australian Economic History Review* for the paper 'Estimating the Aboriginal population in early colonial Australia: The role of chickenpox reconsidered'. He convenes the Bachelor of Philosophy (Honours), or PhB program, for the College of Arts and Social Sciences at ANU.

Kirrily Jordan is a political economist with a particular interest in all aspects of Aboriginal and Torres Strait Islander employment and economic development. Her research includes analysis of various public and private sector programs designed to improve Indigenous employment outcomes, as well as the interaction of these programs with the social security system and new forms of welfare conditionality. Kirrily began investigating the Community Development Employment Projects scheme in 2009 and is currently undertaking research on its replacement—the Community Development Program—as well as other federally funded schemes including the Vocational Training and Employment Centres and Employment Parity Initiative. She is working alongside Lisa Fowkes and Will Sanders as a lead investigator on the Australian Research Council project 'Implementing the remote jobs and communities program: How is policy working in Indigenous communities?'

Will Sanders began studying the Community Development Employment Projects scheme as part of a PhD, undertaken from 1982 to 1985, on the inclusion of Aboriginal Australians in the social security system. Will was an associate of the Centre for Aboriginal Economic Policy Research (CAEPR) from its establishment in 1990 and became a staff member in 1993. During his years of employment at CAEPR, Will has continued to write about the social security system (CAEPR Monograph No. 15, Discussion Paper 212) and about Community Development Employment Projects (Discussion Papers 5, 54, 141, 149, 224, CAEPR Monograph No. 20). Will is now a Chief Investigator on an Australian Research Council Linkage Project with Jobs Australia studying the new remote-area employment and income support program from 2013.

Acknowledgements

Kirrily Jordan would like to thank the many people who have assisted her on the APY Lands and NSW far south coast over the last six years, with special thanks to Wanatjura Lewis and Leah Brady for their support. She is also grateful to Heather Crawford from CAEPR for her help and guidance in preparing statistical data for Chapter 4.

Too many people to name individually have assisted Jon Altman with his research in the Maningrida region over many years since 1979. He would like to specifically thank Dan Gillespie and Ian Munro for checking the factual basis of recollections and providing commentary on Chapter 7; and Kirrily Jordan, Melinda Hinkson, Bree Blakeman and especially Thomas Michel for expert critical commentary on an earlier version.

Will Sanders would like to thank the councillors and staff of both Anmatjere Community Government Council and Central Desert Shire/ Regional Council for their time and openness to his research interests during many visits since 2004.

Boyd Hunter would like to thank Heather Crawford for providing statistical assistance on the geographic concordances and Tablebuilder census data for the south coast study in Chapter 3.

All of the authors are grateful for the advice of the two anonymous reviewers of this manuscript and the expert assistance of the CAEPR Editorial Board (particularly Frances Morphy) and copyeditor Beth Battrick in helping to see the publication through. The assistance of ANU Press has been invaluable and The Australian National University has generously provided financial support for publication through its Publication Subsidy Fund.

Preface

This monograph had its genesis at an annual Centre for Aboriginal Economic Policy Research (CAEPR) strategic research planning retreat at Kialoa on the NSW south coast, way back in November 2009. As I recall, I had just informed my colleagues at CAEPR that I was stepping aside as director and feeling somewhat liberated to focus more on research. At the same time, Kirrily Jordan was increasingly focusing her research interests on Indigenous employment and the major changes to policy in that field that were underway.

Kirrily and I saw a strategic opportunity to collaborate with a number of others at CAEPR to apply for an Australian Research Discovery (ARC) grant that would do two things. First, document a policy history of the Community Development Employment Projects (CDEP) scheme from a number of perspectives, including from communities and regions that had participated in the scheme. Second, ask the question how good is CDEP compared with welfare and what might be at risk if CDEP is abolished, bearing in mind that at that time CDEP was still operating.

At that particular moment, CDEP was in the midst of a series of reforms that had begun in earnest in 2005. And there was a lot more reform to come, even though late in 2009 CDEP still existed as a government program not yet subsumed into the broader frame of the Remote Jobs and Communities Program (RJCP). Nevertheless, CDEP was already a shadow of its former self as an Indigenous-specific program, only available now in remote Australia and cleaved into two forms, those 'grandfathered' as employed wage earners and new entrants deemed unemployed and paid Newstart Allowance from Centrelink.

The project proposal was open to other interested academic colleagues at CAEPR and two others indicated interest: political scientist Will Sanders and labour economist Boyd Hunter. To add to these disciplinary perspectives, I would deploy the lenses of anthropology and economics. Kirrily Jordan, a political economist, undertook the lead research role in the project. A pleasing aspect of this proposed collaboration was that we all had past experience researching and writing about CDEP; and I had actually collaborated in writing about CDEP with all the proposed collaborators, as long ago as 1991 with Will Sanders.

We developed an ARC Discovery Project proposal 'From welfare to work, or work to welfare?: Will reform of the Community Development Employment Program help close the employment gap?' with three of us as chief investigators and Kirrily Jordan named as the dedicated research fellow. We were fortuitously successful in securing funding for a three-year project starting in 2011.

It transpired that due to major illness the project had to be delayed on two occasions for a total of two years. We would like to thank the ARC for its willingness to allow us to extend our completion date owing to these unanticipated circumstances.

From a research perspective, these delays brought successive governments' incremental changes to the scheme to an end point where finally the remnant of CDEP—lingering on as an appendage to the new RJCP—was killed off by the Abbott Government as one of only a few recommendations implemented from the Forrest Review of Indigenous Training and Employment completed in August 2014. Even before the term CDEP was doomed to extinguishment from the policy lexicon from 1 July 2015, it was replaced in December 2014 by the term CDP (Community Development Programme) that was to subsume RJCP inclusive of CDEP. Experimental change was coming thick and fast in the difficult Indigenous employment policy field—indeed, the speed in reform of programs appears to be occurring in a directly inverse relationship to the delivery of successful employment outcomes.

The seven chapters in this monograph are divided between three that provide policy and statistical analysis, mainly from secondary sources, and four chapters that are community-based case studies.

These latter are based on primary data collected on a transect that runs from the south coast of NSW, through the Pitjantjatjara lands and central Australia to the Top End of the Northern Territory. This transect is far from random, it is based on research work that we as academic researchers have undertaken in and with members of selected communities over many years.

As will become apparent to readers, both here and in the past we have observed and documented what we believe were the many positive elements of CDEP, while also recognising that the scheme had shortcomings that needed to be addressed. What has surprised us as this project has progressed is how little ongoing and critical debate there has been, especially among policy academics, about the exceptional resilience of CDEP as an Indigenous-specific program and its demise. And so our intention is to provide some coverage for the historical record of what the abolition of CDEP looked like in some places; and to provide critical engagement with the governmental process that oversaw this abolition irrespective of the wishes of participating communities and community-based organisations. In an academic sense, we are looking to give voice to some of those who have borne the brunt of these reforms, but who lack effective channels to communicate their perspectives, which are far from uniform.

Some of the authors in this volume have made particular acknowledgements to research collaborators. Here, I would just like to acknowledge the wonderful assistance provided by Dr Bree Blakeman as the monograph neared completion; and to the research-supportive environment of CAEPR where the research was undertaken and where many of the ideas in this monograph were discussed and debated, formally at public seminars, less formally in the cafes and corridors with colleagues.

Over a decade ago when I was director of CAEPR, a decision was made to publish our research monograph series with what was then the fledgling ANU E Press; in 2004, the co-edited volume *The Indigenous Welfare Economy and the CDEP Scheme* was one of the first we released in this new arrangement. From the perspective of this monograph, that volume serves as a nice bookend to what we present here in *Better than Welfare? Work and Livelihoods for Indigenous Australians after CDEP*. I would like to take this opportunity to sincerely thank the team at the new ANU Press for all their support, and for making their publications available open access and online as well as in print-on-demand hard copy. This progressive approach certainly makes research outputs readily available to a diversity of stakeholders, including Indigenous Australians sometimes residing very remotely.

Jon Altman
May 2016
Melbourne

1

From welfare to work, or work to welfare?

Kirrily Jordan and Jon Altman

One of the most pressing and enduring concerns in Australian Indigenous policymaking is the employment of Aboriginal and Torres Strait Islander people. It has often been at the top of successive governments' Indigenous affairs agendas and, since 2008, 'closing the gap' in employment rates between Indigenous and other Australians has been a specific policy goal. Yet the employment disparity is growing, not declining. What has been going wrong?

Answering such complex social policy questions is never easy. But any attempt requires much delving into history. It is only since the 1970s that Indigenous engagement in the market economy has been statistically visible, as Aboriginal and Torres Strait Islander Australians have been comprehensively included in the national census. This has roughly coincided with an explicit policy aim of convergence between Indigenous and non-Indigenous people on a range of socioeconomic indicators, including employment. There have been ongoing debates about whether such statistical equality is an appropriate goal, given the diverse livelihood aspirations of Indigenous people, and indeed whether 'improved livelihood' is a more fitting focus for policymaking than 'increased employment'. Nonetheless, the notion of convergence on standard measures like employment has been the cornerstone of a modernisation paradigm that has dominated orthodox economic development thinking from the 1960s.

In broad policy terms, since the 1971 census we have seen two 'waves' in the approach to reduce disparities in the labour market situation of Indigenous and settler Australians. Both have been associated with the core focus of this book: the Community Development Employment Projects (CDEP) scheme. Love it or loathe it, CDEP was an enormously influential Australian Government program that has affected the lives of several generations of Aboriginal and Torres Strait Islander people. In our view, the first major 'wave' in the policy approach to reducing Indigenous employment disparity centred on CDEP's expansion from 1977 to the late 1990s and early 2000s. Taking what was in many ways the opposite approach, the second wave promoted CDEP's subsequent contraction and ultimate demise in mid-2015 as central to improving Indigenous employment outcomes. (Though, as we write this chapter, there is talk about reviving some elements of the scheme even within the political parties that were the architects of its closure—we return to this briefly later.)

CDEP had been introduced in 1977 on a pilot basis to do several things. These included the creation of part-time work for Aboriginal and Torres Strait Islander people in very remote situations where there were few other jobs and unemployment payments were becoming increasingly common. Its basic architecture involved the provision of block grants from the Australian Government to local Indigenous community councils or incorporated organisations. These funds were used to engage participants on a range of projects, from local community development and service provision to social and economic enterprise. The grants were based on the notional amount that participants would have been paid in unemployment benefits, factored up to cover administrative costs and the provision of capital items and equipment to support projects.

CDEP was originally seen as a tool for job creation. Indeed, one of the attractions of the scheme from the outset, for participants as well as communities and governments, was that participants in the scheme were classified as employed. That is, because they were in receipt of a wage they were formally defined as working. This was in accord with the International Labor Organization convention used by the Australian Bureau of Statistics. Because grants were made to community organisations—and local people had substantial control over what work projects were funded—CDEP also facilitated a degree of community self-management. It provided some support for community, social and economic development opportunities in line with local priorities. Initially introduced in just a handful of remote communities, CDEP was assessed quite early on in its history (by what was then the Commonwealth Department of Aboriginal Affairs) as meeting its diverse objectives. Over the next decade, the scheme was incrementally expanded to a growing number of Aboriginal and Torres Strait Islander communities in remote regions.

The first wave of policies seeking to reduce Indigenous employment disparity reached its peak following the comprehensive Hawke Government review of Aboriginal employment and training programs conducted during 1985 and chaired by the late Mick Miller (Miller 1985; see also this volume, Appendix 1). The review's recommendations were operationalised in the Aboriginal Employment Development Policy (AEDP)—officially launched in 1987—which aimed to achieve statistical equality in employment outcomes and income status between Indigenous and other Australians by the year 2000 (Australian Government 1987). CDEP was understood as supporting job creation both directly and indirectly (directly because participants were classified as employed, and indirectly because CDEP funding could also generate more jobs through enterprise development). So it is unsurprising that one of the AEDP's key instruments for achieving its aspirational, but unrealistic, employment target was a substantial expansion of the scheme.

CDEP did indeed begin to expand more rapidly, including into urban and regional areas from 1989. This shift coincided both with a five-year funding commitment to the AEDP (from the Hawke and then Keating governments) and with the establishment of the Aboriginal and Torres Strait Islander Commission (ATSIC). The national representation that ATSIC provided through its elected national board and network of regional councils brought Indigenous-specific program delivery (including CDEP) beyond remote regions and increasingly to more settled areas. CDEP reached a peak of participant numbers in 2003, by which time it employed more than 35,000 Indigenous people Australia-wide. Alongside the Community Housing and Infrastructure Program, CDEP was ATSIC's flagship program.

While the disparity in Indigenous and non-Indigenous employment rates was not eliminated by the expansion of CDEP, the creation of 35,000 jobs funded as part of a principally Indigenous-specific program was of enormous significance, especially given the overall size of the Indigenous population of working age. At its height, CDEP accounted for about one-third of employed Aboriginal and Torres Strait Islander people.

However, in spite of the formal classification of CDEP participants as employed, the scheme was from its establishment rather difficult to define. It fell somewhere between employment and enterprise creation on one hand and community development and empowerment on the other. Moreover, the scheme's notional link to unemployment benefits meant that it sat somewhat uncomfortably between classification as part-time employment and welfare (see Sanders this volume, Chapter 2).

In public debates, the question of whether CDEP participants were productively employed or a special category of welfare recipients became a matter of contested interpretation. To mix metaphors, the tide that had pushed CDEP along was beginning to ebb and then turn. By the late 1990s, during the early years of the Howard Government, CDEP began to be reinterpreted not as a job creation scheme but as primarily a labour market program for welfare recipients from which an exit into other employment was expected. Dominant policy discourse painted CDEP as a failure on these terms (see, for example, Brough 2006; Cape York Institute for Policy and Leadership 2007; Langton 2002; Shergold 2001; also Altman this volume, Chapter 7). There were growing claims from some politicians, bureaucrats and Indigenous spokespeople that it was not enough to engage Indigenous people long-term in what were usually low-paid positions with little opportunity for career and income advancement. The view that CDEP was just a form of welfare came to dominate debate.

This position was associated with what we see as the second 'wave' in the Australian Government's approach to reducing labour market disparities between Indigenous and other Australians. From this perspective, it was argued that an individual's engagement with CDEP should only ever have been temporary, for just as long as was necessary to learn the appropriate skills for moving into a standard job. Although the scheme had, for many years, assisted some people into such mainstream employment, its outcomes on this measure were interpreted as too limited. Broader outcomes of CDEP, including various aspects of community, institutional and economic development, were largely ignored. If policy was to truly 'close the gap' in employment, an argument was mounted that it would be necessary to wind back CDEP and get people into so-called 'real' jobs (Pearson 2000; Rowse 2001).

CDEP has now been closed down, but this imagined transition into 'real' jobs is proving much more elusive than anticipated. Although data are limited, it is clear that a large number of former CDEP participants have not moved into employment (Hunter this volume, Chapter 3). In the name of employment improvement, they have been forced to shift from CDEP work to welfare. The wider goals of CDEP, beyond transitioning participants to employment, have tended to fall off the policy radar.

The architects of CDEP's closure might hope that poor employment outcomes reflect a temporary 'adjustment' period, and that once the dust settles there will be a substantial increase in the number of former CDEP participants moving from welfare back into paid work. However, this argument seems tenuous if one recognises the very significant structural constraints to employment in remote areas, as well as the complex and profound challenges limiting take-up of the few available jobs (see Jordan 2011, and this volume, Chapter 5). None of these issues will be readily resolved by the programs that have replaced CDEP. Even the Minister for Indigenous Affairs, Nigel Scullion, has acknowledged that under current arrangements a likely scenario for many Indigenous people in remote areas is long-term reliance on welfare (in Martin 2015). The same may be true of some regional areas where employment opportunities remain limited (e.g. the south coast of NSW, see Chapter 4).

The history of the rise and fall of CDEP is told here to set the scene for subsequent chapters, but also because it presents an invaluable lens for viewing a number of ongoing and much broader challenges in Indigenous affairs. It highlights the enduring tension about whether 'development' for Indigenous peoples should be about a singular trajectory to 'modernity'—and an associated parity of outcomes on standard socioeconomic measures—or about the opportunity to pursue diverse livelihoods, even if this comes at the expense of such statistical equality.

Perhaps paradoxically, the AEDP sought both statistical equality and the expansion of CDEP in line with a recognition of diverse livelihood aspirations and the dominant rhetoric of self-determination so clearly articulated by the Miller Committee (1985). While the goal of statistical equality was always unrealistic (Altman & Sanders 1991), CDEP did provide options for Indigenous organisations and local community councils to pursue 'development' in line with local aspirations and priorities. This potential for communities to reconfigure CDEP according to local values was an indication of its capacity to allow a degree of self-management, and perhaps even some elements of self-determination (see Rowse 2001, 2002). Certainly, CDEP did initially provide much more local autonomy and authority than programs delivered by some of the contracted 'providers' in recent years, including more recent iterations of CDEP from around 2006 and the schemes that have now replaced it.

By the same token, the shift away from CDEP can be linked to the politically bipartisan Indigenous policy that emerged with the demise of ATSIC from 2004—this saw the explicit rejection of self-determination as a guiding principle or policy goal. The focus of successive governments from around this time was greater emphasis on 'mainstreaming' rather than Indigenous-specific programs, as well as an emphasis on the individual more than the community (Altman 2014; Sanders 2014; Strakosch 2015). In this context, CDEP was seen as an unwelcome hangover from a failed ideology of the past. This substantial change in direction was principally justified by the idea that mainstreaming would be better at reducing statistical gaps on socioeconomic indicators. But on most measures these gaps have stubbornly refused to close (Department of the Prime Minister and Cabinet 2016a), and there are now vocal calls from a range of Indigenous commentators that outcomes will improve substantially only when policymakers take engagement with Aboriginal and Torres Strait Islander people more seriously (see, for example, Dodson in Robinson 2016; Huggins in Gordon & Hunter 2016).

The debate about CDEP also highlights questions about the roles of different kinds of paid work in supporting diverse livelihoods. By initially allowing Indigenous organisations to define and negotiate with officials what constituted CDEP employment, a very broad range of activities could be funded. CDEP was structured around flexibility, with participants usually required to work 15 hours per week at award rates, but given the option of working extra hours for additional pay if financial resources to meet such 'top up' were locally generated.

Some high-profile critiques of the scheme queried whether any of this constituted 'real work', or whether CDEP was in effect a welfare payment for doing 'make work' activities that provided little enduring benefit to individuals or their communities (see Hudson 2008; Hughes 2007; Hughes & Hughes 2010). A number of studies, though, over many years have shown that CDEP participants on average fared better on a range of socioeconomic indicators than welfare recipients who were not in receipt of CDEP wages (Altman & Daly 1992; Altman & Hunter 1996; Altman, Gray & Levitus 2005; Hunter 2009). That is, while CDEP was highly unlikely to deliver statistical equality—which is arguably impossible owing to structural, cultural and locational factors—it does not follow that it condemned participants to a second-rate livelihood.

In addition, critiques of CDEP as 'pretend work' ignored the possibility that the flexibility it offered could be valued by participants and encourage productive activity by matching work routines to local needs (see Jordan this volume, Chapter 4). The most recent government review of Indigenous employment and training programs has promoted a much less flexible approach: it suggested hastening the end of CDEP and focusing on 26-week employment outcomes with mainstream employers (Forrest 2014). Post-CDEP, the rules for welfare recipients in remote areas have also changed, with many people now required to engage in Work for the Dole five hours a day, five days per week, with little room for flexibility to account for local circumstances. This narrower focus not only understates the major structural constraints on employment opportunity in remote areas, it also overlooks the current reality that many Indigenous people, especially in remote locations, are unlikely to adopt the regular work routines envisaged (Jordan this volume, Chapter 5).

In the end, key policymakers did judge CDEP to be 'pretend work' incapable of meeting the challenge to close statistical employment gaps and prepare Aboriginal and Torres Strait Islander people for lives in the Australian 'mainstream'. To this extent, the critique of CDEP was caught up in broader debates about the dysfunction of remote Indigenous communities (Cape York Institute for Policy and Leadership

2007; Hughes 2007; Pearson 2009; Sutton 2009). While CDEP often had local support, participants and their organisations lacked sufficient influence in policy decisions, even when engaging with debates with parliamentarians (see Altman this volume, Chapter 7). In our view, the decision to abolish the scheme gave inadequate attention to concerns raised by many CDEP providers with experience on the ground. It also gave much too little consideration to what would replace the scheme beyond 'imagined' real jobs.

Fundamentally, the contestation over CDEP is also a debate about welfare. The notional link of CDEP to social security entitlements was a strength in that it constituted a cost offset and the scheme was thus relatively cost-neutral for the Australian Government. But it was also a weakness in the sense that it allowed critics to conflate CDEP wages with welfare payments (see especially Cape York Institute for Policy and Leadership 2007; Langton 2002). CDEP became seen as synonymous with 'welfare' in the minds of most policymakers, so much so that it seems to have surprised Mal Brough, then Minister for Indigenous Affairs, when he discovered in July 2007 that CDEP payments could not be subjected to income management under the Northern Territory National Emergency Response because they were wages. This set the scene for the sudden abolition of CDEP in parts of the Northern Territory from September 2007, before its temporary reinstatement under the Rudd Government in 2008.

Representing CDEP as welfare also served to focus policy on the individual (see Rowse 2002). Here Brough's 'Blueprint for Action in Indigenous Affairs' (2006) is instructive. It reflects the emerging neoliberal trope that increasingly influenced Indigenous policymaking after ATSIC (Altman 2014; Strakosch 2015). This neoliberal turn proposed that state agencies should bypass community organisations that played a crucial brokerage role and instead deliver training and employment services to individual 'clients' directly—although in reality this role was performed by a mix of organisation types including community organisations, not-for-profit NGOs and for-profit business entities external to communities. It also reflected a broader welfare policy shift encapsulated in the 2000 McClure reform proposals that borrowed from the United Kingdom to establish a very different relationship between the state and 'unemployed' clients/ individuals. A narrative was vigorously promoted that if people were not engaging with the mainstream economy it was principally because of individual behavioural deficiencies; the discipline of tough love 'mutual obligation' requirements would compel the unemployed to engage in 'real' work or in structured training for future real work, always just around the corner.

A series of Australian Governments incrementally dismantled CDEP using such logic to propose that they would move participants from what was deemed an overly permissive form of welfare, first into the mainstream welfare system with tougher mutual obligation requirements, and then into mainstream jobs. The Remote Jobs and Communities Program (RJCP) that replaced CDEP in remote areas from 1 July 2013 required participants to continue turning up for 'work-like' activities in return for welfare payments, but with less prospect for extra payments in return for additional work (as previously available under CDEP top up). RJCP was branded a failure by the Abbott Government soon after coming into office in September 2013, and from July 2015 it was replaced by CDP (the Community Development Programme). This seemed to rhetorically allude to CDEP and to acknowledge that something important had been lost. More recently, Indigenous Affairs Minister Nigel Scullion has tabled a new proposal in parliament that he says will resurrect the 'positive elements' of CDEP (Scullion 2015).

But CDP—and its proposed replacement—are vastly different to CDEP and remain firmly within the welfare system. They are fundamentally Work for the Dole schemes, with participants required to work more hours for a social security payment than they did for the equivalent CDEP wage. At the same time, the application of income penalties (called breaching) for non-attendance at appointments and activities has increased (Fowkes & Sanders 2016; Haughton 2016). Evidence suggests that social security recipients in remote areas (most of whom are Indigenous) are now experiencing serious income penalties at much higher rates than non-Indigenous people, principally because their Work for the Dole obligations are more onerous (Fowkes & Sanders 2016). This is supposedly to promote 'work-like behaviour' that will assist people in securing a job. The message is contradictory, though: as noted earlier, Nigel Scullion has acknowledged that for many Indigenous people in remote areas there may be 'no alternative' to long-term Work for the Dole (in Martin 2015).

This highlights a fundamental tension in the prevailing approach: if one acknowledges the major structural barriers to employment opportunity, it is difficult to accept that withholding welfare payments unless recipients display the 'correct' behaviours (judged according to mainstream Australian norms) will be sufficient to lead to a job. Policymakers and public commentators have sometimes proposed that the solution is migration of remote-living Indigenous people to take up employment opportunities elsewhere—and cautioned that those remaining in remote communities should no longer expect public funding for services there (see Brough 2006; Abbott in Medhora 2015). In practice, though, this makes little sense to many people who have only recently had their land returned via land rights and native title laws, and there has been strong resistance to this approach (Davey 2015). In addition, assumptions that migration to areas with stronger labour markets improves outcomes for Aboriginal and Torres Strait Islander people from remote locations may be misguided. There is evidence to suggest that inward migration of Indigenous people from remote regions may instead be associated with declining employment rates for Aboriginal and Torres Strait Islander people in the destination locations overall (Biddle 2009).

Indigenous employment policy has evolved into an intractable 'wicked problem' in part because there is ongoing disputation about how outcomes can be improved, and little genuine consultation with Indigenous people. The language of improvement gives proponents of reform the high moral ground: if one criticises the dominant approach one must be content to endorse the status quo and be tolerant of continued deeply entrenched Indigenous poverty and social exclusion. Policymaking becomes less about evidence than 'belief' and 'conviction', and discourse becomes naturalised around the abstract notion of 'closing the gap'.

It is in this heavily value-laden space of 'politics' (not just 'policy') that this volume is written. It presents the main findings from an Australian Research Council Discovery Project 'From welfare to work, or work to welfare?: Will reform of the Community Development Employment Program help close the employment gap?' The project was undertaken between 2011 and 2015 by four researchers at the Centre for Aboriginal Economic Policy Research (CAEPR) at The Australian National University. CAEPR researchers have a track record of consistently examining CDEP over time, with over

60 publications about aspects of the scheme since 1990 (some of which are documented in Appendix 2) and a major conference in 2000 that brought together academic, community and public policy perspectives on the scheme (see Morphy & Sanders 2001). We are surprised at the absence of research from other quarters on the demise of CDEP, given its significance and longevity over so many decades. Perhaps this reflects a rational choice if research findings are consistently ignored by those making policy; it does appear that much research that does not accord with the dominant government focus on convergence has been ignored in recent years.

In the absence of substantial alternative analysis, a key research question is what have been the consequences of CDEP's closure for Indigenous people, communities and organisations? This monograph does not provide the definitive answer—the experiences of CDEP, and its closure, have been so complex and varied that no single volume could do that. Instead, it focuses in depth on the consequences of change in four case study communities, as well as giving an overview of the national policy context and the broader implications for employment and other socioeconomic indicators as far as available statistical data will allow. Each chapter in effect tells the story of CDEP's decline from a different perspective, variously focusing on the consequences of change in the case study regions for community and economic development, individual work habits and employment outcomes, and institutional capacity within the Indigenous sector. Taken together, these various perspectives suggest that CDEP could be 'better than welfare' in many ways.

The contributors to this book are not disinterested parties. We have actively researched and published on aspects of CDEP, some of us for almost four decades. Four of the five contributors have also made public submissions or statements of concern when CDEP closures and the removal of CDEP wages have been announced (see, for example, Altman, Hunter & Sanders 2006; Altman 2008; Altman & Sanders 2008; Altman & Jordan 2009). We have encouraged governments of all political persuasions to modify CDEP and appreciate its value rather than abolish it. This is not to suggest that we all share the same views, but to demonstrate that we all have an enduring interest in the legacy of CDEP and the livelihood and development options for Indigenous Australians that CDEP could, and often did, support.

For all of us, this interest is more than scholarly. For some of us it is also personal and emotional, as people we have known for a long time have been directly affected by the changes and have asked for assistance in assessing their concerns. To some extent, this also reflects the choice of the four case studies. In Chapter 3, Hunter shows that, for the most part, these cases fit neatly into what he calls 'CDEP intense' areas and so would number among the locations where the effects of change are most keenly felt. But the case studies are also in areas where the researchers either had longstanding relationships or other connections that provided initial conduits for community-based investigation. In each, research occurred over several visits and years, demonstrating both an ongoing commitment to these regions (even if on a 'fly-in, fly-out' basis) and a determination to understand, as clearly as possible, a complex and rapidly changing policy arena that has been in a continual state of flux during the period of investigation.

Focus of contributions

Each chapter in this volume takes a different disciplinary perspective to present insights into the origins and effects of the dramatic changes to the program over the last decade. Some chapters suggest lessons from the demise of CDEP for future policymaking to improve Indigenous livelihoods. There is an adage drawn from the work of Aldous Huxley (1959: 222): 'That men do not learn very much from the lessons of history is the most important of all the lessons that history has to teach.' It is our optimistic hope that this adage will not apply on this occasion and that the policy history we grapple with here will prove of some value for Aboriginal and Torres Strait Islander people and policymakers in the future.

Chapter 2 provides an overview of the changes to CDEP from the perspective of bureaucratic politics. Its principal focus is the way in which a once positively regarded program that was designed to avoid reliance on social security payments (and associated passivity and disengagement) became reframed as a Work for the Dole scheme within the welfare system. As Sanders asks, 'How does a popular and successful solution to a significant public policy problem come, over time, to be seen as part of that problem?' Later chapters suggest this recasting of CDEP was partly political and ideological, occurring alongside a more general policy shift towards 'mainstreaming' and contestation over the merits of 'self-determination'. Here, though, Sanders makes the compelling case that a key factor was the more mundane influence of administrative decisions, often made in response to reviews of the scheme or to align it with the dominant mode of administration in the very different government departments that delivered CDEP throughout its history. Since ATSIC, this has involved a revolving door of departments lacking adequate expertise or corporate memory about CDEP and only limited accountability where outcomes of program changes have been poor.

Looking back further, some changes—like the 1998 decision to allow CDEP participants a $20 per fortnight 'participant supplement'— might have seemed routine at the time but, on Sanders' analysis, become key events without which the eventual reframing of CDEP as a form of welfare may never have happened. Other decisions, such as moving CDEP into the Australian Government employment department when ATSIC was closed in 2004, had a profound effect as the program was actively reformulated to align with that department's institutional culture and practices and the ideological leanings of its powerful bureaucratic leadership (see also Altman 2014). A new mode of program delivery based on competitive contractualism, and a new view of participants as unemployed jobseekers, were arguably the inevitable result. It is unclear whether this change was an unintended consequence of the abolition of ATSIC or part of a more deliberate strategy, but it neatly aligned with the ideological position of the government of the day. From 2008, this 'logic' of seeing CDEP participants as unemployed was taken to its ultimate conclusion when FaHCSIA—CDEP's new institutional guardian from late 2007— determined to 'equalise' treatment between CDEP participants and unemployed welfare recipients by phasing out the payment of CDEP as wages. When viewed alongside the broader ideological shift among politicians that reframed CDEP as part of the 'welfare problem', Sanders' analysis contributes to the sense of a 'juggernaut' of change that was relatively impervious to either caution or critique.

Continuing this broad overview of the changes to CDEP, Chapter 3 takes a labour market perspective, gathering available statistical evidence and speculating on some possible outcomes of the scheme's closure. It also introduces a general statistical context for the more localised analysis in the case studies. Hunter reminds us of evidence that CDEP participants in receipt of wages had significantly better socioeconomic outcomes than the unemployed on a range of measures. To that extent, CDEP was evidently 'better than welfare'. Of course, successive governments argued that closing CDEP would facilitate the movement of former participants into non-CDEP jobs, where socioeconomic outcomes could be better still. If, however, many former participants have moved into unemployment or left the labour force, Hunter's analysis shows considerable cause for concern.

Unfortunately, there is no comprehensive longitudinal data available to show whether the bulk of former CDEP participants have moved into other employment or have found themselves without a job. In the absence of such data, Hunter presents us with two stylised scenarios. The first is the 'pessimistic' case in which no former participants have found alternative employment; the second is the 'optimistic' case based on longitudinal data from the 1990s Indigenous Job Seeker Survey that recorded transitions of CDEP participants into other jobs. Unsurprisingly, given that CDEP participation was associated with better socioeconomic outcomes than welfare, the 'pessimistic' scenario would see substantial declines across all the domains measured, including income, health and interactions with the criminal justice system. Perhaps more surprisingly though, even the 'optimistic' scenario would see higher rates of arrest, violence and crime, declining health and an increase in the number of people living in low-income households, since the improved outcomes of those assumed to find mainstream jobs would be offset by the larger number moving into unemployment or exiting the labour force. This raises important questions about the net effects of the CDEP reform process inclusive of social and wider societal costs.

Hunter's chapter also identifies the limitations of many existing data sources for tracking the outcomes of closing CDEP.[1] Nonetheless, available data can provide some statistical context for the case studies

---

1   Some data are difficult to interpret at the national level, for example, where census and administrative data suggest vastly different numbers of CDEP participants. Such problems come into even sharper relief at the local level, particularly where administrative data are also complicated by the changing institutional arrangements for delivering CDEP (with different providers, and different regional boundaries, for individual schemes over time). The problem of accessing useful data appears to have gotten worse, not better. For example, the ABS publication *Aboriginal and Torres Strait Islander Labour Force Characteristics* seems to have disappeared off the statistical landscape since 2011. This was the only annual source of data on Indigenous labour force status that was inclusive of CDEP as an employment category.

presented in this book. While individual cases should never be assumed as representative of the totality of over 200 CDEP organisations, the analysis presented here suggests that the three remote case studies (Chapters 5 to 7) sit well within the range of typical 'CDEP intense' regions—that is, regions where a high proportion of the working age population were participating in the scheme before its closure. In these areas, the effects of closing the scheme are likely to be the most pronounced. As Hunter suggests, this provides some rationale for the choice of organisations and areas selected for closer analysis. Similarly, although the regional case study of southeastern NSW (Chapter 4) is comparatively closer to urban centres and employment opportunities, the high proportion of the Indigenous working age population who were engaged in CDEP suggests that closing the scheme was also likely to be keenly felt there.

This proposition is tested in Chapter 4. The first of four case studies, it focuses on the 'Wallaga Lake CDEP' on the far south coast of NSW—the region from Wallaga Lake in the north to Eden, 100 km south (the subsequent case studies are organised geographically from south to north). The presence of CDEP in regional and urban areas might already seem like ancient policy history, having been phased out by the end of 2009. But these regional and urban schemes existed for nearly 20 of CDEP's 38 years. Being closer to established labour markets, they were also subject to the most strident and protracted criticism that they were 'failing employment programs' for otherwise unemployed jobseekers who should have been transitioned into other jobs (see, for example, DEWR 2006; Hockey in Karvelas 2007; also Smith 1994, 1995, 1996). Such criticism helps explain why these CDEPs were closed much earlier, and much more suddenly, than the schemes in more remote locations. This was despite an Office of Evaluation and Audit review of non-remote CDEPs in 1997 that found a range of positive social impacts arising from these schemes (Office of Evaluation and Audit 1997).

Taking a political economy perspective, Jordan argues that defining CDEP as 'just an employment program' was much too narrow. In contributing to the sudden closure of the Wallaga Lake CDEP scheme, this definition was extremely counter-productive for the welfare and well-being of local residents. She shows that CDEP did support employment and economic development on the NSW south coast—especially by subsidising small commercial and social enterprises—but also notes its broader social and community development functions that improved a range of hard-to-measure outcomes. Jordan makes the case that these social and community development functions were not peripheral to job outcomes but central to addressing some of the significant barriers to mainstream work. While CDEP in the region is now long gone, many of these barriers to mainstream employment remain. As a consequence, many former CDEP participants have joined the ranks of the long-term unemployed or given up looking for work altogether. Jordan argues that the lessons from CDEP's closure remain as pertinent as ever, with mainstream employment services and providers failing to substantially improve outcomes and new strategies needed if governments are serious about improving either employment rates or livelihoods for Koori residents of the region.

The picture looks no better in Jordan's second case study (Chapter 5) focusing on the Aṉangu Pitjantjatjara Yankunytjatjara (APY) Lands in the remote far north of South Australia. Jordan briefly touches on evidence (presented more fully elsewhere, see Jordan 2011) that the move away from CDEP wages to income support payments has been associated with decreased engagement in productive activity on the APY Lands—a similar scenario to the far south coast of NSW and the very opposite of what governments set out to achieve at least discursively. To paraphrase American political scientist Murray Edelman (1977), this appears to be a case of words that succeed and policies that fail. As in the previous chapter, Jordan explores why the dominant approach might have failed, and attempts to distil useful insights for future policy directions.

She suggests, in particular, that contrasting CDEP to supposedly more favourable 'real jobs' exposes a lack of understanding about the nature of employment in the APY Lands. She advocates instead for a more realistic appraisal that recognises the common practice of 'intermittent working'. This might involve 'target working'—previously identified by Peterson (2005: 15) as 'working for short periods to acquire money for specific purposes'. But it might also involve periodic alternation between paid work and other activity for a variety of reasons (such as ill health, caring responsibilities, variable relations with supervisors and colleagues or competing cultural and familial responsibilities and obligations).

According to Jordan, any assumption by those calling for CDEP's closure that intermittent working was only present among CDEP participants—and not among other Aboriginal workers in the APY Lands—was always fictitious, as was any notion that the complex barriers to mainstream employment could be better addressed by shifting participants onto income support payments. Similarly, Jordan suggests, there is little evidence that increasing 'breaching' for lack of participation in activities, or attendance at appointments, will force Anangu on welfare to abandon patterns of intermittent working. Indeed, there is some concern that this will further entrench disengagement and a distrust of government, where people see it as an unwelcome attempt at external control of their day-to-day lives. As in Chapter 4, Jordan's concern is that policymakers take a more realistic view of what might improve livelihoods—as well as mainstream employment outcomes—for Aboriginal residents of this region.

In Chapter 6, Sanders examines the impacts of changes to CDEP in the Anmatjere region of the Northern Territory, just north of Alice Springs. Taking a political science perspective, he critiques what he sees as the dominant mode of policymaking in Indigenous affairs, which is premised on a 'failure and change' style of analysis. That is, if policies and programs do not meet the high expectations placed upon them, they can quickly become labelled as failures and subject to major institutional change. While this approach is understandable, Sanders suggests that there is also 'a downside to this well intentioned dynamic' in that existing good practice and corporate capacity can be lost. This is clearly apparent in Sanders' analysis of the Anmatjere region CDEPs.

The Anmatjere story is partly one of rapid administrative change as the CDEP organisation—Anmatjere Community Government Council (ACGC)—was first asked to expand its coverage into additional communities in 2006, only to be subsumed into the Central Desert Shire Council in 2008. Central Desert Shire delivered CDEP across its nine service centres until the scheme's closure in 2013, but then won the RJCP contract for only five of those locations. All of this can be seen as major institutional change, but Sanders argues that until the closure of CDEP and introduction of RJCP, existing good practice of regular work patterns and localised authority was maintained. With the shift to RJCP, he suggests, two things occurred.

First, those delivering the program at Central Desert Shire were too willing to accept the government's argument that the established system had been a 'failure'. As a consequence, they were not protective enough of aspects of their existing practice that had been working well. Second, RJCP program rules created an administrative upheaval that encouraged a new model of participant engagement centred on monthly appointments. These were prioritised over the old 'CDEP model' of participants turning up for activities four days per week, such that the regular work habits of participants were undermined. As also noted in the preceding chapter, this outcome was the opposite of what 'reforming' governments intended.

In the final case study (Chapter 7), Altman also raises serious concerns about the ways in which 'local success can be jeopardised as part of a broader national agenda of imagined improvement'. Focusing on the Maningrida region of remote central Arnhem Land, Altman takes an institutional approach to examine the changing fortunes of the Bawinanga Aboriginal Corporation, the organisation formerly delivering CDEP in Maningrida and to associated outstations located across a massive hinterland covering 10,000 sq km. One of the abiding paradoxes of this case is that Bawinanga (which had delivered CDEP flexibly and effectively to 600 participants and had championed the program) was from 2013 charged with delivering RJCP services to 950 'job seekers', a task that was recognised as an impossible challenge by all concerned—from the responsible minister for Indigenous affairs to local service providers and participants.

For at least 10 years prior to 2009 when the phasing out of CDEP wages commenced, Bawinanga was a successful regional development corporation without peer in remote Indigenous Australia. It delivered a range of community services, ran productive regional businesses and enhanced the livelihoods of community members underwritten by CDEP. At outstations, and to some extent elsewhere, CDEP operated as a basic income scheme (Altman 2016). This, in turn, allowed the generation of additional income that was earmarked for additional employment or utilised as investment in local initiatives or to increase individual and household income.

Altman documents Bawinanga's activities during this period, noting that despite operating in very difficult circumstances with enduring structural challenges, the organisation became one of the biggest and best performing Indigenous corporations in the country, with annual turnover exceeding $30 million. From this position, Bawinanga's rapid decline into special administration in 2012—from which it emerged deeply indebted in mid-2014—appears particularly dramatic. Altman argues that while several factors contributed to this greatly weakened position, principal among them were two key changes to CDEP: doing away with the annual grants model and incrementally making new participants ineligible for CDEP wages and 'top up'.

These changes, according to Altman, reflected 'metropolitan managerialism' as politicians and bureaucrats in faraway Canberra sought to impose their particular vision of CDEP as a failing employment program, while ignoring expert local knowledge and much published information about how the program was being deployed for substantial—and much broader—community benefit. Altman sees this bureaucratic vision as linked to the wider discourse, dominant for the last decade and half, that has represented 'self-determination' as a failure and imagined that socioeconomic outcomes will improve for Indigenous people if programs and services are 'mainstreamed' and placed on a competitive service provider basis. In this process, Altman argues that an effective operator in the Indigenous sector was undermined, to the detriment not only of Bawinanga's members but also the broader region. A program that had clearly proven much better than welfare was destroyed. The net impact on individuals and families was deep impoverishment.

Conclusion

The research for this volume began in 2011. As we have been preparing chapters for this volume, we have become acutely aware that the inherent dynamism of the policy cycle has seen some developments that warrant comment.

First, the proposed next round of changes to CDP have been examined by a senate committee of inquiry (Haughton 2016), and become the subject of a public consultation process under the Department of the Prime Minister and Cabinet.[2] As this monograph is being completed,

---

2   The submissions to the senate inquiry (Social Security Legislation Amendment (Community Development Program) Bill 2015) and final report from the committee are available online.

it is unclear if required amendments to the Social Security Act will be passed in the immediate future, with a new Senate after the federal double dissolution election of July 2016.

If passed by parliament, the changes would give substantial powers to the Minister of Indigenous Affairs to determine the social security arrangements for remote income support recipients for a period of two years—at least at first in four trial regions. Many of the submissions to the senate inquiry raised concerns that the proposed changes could be detrimental to remote-living Indigenous people, and did not reflect adequate consultation with those likely to be most affected (for transparency we note that two such submissions were made independently by Jordan and Altman, both of which are on the public record).

Nonetheless, the majority report of the senate committee recommended the changes be approved by parliament.[3]

Although the Bill has not yet been passed, in early 2016 the Department of the Prime Minister and Cabinet (2016b) released a consultation paper suggesting that the new arrangements would commence from 1 July. This did not occur; but, having retained government in the July 2016 federal election, the Coalition may continue to pursue the proposed changes. We remain concerned that an effective solution to what has become such a seemingly intractable policy problem will not be developed until a diverse range of Indigenous people are more fully included in the policymaking process.

The second issue that has emerged as we write is the change of Prime Minister with the deposing of Tony Abbott by Malcolm Turnbull, and the subsequent election of the Turnbull Government. While advocating for more nuanced policy debate that moves beyond slogans, a word that initially appeared again and again in the new Prime Minister's lexicon was 'innovation'. With that in mind, we think back to the policy innovation embedded in the establishment of CDEP nearly 40 years ago, the very original idea that notional links to welfare could be utilised to create productive opportunity for employment, community development, commercial and social enterprise and basic

---

3   Two dissenting reports—from the Australian Labor Party and Australian Greens—recommended the legislation be withdrawn.

income support. The idea was clever, it was carefully trialled and, then on the basis of evidence of success, expanded. We challenge those in power in Australia today to contrast the emergence of CDEP with that of RJCP and now CDP. These new approaches lack a coherent policy logic, unless one assumes that income penalties will ensure the supply of labour, and that such a supply will generate demand. The evidence from mainstream Work for the Dole programs suggests the new approach is misguided at best (see, for example, Borland & Tseng 2011), and it is notable that the recently released federal budget for 2016–17 proposes to scale back Work for the Dole programs for unemployed job seekers, except those participating in CDP.

Third, and linked to the change in national leadership, is the emerging realisation that Australia's long economic boom is slowing and may be over. This, too, is inevitable but long periods of sustained economic growth can make nations complacent to the reality that market capitalism is inherently subject to fluctuating business cycles, and increasingly so during the age of neoliberal globalisation. These fluctuations have already impacted on the Australian labour market, with the unemployment rate now trending close to 6 per cent compared to lows of just over 4 per cent before the 2008 global financial crisis. This is a time when government support for the productive use of welfare or welfare equivalent support would be preferable to berating the unemployed for their collusion in the production of their unfortunate circumstances.

A principal element of the Australian Government's response during this period of economic slowing has been to commission the Forrest Review of Indigenous training and employment programs (Forrest 2014). The Forrest Review reinforced recommendations for the end of CDEP and anticipated that new 'Vocational Training and Employment Centres' (VTEC), combined with pledges by corporations to employ more Indigenous staff, would be key to solving high Indigenous unemployment rates (see Jordan 2014). While VTEC services have some merits, we remain adamant that a diversity of approaches is needed to address the diversity of Indigenous circumstances, and that a wages-based program like CDEP as originally constituted could make important and cost-effective contributions as a part of the policy mix.

Fourth, we note the celebration in late September 2015 of the 8th International Basic Income Week. There is a growing global interest in universal basic income as an alternative to punitive welfare approaches that seek to demonise the undeserving poor for being individually responsible for their socioeconomic marginality (Standing 2014). Some elements of CDEP always operated like basic income, especially when delivered in the remotest outstation situations beyond mainstream labour market opportunity. This was reflected in CDEP guidelines that, when operating under community control, did not compel participants to fulfil meaningless work tests where there was no work available. Instead, they allowed for flexibility in determining appropriate obligations of those receiving a CDEP wage. Importantly, the guidelines also allowed the payment of wages and substantial additional top up without a requirement for income testing, meaning that some participants could earn well above the rate of social security payments (see Altman 2016).

This was a level of innovation that was unacceptable to powerful political, bureaucratic and corporate interests, and arguably also to some in the wider Australian community who subscribed to the false view that Indigenous Australians have been content to exist on 'handouts'—a particularly unfortunate version of the 'dole bludger' stereotype that has often found traction in the tabloid media. The basic income element to CDEP could have been better designed and managed, especially to reflect the very different circumstances of different regions. Again, though, there is no evidence that what has replaced this system has generated superior outcomes even according to the mainstream employment priorities of the architects of change.

Yet another judgement day approaches as information will be collected in August 2016 in the national census on employment status. There is little doubt in our minds (but we would be pleased to be proved wrong) that the disparity in employment rates between Indigenous and other Australians is likely to expand rather than contract, a view that is shared with the Productivity Commission (2015). It is hard to envisage what might change this prediction in the near future as the relentless pressure of Indigenous population growth and demographic transitions see more and more Indigenous people of working age, alongside more and more Aboriginal-owned land in remote and regional Australia, and possibly more and more disenchantment with 'work-like' activity and the punitive and bureaucratic welfare system.

At the same time, it is unclear how community development will occur, overseen from outside, allowing little community autonomy. Where are the new mechanisms to create opportunity for community-driven innovation and development? Or to facilitate genuine consultation with Indigenous people about the way forward? We see less autonomy at an individual and community level and less opportunity, especially at outstations and homelands, to pursue lifeways in accord with local undeniably diverse aspirations.

We lament that CDEP has been closed without any clear vision or assessment of what productive activity will replace it beyond a mix of welfare and some government-underwritten jobs. We see this decision as disconnected from the local realities that the case studies in this volume seek to document. In a way, we are looking to record what has actually happened 'out there' as CDEP has been closed, at least in our case study regions. Everything we have seen and documented suggests that CDEP was better than welfare. This is a view that is shared with many of our interlocutors. It is also supported by official statistics. The challenge we pose for the emerging crop of policy reformers and politicians is to ensure that what is being implemented is in fact better than CDEP.

References

Altman JC (2007). Neopaternalism and the destruction of CDEP. *Arena Magazine* 90 (August–September): 33–35.

Altman JC (2008). Submission to Increasing Indigenous Economic Opportunity: a discussion paper on the future of the CDEP and Indigenous Employment Programs. *CAEPR Topical Issue No. 14/2008*, Centre for Aboriginal Economic Policy Research, The Australian National University, Canberra.

Altman JC (2014). Indigenous Policy: Canberra consensus on a neoliberal project of improvement. In Miller C & Orchard L (eds), *Australian Public Policy: Progressive Ideas in the Neoliberal Ascendency*, Policy Press, Bristol.

Altman JC (2016). Basic income for remote Indigenous Australia: prospects for a livelihoods approach in neoliberal times. In Mays J, Marston G & Tomlinson J (eds), *Basic Income in Australia and New Zealand: Perspectives from neoliberal frontiers*, Palgrave, London.

Altman JC & Daly AE (1992). *The CDEP scheme: a census-based analysis of the labour market status of participants in 1986*, CAEPR Discussion Paper No. 36, Centre for Aboriginal Economic Policy Research, The Australian National University, Canberra.

Altman JC, Gray MC & Levitus R (2005). *Policy issues for the Community Development Employment Projects scheme in rural and remote Australia*, CAEPR Discussion Paper No. 271, Centre for Aboriginal Economic Policy Research, The Australian National University, Canberra.

Altman JC & Hunter B (1996). *The comparative economic status of CDEP and non–CDEP community residents in the Northern Territory in 1991*, CAEPR Discussion Paper No. 107, Centre for Aboriginal Economic Policy Research, The Australian National University, Canberra.

Altman JC, Hunter B & Sanders W (2006). *Submission on Indigenous Potential meets Economic Opportunity Discussion Paper*, 13 December.

Altman JC & Jordan K (2009). *Submission to Senate Community Affairs Committee inquiry into the Family Assistance and Other Legislation Amendment (2008 Budget and Other Measures) Bill 2008*, 20 April.

Altman JC & Sanders W (1991). Government initiatives for Aboriginal employment: equity, equality and policy realism. In Altman JC (ed.), *Aboriginal Employment Equity by the Year 2000*, Research Monograph No. 2, Centre for Aboriginal Economic Policy Research, The Australian National University, Canberra.

Altman JC & Sanders W (2008). Re-vitalising the Community Development Employment Program in the Northern Territory: Submission prepared in response to the Northern Territory Government's Review of Community Development Employment Program Discussion Paper. *CAEPR Topical Issue No. 05/2008*, Centre for Aboriginal Economic Policy Research, The Australian National University, Canberra.

Australian Bureau of Statistics (2002). *National Aboriginal and Torres Strait Islander Social Survey*, Catalogue No. 4714.0, www.abs.gov.au/ausstats/abs@.nsf/mf/4714.0/.

Australian Government (1987). *Aboriginal Employment Development Policy statement: Policy paper no. 1*, Australian Government Publishing Service, Canberra.

Biddle N (2009). *The geography and demography of Indigenous migration: insights for policy and planning*, CAEPR Working Paper No. 58, Centre for Aboriginal Economic Policy Research, The Australian National University, Canberra.

Borland J & Tseng Y (2011). Does 'Work for the Dole' work? An Australian perspective on work experience programs. *Applied Economics*, 43(28): 4353–4368.

Brough M (2006). *Blueprint for Action in Indigenous Affairs*, Speech delivered to the National Institute of Governance, University of Canberra, 5 December.

Cape York Institute for Policy and Leadership (2007). *From hand out to hand up. Cape York Welfare Reform Project: Aurukun, Coen, Hope Vale, Mossman Gorge. Design recommendations*, Cape York Institute for Policy and Leadership, Cairns.

Champion M (2002). *Urban CDEPs as Indigenous Employment Centres: policy and community implications*, CAEPR Discussion Paper No. 228, Centre for Aboriginal Economic Policy Research, The Australian National University, Canberra.

Clark M (1963). *A short history of Australia*, 4th revised edition, Penguin Books, Camberwell, Victoria.

Davey M (2015). Thousands join protests against WA Indigenous community closures. *The Guardian*, 1 May, www.theguardian.com/australia-news/2015/may/01/thousands-join-protests-against-wa-indigenous-community-closures.

Department of the Prime Minister and Cabinet (2016a). *Closing the Gap Prime Minister's report 2016*, Commonwealth of Australia, Canberra.

Department of the Prime Minister and Cabinet (2016b). *Consultation paper: changes to the Community Development Programme*, Commonwealth of Australia, Canberra.

DEWR (Department of Employment and Workplace Relations) (2006). *Indigenous potential meets economic opportunity*, Discussion paper, Department of Employment and Workplace Relations, Canberra.

Edelman M (1977). *Political language: words that succeed and policies that fail*, Academic Press, New York.

Forrest A (Chair) (2014). *Creating parity – The Forrest Review*, Commonwealth of Australia, Canberra.

Fowkes L & Sanders W (2016). *Financial penalties under the Remote Jobs and Communities Program*, CAEPR Working Paper No. 108, Centre for Aboriginal Economic Policy Research, The Australian National University, Canberra.

Gordon M & Hunter F (2016). Closing the Gap: Indigenous leaders appeal to Turnbull for engagement amid crisis. *The Sydney Morning Herald*, 10 February, www.smh.com.au/federal-politics/political-news/closing-the-gap-indigenous-leaders-appeal-to-turnbull-for-engagement-amid-crisis-20160209-gmpqf2.html.

Haughton J (2016). Social Security Legislation Amendment (Community Development Program) Bill 2015. *Bills Digest No. 93, 2015–16*, Parliamentary Library, Canberra.

Hudson S (2008). CDEP: help or hindrance? The Community Development Employment Program and its impact on Indigenous Australians, *CIS Policy Monograph 86*, Centre for Independent Studies, Sydney.

Hughes H (2007). *Lands of shame: Aboriginal and Torres Strait Islander 'Homelands' in transition*, Centre for Independent Studies, Sydney.

Hughes H & Hughes M (2010). Indigenous employment, unemployment and labour force participation: Facts for evidence based policies, *CIS Policy Monograph 107*, The Centre for Independent Studies, Sydney.

Hunter BH (2009). A half-hearted defence of the CDEP scheme. *Family Matters*, 81: 43–54.

Huxley A (1959). A Case of Voluntary Ignorance. In *Collected Essays*, Harper, New York.

Jordan K (2011). *Work, welfare and CDEP on the Aṇangu Pitjantjatjara Yankunytjatjara (APY) Lands: first stage assessment*, CAEPR Working Paper No. 78, Centre for Aboriginal Economic Policy Research, The Australian National University, Canberra.

Jordan K (2014). Andrew Forrest's Indigenous employment project: Do the arguments stack up? *Australian Review of Public Affairs*, October 2014.

Karvelas P (2007). Thirty-year Aboriginal work-for-dole scheme cut. *The Australian*, 17 February.

Langton M (2002). *A New Deal? Indigenous development and the politics of recovery*. Dr Charles Perkins AO Memorial Oration, The University of Sydney, 4 October.

Macklin J & O'Connor B (2008). *Strengthening Indigenous employment opportunities*, media release, 19 December, www.formerministers. dss.gov.au/14806/strengthening-indigenous-employment-opportunities/.

Martin S (2015). 30 years working for dole a reality. *The Australian*, 2 March, www.theaustralian.com.au/national-affairs/indigenous/years-working-for-dole-a-reality/story-fn9hm1pm-1227243883240.

Medhora S (2015). Remote communities are 'lifestyle choices', says Tony Abbott. *The Guardian*, 10 March, www.theguardian.com/australia-news/2015/mar/10/remote-communities-are-lifestyle-choices-says-tony-abbott.

Miller M (Chair) (1985). *Report of the Committee of Review of Aboriginal Employment and Training Programs*, Australian Government Publishing Service, Canberra.

Morphy F & Sanders F (eds) (2001). *The Indigenous Welfare Economy and the CDEP Scheme*, CAEPR Research Monograph No. 20, ANU E Press, Canberra.

Office of Evaluation and Audit (1997). *Evaluation of the Community Development Employment Projects*, Aboriginal and Torres Strait Islander Commission, Canberra.

Pearson N (2000). *Our right to take responsibility*, Noel Pearson and Associates, Cairns.

Pearson N (2009). *Up from the mission: selected writings*, Black Inc., Melbourne.

Peterson N (2005). What can the pre-colonial and frontier economies tell us about engagement with the real economy? Indigenous life projects and the conditions for development. In Austin-Broos D & Macdonald G (eds), *Culture, economy and governance in Aboriginal Australia*, Sydney University Press, Sydney.

Productivity Commission (2015). *National Indigenous Reform Agreement, performance assessment 2013–14*, Productivity Commission, Canberra.

Robinson N (2016). Closing the Gap 'doomed to fail' without more Indigenous input, activist Patrick Dodson says. *ABC News Online*, 9 February, www.abc.net.au/news/2016-02-09/closing-the-gap-doomed-to-fail-without-more-indigenous-input/7149442.

Rowse T (2001). The political dimensions of community development. In Morphy F & Sanders W (eds), *The Indigenous welfare economy and the CDEP scheme*, CAEPR Research Monograph No. 20, ANU E Press, Canberra.

Rowse T (2002). *Indigenous futures: choice and development for Aboriginal and Islander Australia*, UNSW Press, Sydney.

Sanders W (2014). *Experimental governance in Australian Indigenous Affairs: from Coombs to Pearson via Rowse and the competing principles*, CAEPR Discussion Paper No. 291, Centre for Aboriginal Economic Policy Research, The Australian National University, Canberra.

Scullion N (2015). Second reading speech, Social Security Legislation Amendment (Community Development Program) Bill 2015, Senate Official Hansard, 2 December, Commonwealth of Australia.

Shergold P (2001). The Indigenous Employment Policy: a preliminary evaluation. In Morphy F & Sanders W (eds), *The Indigenous welfare economy and the CDEP scheme*, CAEPR Research Monograph No. 20, ANU E Press, Canberra.

Smith DE (1994). *Working for CDEP: a case study of the Community Development Employment Projects scheme in Port Lincoln, South Australia*, CAEPR Discussion Paper No. 75, Centre for Aboriginal Economic Policy Research, The Australian National University, Canberra.

Smith DE (1995). *Redfern works: the policy and community challenges of an urban CDEP scheme*, CAEPR Discussion Paper No. 99, Centre for Aboriginal Economic Policy Research, The Australian National University, Canberra.

Smith DE (1996). *CDEP as urban enterprise: the case of Yarnteen Aboriginal and Torres Strait Islanders Corporation, Newcastle*, CAEPR Discussion Paper No. 114, Centre for Aboriginal Economic Policy Research, The Australian National University, Canberra.

Standing G (2014). *A precariat charter: from denizens to citizens*, Bloomsbury Academic, London.

Strakosch E (2015). *Neoliberal Indigenous policy: settler colonialism and the post-welfare state*, Palgrave Macmillan, London.

Sutton P (2009). *The politics of suffering: Indigenous Australia and the end of the liberal consensus*, Melbourne University Press, Melbourne.

.

2

Reframed as welfare: CDEP's fall from favour

Will Sanders

Introduction

Discussion of welfare and work for Indigenous Australians leads quickly to the Community Development Employment Projects scheme (CDEP). Introduced by the Fraser Coalition Government in 1977, CDEP was both a response and an alternative to increasing eligibility for social security unemployment payments among Indigenous people in remote areas (Sanders 1985). The idea was to make grants to Indigenous community organisations to employ community members part-time who would otherwise be eligible for unemployment benefits. CDEP was not itself part of the social security system. It was an employment scheme, administered by the Commonwealth Department of Aboriginal Affairs with funding notionally offset against social security entitlements. CDEP proved very popular, with many Indigenous community organisations in remote areas asking to be included (Sanders 1988). From 1987, after a review process by the Hawke Labor Government, CDEP also spread to more regional and urban areas (Australian Government 1987: 6). From 1990, CDEP became a major nationwide program of the Aboriginal and Torres Strait Islander Commission (ATSIC) and continued to grow strongly (Sanders 1993). By the late 1990s, CDEP was coming under greater scrutiny and essentially stopped growing. In 2004, when the Howard

Coalition Government abolished ATSIC, CDEP was transferred to the Commonwealth Department of Employment and Workplace Relations (DEWR), which presided over a process of reform and shrinkage back to remote areas. From late 2007 under the Rudd Labor Government, CDEP became the responsibility of the Department of Families, Housing, Community Services and Indigenous Affairs (FaHCSIA), which reformed it further. This led to new CDEP participants from July 2009 becoming social security payment recipients undertaking required activities in return for welfare.

How is it that an employment program designed to avoid Indigenous reliance on social security payments in 1977 became reframed as part of the welfare system 32 years later? How does a popular and successful solution to a significant public policy problem come, over time, to be seen as part of that problem? These questions are explored below in seven sections of analysis. The reframing of CDEP from employment to welfare did not occur all at once. It proceeded through diverse events over a 20-year period from seemingly innocuous beginnings, and it led in the end to the destruction of CDEP. Some of the reframing was legislative, but much was administrative. Only occasionally did the reframing become a matter of public debate between politicians and in the media. Such was the power of routine decisions within government that cumulatively they did most of the reframing of this once positively regarded program. This is the story of CDEP's fall from favour.

Legislative recognition and complaints of discrimination

During its first decade, CDEP was unequivocally a part-time employment program funded by the Department of Aboriginal Affairs. In 1988, a broad-ranging official review of the social security system observed that, as low income part-time workers still available for additional employment, CDEP participants could theoretically be eligible for part unemployment payments (Cass 1988: 251). As a consequence, two new sections were added to the Social Security Act in 1991 that clearly ruled out this possibility. Subsection 23(1) spoke of a 'Commonwealth funded employment program' based on 'the number of people in that community or group who are, or are likely to be qualified for new start allowance'.[1] Without naming it, this was CDEP and in section 614A it was subject to a 'multiple entitlement exclusion'. This meant that CDEP participants were now legislatively barred, even in theory, from also receiving part Newstart Allowance. CDEP was recognised in the Social Security Act as based indirectly on eligibility for Newstart Allowance, even though it was at that time entirely administered by the Commonwealth's Aboriginal and Torres Strait Islander affairs portfolio.

With legislative recognition, CDEP had moved ever so slightly from being unequivocally an employment program towards being part of the social security system. In remote areas, where CDEP had started and was most prevalent, this change seemed to pass unnoticed. By contrast, in urban areas, to which CDEP had recently spread, the change provoked a series of complaints to the Human Rights and Equal Opportunity Commission. The basis of these complaints was that CDEP participants were not able to access add-on social security entitlements, as could Newstart Allowance recipients. This was seen by complainants as a form of racial discrimination that denied Indigenous Australians their rights within the social security system (Sanders 1997).[2]

When the Race Discrimination Commissioner within the Human Rights and Equal Opportunity Commission published a report investigating these complaints and allegations, she did not find 'any significant issue of racial discrimination' (Antonios 1997: vii). She did, however, express 'concern' about a 'lack of consistency in the treatment of CDEP participants by the Commonwealth Government' (Antonios 1997: viii). This lack of consistency was traced back to section 614A of the Social Security Act, which the Race Discrimination Commissioner saw as in need of amendment so that CDEP participants could be treated 'as ordinary wage earners' (Antonios 1997: ix). This would have returned CDEP to its pre-1991 status of being an employment program without formal links to the social security system. In the event,

---

1 New start allowance was the new name for unemployment benefits in the Social Security Act from 1991. I use the generic term unemployment payments to refer to both the pre-1991 and post-1991 income support provisions. Newstart quickly became a single word within the Australian social security system.

2 This 1997 paper grew out of a consultancy report undertaken for the Human Rights and Equality Opportunity Commission in 1995, which provided background analysis for the Commission's own report in 1997.

the Commonwealth Department of Social Security (DSS) and ATSIC moved in the opposite direction, drawing CDEP closer to the social security system.

Administrative inclusion alongside Work for the Dole

During 1997 the new Howard Coalition Government introduced a scheme under which some Newstart Allowance recipients were asked to undertake community work and in return received a $20-per-fortnight supplement to their social security payment. This general Work for the Dole initiative allowed ATSIC and DSS new room to manoeuvre in relation to CDEP. The 1998 Commonwealth budget announced that legislation would be introduced for a CDEP participant supplement of $20 per fortnight, much like that for Work for the Dole. Because this was done under social security legislation, it also allowed CDEP participants to qualify for add-on social security entitlements like rent assistance, telephone allowance and health care concession cards (Newman 1998). This legislation came into effect in September 1999 and began a process of inclusion of CDEP participants in social security administration, by then the province of Centrelink.

During the latter months of 1999, Centrelink began to sign up CDEP participants for their $20 supplement and other add-on entitlements, in the process giving them a Customer Reference Number. This brought CDEP participants into the individualised world of social security administration, though their basic CDEP wage was still paid by an Indigenous community organisation funded by ATSIC. This hybrid administrative arrangement was highly unusual, quite different from Work for the Dole although made possible by it. CDEP participants were still very clearly employees of their provider organisations, but they also had a presence within social security administration. They were, in retrospect, already starting to be reframed as welfare recipients.

Employment in and out of CDEP: ATSIC's balancing act after Spicer

The Howard Coalition Government commissioned a more broad-ranging review of CDEP during 1997. Completed by a former chief executive of the Australian Chamber of Commerce and Industry, Ian Spicer, this self-proclaimed 'independent' review opened by stating that:

> The importance of CDEP to governments and the 30,000 indigenous Australians involved cannot be overstated. In some localities, CDEP often represents the community itself. Without it some remote communities would simply not exist (Spicer 1997: 1).

After this enthusiastic opening, Spicer went on to identify some problems within the 20-year-old program. One was that 'up to a third of CDEP participants' were not working and some were receiving 'as little as $30–40 per week'. Spicer suggested that this 'sit-down money' aspect of CDEP should be removed over time, with participants not working and on very low incomes being returned to the social security system where they would be 'financially better off'. This would also free up places for 'waiting lists of people wishing to join' CDEP and work (Spicer 1997: 3). Another problem identified by Spicer was that there were not enough participants moving out of CDEP into other employment. This called for greater skills development and 'individual case management', which Spicer encouraged through greater 'linkages with employment placement providers' or even CDEPs becoming such providers themselves (Spicer 1997: 6).

Although independent, the Spicer Review had been carried out with the assistance and cooperation of ATSIC staff. As a consequence, ATSIC was comfortable working with Spicer's recommendations over the next few years and pushed to get more Indigenous people working both in and out of CDEP. In this, ATSIC was assisted by its ex-CEO, Peter Shergold, who had become Secretary of the Commonwealth's employment department. In this new role, Shergold worked hard on an Indigenous Employment Policy (IEP) that provided wage subsidies for up to 26 weeks for Indigenous people placed in non-CDEP employment. In 2000, he reported that 1,600 Indigenous Australians had been assisted with wage subsidies in the first year and that placements were then running at between 200 and 250 per month

(Shergold 2001: 69). Another part of IEP provided for payments of $2,000 to CDEP organisations who placed a participant in 'mainstream employment'. However, this part of IEP was not performing so strongly, with only 180 such placements over 12 months. Shergold (2001: 71) believed that the IEP 'incentives' for moving participants out of CDEP needed 'rethinking'.

While the employment department was slowly becoming interested in CDEP through its IEP, it was still ATSIC that owned and was enthusiastic about the CDEP scheme. ATSIC's balancing act around CDEP could be seen in its annual reporting, which in 2002–03 for the first time placed CDEP activities in three 'output groups': 'promotion of cultural authority', 'improvement to social and physical wellbeing' and 'economic development'. Previously CDEP had been reported solely under 'employment and training' within ATSIC's 'economic development' output group, although clearly CDEP's significance had always been much broader than that.

DEWR's contractualism and employment service model

In 2004, with the abolition of ATSIC, CDEP was transferred to DEWR. Employment had, over the previous decade, become a leading Commonwealth portfolio in the contracting out of government services (Considine 1999). From 2006, CDEP was also subjected to this competitive contractualism. Organisations had to formally express interest in being a provider and, if successful, were given a three-year contract. This was quite different from ATSIC's former annual grants program, which had loyally funded Indigenous community-based organisations from year to year, unless their CDEP was going badly awry. Through DEWR's competitive contractualism, some non-Indigenous organisations became providers of CDEP and some Indigenous organisations competed with each other outside their established service regions, as seen in some of our case studies.

DEWR also subjected CDEP to two rounds of more substantive policy review. This involved discussion papers suggesting changes, followed by community consultations and ministerial announcements that largely confirmed earlier suggestions (Andrews 2005; DEWR 2005,

2006; Hockey 2007). One result was the closure from July 2007 of CDEPs in over 60 urban areas seen as having 'strong labour markets'. The 7,000 participants in these CDEPs were referred on closure to a specialised Indigenous 'job brokerage service' called STEP and to general Job Network employment service providers in their areas.[3] For the remaining regional and remote CDEPs and their 28,000 participants there would be incentive payments 'for getting people into real work for 26 weeks' and some lowering of allowable additional income while on CDEP. There was even talk of restricting new entrants to CDEP to 12 months participation (Hockey 2007; see also DEWR 2007).

Analytically, I argue, what was occurring through these reform processes was a move towards DEWR's preferred employment service model. DEWR worried that employment in CDEP could continue indefinitely and that participants were not sufficiently encouraged into the larger labour market. They wanted CDEP participants to link in with the larger general employment services providers, the Job Network, and with other (non-CDEP) employers. Pushing in this direction involved DEWR reframing CDEP participants as still unemployed jobseekers, even though they had some continuing part-time employment. Indeed, through CDEP's generous allowable additional income rules, over half of CDEP participants in 2002 worked more than the minimum 15 hours per week and their average weekly income was over $100 more than that of the unemployed (Altman et al. 2005: 11).

DEWR's reframing of CDEP participants as still unemployed jobseekers meant also encouraging a greater presence in remote areas for Job Network providers, which in the previous decade had not been strong (Shergold 2001: 67–8). This increasing presence of general employment services in remote areas highlighted their very different mode of operation from CDEP, sometimes leading to cooperation but more often to tension, as again seen in some of our case studies (see also Jordan 2011: 46).

---

3   STEP stood for Structured Training and Employment Projects. A catchy acronym sometimes appears a requirement for a government program.

Pearson's 2007 reversal and the Northern Territory Intervention

During 2007, two other events contributed to the gradual reframing of CDEP from work to welfare. The first was a reversal in the analysis and public position on CDEP of prominent north Queensland Aboriginal commentator, activist and lawyer, Noel Pearson. The second was the Howard Coalition Government's decision to override Northern Territory self-government and intervene in Territory Aboriginal communities, which belatedly included an intention to abolish CDEP in the Territory. Both were more public, high-profile contributions than the administrative, budgetary and legislative manoeuvres analysed in other sections. But they were nonetheless an important part of the extended process of reframing CDEP.

Around the turn of the millennium, when Noel Pearson began focusing on the problem of 'passive welfare' in Aboriginal communities, he did not include CDEP in that rubric. Rather, he argued that CDEP reflected the 'principles' of 'responsibility and reciprocity' instituted at the 'local level', which he saw as the way forward (Pearson 2000: 84–6). While noting that in some smaller communities CDEP was 'very successful', Pearson also observed that in 'particularly larger' communities CDEP was 'often not very distinguishable from the dole—in terms of achieving the reciprocity principle' (Pearson 2000: 87). This qualifying subordinate statement in 2000 was perhaps a foretaste of what was to come. In February 2007, Pearson very publicly reversed his position on CDEP. In one of his regular opinion pieces in *The Weekend Australian* newspaper, Pearson developed the idea of a 'welfare pedestal' and a 'staircase of opportunity' driven mainly by 'economic incentives'. He now saw CDEP as part of the welfare pedestal from which Indigenous people 'must first … step down before the process of climbing the staircase can begin'. Slightly changing the metaphor, Pearson argued that 'CDEP was intended to be a stepping stone to a real job', but had in 'reality … become a permanent destination' (Pearson 2007). Pearson's reframing of CDEP in February 2007 sat comfortably with Minister Hockey's a week later. In May 2007, this reframing also became the declared position of the Cape York Institute for Policy and Leadership, the think tank offshoot of Griffith University that Pearson had created in 2004 to help progress his welfare reform agenda (Cape York Institute for Policy and Leadership 2007).

In June 2007, when the Howard Coalition Government launched its 'Intervention' into Northern Territory Aboriginal communities, changes to CDEP were not initially part of this 'emergency response'. But in July, ministers Hockey and Brough argued that CDEP had 'become a destination for too many' and that 'measures' already 'successfully introduced in urban and regional areas' were now to be implemented across the Northern Territory. This meant closing CDEPs and 'converting CDEP positions that support Government service delivery into real jobs wherever possible'. With the help of both government and other employers, the ministers 'expected that some 2,000 people will be assisted off CDEP into real work'. For the rest of the Territory's 8,000 CDEP participants, there would be social security 'income support, with normal participation requirements including access to Job Network services, Structured Training and Employment Projects (STEP) or Work for the Dole', plus the Intervention's new income management arrangements. This was to be rolled out 'on a community by community basis' commencing in September 2007 (Brough & Hockey 2007).

In tandem with this Coalition Government announcement in July 2007, four Opposition Labor members of the House of Representatives were putting their names to a minority parliamentary committee report entitled *Indigenous Australians at Work*. They identified the reframing of CDEP when they observed that in its 'original form' the 'emphasis' had been 'on community development which generated employment, not just on individual employment readiness' (HRSCATSIA 2007: 216). Labor was clearly internally divided over how to respond to the Coalition's July announcement to close CDEPs across the Northern Territory. Opposition leader Rudd was more supportive than his parliamentary colleagues from the Northern Territory, as the Coalition's Minister for Workforce Participation took delight in pointing out during September (Stone 2007). By October, Labor had reunited around an 'Indigenous Economic Development Strategy', which involved 'reforming and improving CDEP' rather than abolishing it. Reforms would 'apply nationally in remote areas, including in the Northern Territory' (Garrett et al. 2007). This position clearly differentiated Labor from the Coalition on CDEP in the November 2007 election and when Labor won, it meant that the Rudd Labor Government placed an immediate moratorium on further closures of CDEPs in the Northern Territory. About 20 CDEPs had already been closed across the Northern Territory, while some 30 remained. The Rudd Labor Government also immediately moved CDEP administratively from the employment portfolio to the Department of Families, Housing, Community Services and Indigenous Affairs (FaHCSIA).

Equalising CDEP and income support: FaHCSIA's contribution

In April 2008, Rudd's Indigenous affairs and employment ministers announced that CDEP would be offered back to Northern Territory communities in which it had been closed in 2007 as a 12-month 'interim measure' while the government progressed reform (Macklin & O'Connor 2008a). In May 2008, under the names of these two ministers and the Deputy Prime Minister, the Rudd Government released a discussion paper on 'the future of the CDEP and Indigenous Employment Programs'. This asked respondents to make 'suggestions' about how CDEP and IEP could be 'better linked to the Government's new universal employment services model to be implemented from July 2009'. It also asked for 'views on what works now' and 'fresh innovative ideas to ensure both programs meet Indigenous people's needs into the future' (Gillard et al. 2008a: 1). This discussion paper went on to identify some 'reform principles and difficult questions' already understood. One was 'unequal treatment' between 'CDEP and income support' for the unemployed, both in activity requirements and in allowable additional earnings. Following a tabular presentation of these differences, the suggestion was 'to move away from the system of CDEP wages and move participants into the income support system' as a 'way of fixing these inequalities' (Gillard et al. 2008a: 4–5). While there was much else in this discussion paper, this concern with equalising CDEP and social security income support was a new contribution, probably reflecting FaHCSIA's perspective and influence as the new departmental guardian of CDEP.

In October 2008, these same three ministers issued an expanded paper that both reported on 'consultations' and progressed 'suggestions' to 'proposed reforms' for implementation in July 2009. CDEP would cease to operate 'in non-remote regions'. In remote areas, new CDEP participants would 'access the program while on relevant income support payments rather than be paid CDEP wages', while existing participants could continue to 'receive CDEP wages' during an 'adjustment period' extending to March 2010 (Gillard et al. 2008b: 6–7). In December, two of these ministers announced that these CDEP reforms would indeed 'begin on 1 July 2009', together with a $764 million injection into IEP over five years. The adjustment period for existing CDEP participants to continue receiving wages would be extended to June 2011 and 'reformed universal employment services' from July 2009 would also provide Indigenous job seekers 'with more tailored assistance' (Macklin & O'Connor 2008b).

These reforms, developed during 2008 and implemented from July 2009, amounted to a further inclusion of CDEP in the social security system. Politically, within the Rudd Government, the southern leaders (Rudd, Gillard and Macklin) had prevailed over their Northern Territory colleagues and some others who were more supportive of the existing wages-based CDEP. Administratively over time, increasing numbers of CDEP participants were becoming income support recipients subject to precise legislative eligibility requirements, like the activity test and restricted allowable additional income rules. Conversely, decreasing numbers of CDEP participants from before July 2009 were being paid wages and allowed the generous additional income rules referred to as 'top-up'. CDEP was by 2009 more within the social security system than outside it, and becoming more so all the time as pre-July 2009 participants fell away. The old framing of CDEP as part-time employment was rapidly fading. The dominant reframed view from July 2009, both politically and administratively, was that CDEP participants were just another group of unemployed welfare recipients undertaking required activities in return for income support.

From CDEP to RJCP: Service integration and reframing confirmed

In 2011, the Gillard Labor Government initiated a broad-ranging review of 'remote participation and employment servicing arrangements'. Among Indigenous-specific programs, this covered both CDEP and IEP. In general employment programs, it covered Disability Employment Services and the much larger universal employment services, renamed Job Services Australia (JSA) in the process of awarding contracts for 2009–12. With these four programs to consider, the discussion paper for this review highlighted the 'fragmented' nature of existing services in which 'goals are not always aligned' (Arbib et al. 2011: 7). It then argued for a 'new model' that would involve a 'single provider' in each remote region, arguing that this would be 'simpler, more integrated and more flexible' (Arbib et al. 2011: 8). With this framing of existing services and the suggested new model, change seemed unexceptional and hard to resist. However, as some of our case studies show, CDEP and JSA operated in quite different ways in the same geographic area and placing them together would raise important questions about the mode of operation of the new single provider.

In May 2012, a new troika of ministers announced the Remote Jobs and Communities Program (RJCP), which would replace all four existing programs, including CDEP. From July 2013, RJCP would offer 'a more integrated and flexible service to people in remote Australia and help to build sustainable communities' (Macklin et al. 2012). A 'Job Seeker Compliance Framework' would 'provide a direct connection between attending employment or community projects and receiving income support payments', while a 'Community Development Fund' would support projects identified in 'Community Action Plans', which would 'provide employment and participation opportunities for local people' (Macklin et al. 2012). For 'grandfathered' CDEP participants from before July 2009, wages could now continue until June 2017 to 'provide stability and familiarity' (Macklin et al. 2012).[4]

---

4   'Grandfathered' participants were those who had joined CDEP prior to 1 July 2009 who, as explained above, could continue to receive a CDEP wage for the specified 'adjustment' period.

Expressions of interest in being a RJCP provider were due in November 2012 and successful applicants across 60 regions were announced in April/May 2013. A little more than 3,000 grandfathered CDEP wages participants were passed to the new RJCP providers in July 2013, which was less than 10 per cent of their anticipated case load of 35,000 jobseekers across 60 regions. Wage-based CDEP was fading away, with just three or four providers hanging on tenaciously to grandfathered positions, including in one of our case studies. Among almost 50 RJCP providers, about 40 per cent had past experience delivering both CDEP and JSA, with two more groups of 20 per cent each having experience delivering one of these major programs or the other. The successful competitors for these new five-year government service contracts were a mix of local Indigenous, national non-government welfare and for-profit organisations. Many were operating in new organisational partnerships encouraged during the contracting process, but almost all had past experience as employment service providers of one sort or another (Fowkes & Sanders 2015).

As RJCP began during the second half of 2013, the Abbott Coalition Government won office in Canberra. With RJCP being a Gillard Labor Government creation, the new government was not always supportive. It did, however, include RJCP in an election promise to move 'Indigenous programmes to the Department of the Prime Minister and Cabinet' (Loughnane 2013: 2). Strictly speaking, this was not necessary, since RJCP covered *all* people in remote areas, not just the Indigenous. RJCP was clearly seen by the incoming Abbott Government as a very important program for remote Indigenous people, which it wanted centrally located in its new Indigenous affairs administrative arrangements.

Two years on, the Abbott Coalition Government had reworked the activity and funding model for RJCP. From July 2015, CDEP wages ceased and all participants became social security income support recipients who were asked to undertake up to 25 hours per week of work-like activity. This confirmed the reframing of RJCP participants as unemployed job seekers doing required activities in return for income support. However, the Abbott Government also renamed the new arrangements from July 2015 the Community Development Programme (CDP), which is bound to cause confusion and perhaps lead some to think that there is movement back towards an employment and wages-based program. This is not the case.

Conclusions

The story of CDEP's fall from favour suggests, on my reading, three conclusions. The first is that the framing of government programs is very powerful. The second is that reviews of government programs almost always change them. The third is that administrative arrangements within government are as important as politicians in changing the framing of programs (Sanders 2012). It is through reframing, predominantly within government, that a program designed as a solution to a policy problem can, three decades later, be cast as part of that problem. This accords with a large recent literature on the power of framing within public policy (Fischer 2003).

In its original form in 1977, CDEP was all about Aboriginal people in remote areas not being on social security unemployment payments and instead being in part-time employment. There was no concern that this might become a long-term arrangement and there was only a notional offset-funding link back to the social security system. This was captured in original guideline 5, which stated that these grants 'to provide employment opportunities' would be 'at a cost approximating unemployment benefits', 'thereby reducing the need for unemployment benefit for unemployed Aboriginals within the community' (Commonwealth of Australia 1977: 1922). After the social security review, which ran from 1986 to 1988, this notional funding link was changed in 1991 to a direct legislative link, albeit a minor one for the purposes of a multiple entitlement exclusion seemingly unnoticed in remote areas. The Race Discrimination Commissioner's review in 1997 suggested going back to treating CDEP participants as 'ordinary wage earners', but all other reviews in this seven-section analysis have pushed in the opposite direction. Each review brought CDEP participants a step closer into either the social security system or associated employment services. ATSIC's deal with DSS in the 1998 budget to pay CDEP participants and Work for the Dole participants a similar supplement seemed logical and sensible at the time, but in the long run it probably killed CDEP as an employment and wages-based program. Subsequent reviews by DEWR and FaHCSIA would, with the help of politicians of both major parties, move CDEP more and more into the income support and employment services systems. From July 2009, new CDEP participants were clearly part of social security administration and existing CDEP participants were a doomed, grandfathered cohort, slowly fading away. CDEP died as a program in 2013 with the move to RJCP, and the last of its grandfathered participants lost that status in 2015. A good idea for Indigenous employment from 1977 had been reframed as welfare and comprehensively destroyed 38 years later.

References

Altman JC, Gray M & Levitus R (2005). *Policy issues for the Community Development Employment Projects scheme in rural and remote Australia*, CAEPR Discussion Paper No. 271, Centre for Aboriginal Economic Policy Research, The Australian National University, Canberra.

Andrews K (2005). *CDEP future directions*, media release, Minister for Employment and Workplace Relations, Canberra, 10 May.

Antonios Z (Race Discrimination Commissioner) (1997). *The CDEP scheme and race discrimination*, Human Rights and Equal Opportunity Commission, Sydney.

Arbib M, Macklin J & Ellis K (2011). *The future of remote participation and employment servicing arrangements: discussion paper*, Minister for Indigenous Employment and Economic Development, Minister for Families, Housing Community Services and Indigenous Affairs, Minister for Employment Participation and Childcare, Australian Government, Canberra.

Australian Government (1987). *Aboriginal employment development policy: community-based employment, enterprise and development strategies*, Australian Government Publishing Service, Canberra.

Brough M & Hockey J (2007). *Jobs and training for Indigenous people in the NT*, media releases, Minister for Families, Community Services and Indigenous Affairs, Minister for Employment and Workplace Relations, Canberra, 23 July.

Cape York Institute for Policy and Leadership (2007). *From hand out to hand up: Cape York welfare reform project, Aurukun, Coen, Hope Vale and Mossman Gorge – Design recommendations*, Cape York Institute for Policy and Leadership, Cairns.

Cass B (1988). *Income support for the unemployed in Australia: towards a more active system,* Social Security Review, Issues Paper No. 4. Australian Government Publishing Service, Canberra.

Commonwealth of Australia (1977). *Parliamentary debates: House of Representatives (official Hansard),* 26 May, Australian Government Publishing Service, Canberra, 1922.

Considine M (1999). Markets, networks and the new welfare state: employment assistance reform in Australia. *Journal of Social Policy* 28: 183–203.

DEWR (Department of Employment and Workplace Relations) (2005). *Building on success: CDEP discussion paper,* Australian Government, Canberra.

DEWR (Department of Employment and Workplace Relations) (2006). *Indigenous potential meets economic opportunity: discussion paper,* Australian Government, Canberra.

DEWR (Department of Employment and Workplace Relations) (2007). *Questions and answers for the outcome of the Indigenous potential meets economic opportunity consultation,* Australian Government, Canberra.

Fischer F (2003). *Reframing public policy: discursive politics and deliberative practices,* Oxford University Press, Oxford.

Fowkes L & Sanders W (2015). *A survey of remote jobs and communities program(me) providers: one year in,* CAEPR Working Paper No. 97, Centre for Aboriginal Economic Policy Research, The Australian National University, Canberra.

Garrett P, Macklin J & Snowdon W (2007). *Federal Labor to create 300 rangers as part of Indigenous economic development strategy,* joint statement, Shadow Minister for Environment and Heritage, Shadow Minister for Indigenous Affairs and Reconciliation, Shadow Parliamentary Secretary for Northern Australia and Indigenous Affairs, Canberra, 5 October.

Gillard J, Macklin J & O'Connor B (2008a). *Increasing Indigenous economic opportunity: a discussion paper on the future of the CDEP and Indigenous Employment Programs,* Deputy Prime Minister, Minister for Families, Housing, Community Services and Indigenous Affairs, Minister for Employment Participation, Australian Government, Canberra.

Gillard J, Macklin J & O'Connor B (2008b). *Increasing Indigenous employment opportunity: proposed reforms to the CDEP and Indigenous Employment Programs,* Deputy Prime Minister, Minister for Families, Housing, Community Services and Indigenous Affairs, Minister for Employment Participation, Australian Government, Canberra.

Hockey J (2007). *Indigenous employment services reforms announced,* media alert, Minister for Employment and Workplace Relations, Canberra, 17 February.

HRSCATSIA (House of Representatives Standing Committee on Aboriginal and Torres Strait Islander Affairs) (2007). *Indigenous Australians at work: successful initiatives in Indigenous employment,* Parliament of the Commonwealth of Australia, Canberra.

Jordan K (2011). *Work, welfare and CDEP on the Aṉangu Pitjantjatjara Yankunytjatjara Lands: first stage assessment,* CAEPR Working Paper No. 78, Centre for Aboriginal Economic Policy Research, The Australian National University, Canberra.

Loughnane B (2013). *The Coalition's policy for Indigenous Affairs,* Barton, September.

Macklin J & O'Connor B (2008a). *Government timetable for Indigenous employment reforms announced,* media release, Minister for Families, Housing, Community Services and Indigenous Affairs, Minister for Employment Participation, Canberra, 30 April.

Macklin J & O'Connor B (2008b). *Strengthening Indigenous employment opportunities,* media release, Minister for Families, Housing, Community Services and Indigenous Affairs, Minister for Employment Participation, Canberra, 12 December.

Macklin J, Shorten B & Collins J (2012). *Remote Jobs and Communities Program: jobs and stronger communities for people in remote Australia,* Minister for Families, Community Services and Indigenous Affairs, Minister for Employment and Workplace Relations, Minister for Indigenous Employment and Economic Development, Australian Government, Canberra.

Newman J (1998). Fairer treatment for CDEP participants, *News Release Budget 1998/99,* Minister for Social Security, Canberra.

Pearson N (2000). *Our right to take responsibility.* Noel Pearson and Associates, Cairns.

Pearson N (2007). Stuck on the welfare pedestal. *The Weekend Australian,* 10–11 February.

Sanders W (1985). The politics of unemployment benefit for Aborigines: some consequences of economic marginalisation. In Wade-Marshall D & Loveday P (eds), *Employment and unemployment: a collection of papers,* The Australian National University North Australia Research Unit, Darwin.

Sanders W (1988). The CDEP scheme: Bureaucratic politics, remote community politics and the development of an Aboriginal 'workfare' program in time of rising unemployment. *Politics* 23(1): 32–47.

Sanders W (1993). *The rise and rise of the CDEP scheme: an Aboriginal 'workfare' program in times of persistent unemployment,* CAEPR Discussion Paper No. 54, Centre for Aboriginal Economic Policy Research, The Australian National University, Canberra.

Sanders W (1997). How does (and should) DSS treat CDEP participants? What are these allegations of racial discrimination? *Social Security Journal,* December, 19–30. (Also available as CAEPR Discussion Paper 149/1997.)

Sanders W (2012). Coombs' bastard child: the troubled life of CDEP. *Australian Journal of Public Administration,* 71(4): 371–391.

Shergold P (2001). The Indigenous employment policy: a preliminary evaluation. In Morphy F & Sanders W (eds), *The Indigenous welfare economy and the CDEP scheme,* CAEPR Research Monograph No. 20, ANU E Press, Canberra, 67–74.

Spicer I (1997). *Independent review of the Community Development Employment Projects (CDEP) scheme,* Office of Public Affairs, ATSIC, Woden ACT.

Stone S (2007). *Labor MP Warren Snowdon splits with Rudd on CDEP,* media release, Minister for Workforce Participation, Canberra, 7 September.

3

Some statistical context for analysis of CDEP

Boyd Hunter

Introduction

This volume includes four case studies of communities that have been affected by the reforms to the Community Development Employment Projects (CDEP) outlined in the previous chapters. The first three case studies are based in very remote parts of Australia where the scheme was a prominent feature of the Indigenous labour market between its inception in 1977 and closure in 2015. Those sites are based in the Aṉangu Pitjantjatjara,[1] Anmatjere and Maningrida census regions. The other case study site is based on the far south coast of NSW. This chapter will provide rudimentary information on CDEP scheme employment for those areas, as well as some broader statistical context on the CDEP scheme derived from administrative, survey and census data.

Chapter 2 comprehensively documented the significant changes in the CDEP scheme rules and administration over the last decade; however, this chapter provides statistical analysis to provide some insights into likely impacts of these reforms. Looming large among these changes is

---

1   Note that 'Aṉangu Pitjantjatjara' is the statistical region as defined by the Australian Bureau of Statistics, but this corresponds in practice to the Aṉangu Pitjantjatjara Yankunytjatjara Lands.

the fact that CDEP jobs have disappeared since 2006. From its height in 2002–03 when it had over 35,000 participants, the CDEP scheme declined slowly to around 32,800 around the time of the 2006 census, after which it was soon cut to less than a third of its former size. At the time of the 2011 census, administrative records indicated that only 10,700 participants remained on the scheme (Gray et al. 2014). While CDEP continued in remote areas until June 2015 (albeit with such reduced numbers), the analysis here focuses on the intercensal period between 2006 and 2011, the most recent year for which there are available data from statistical collections.

The substantial policy changes relating to CDEP have been disproportionately felt in certain areas. As noted above, the scheme was eliminated in most non-remote areas in 2007, but this chapter will illustrate that between 2006 and 2011 some remote areas experienced greater reduction in CDEP participation than others. The extent to which changes in CDEP affected local communities during that intercensal period should be greatest in the areas that lost most CDEP participants.

There has been considerable research into 'Coombs' bastard child' since its inception in 1977 (Sanders 2012). Ironically, the zenith of understanding about the composition of the CDEP workforce was probably reached just after the scheme entered its declining years (or what Sanders called its 'lingering old age'). It is well documented that CDEP was historically associated with working part-time, while participation tended to be disproportionately male and focus on employing younger people (Altman et al. 2000). On average, CDEP participants had a higher income than people who were unemployed or not in the labour force (NILF), but a substantially lower income than people employed in mainstream jobs outside of CDEP (i.e. the non-CDEP employed).

Hunter and Gray (2013) build on these facts and confirm that CDEP participants experienced significantly better socioeconomic outcomes than the unemployed in a wide range of issues (including crime, health, financial stress, and community security). CDEP participation was also strongly associated with the maintenance of language and culture as well as an ongoing connection to traditional lands.

One particularly salient finding in Hunter and Gray (2013) is that the main characteristics of remote CDEP jobs did not change between 1994 and 2008. That is, if a person was employed in a CDEP job during both 1994 and 2008, they could have expected to receive similar employment outcomes for themselves and for their local communities. Given that CDEP schemes were closed in most non-remote areas in 2007, these changes would have had a significant effect on regions like the far south coast of NSW (see Chapter 4). The size of any such effect will depend on the number of jobs lost as a proportion of the resident population.

Of course, former CDEP scheme workers may find other jobs, may become unemployed, may leave the labour force or may even leave the local area. This chapter will provide some bounds on the likely effect of the loss of 35,000 CDEP jobs by estimating the marginal effects of former workers entering various labour force states using Hunter and Gray (2013).

Commonly, case studies are conducted in areas where researchers have existing connections and social links that allow the research to be undertaken. This is clearly a sensible strategy designed to maximise the amount of usable information collected in a qualitative study. There is always a question as to how representative the case studies are of the circumstances they seek to characterise. However, qualitative research does not usually attempt to generalise its findings in terms of the representativeness of the information provided, but rather appeals to the depth or quality of information attained from particular individuals or case studies. This chapter also attempts to situate the remote case studies in terms of location and some broad census characteristics as well as limited information provided from administrative sources.

The next section introduces the administrative data on CDEP employment after 1997 to illustrate the magnitude of the loss of CDEP scheme work. The third section revisits some salient findings from Hunter and Gray (2013) and reflects on the consequences of the decline and demise of CDEP since 2006. The fourth section uses some little-known data from the first longitudinal analysis of Indigenous jobseekers to reflect on the transition of CDEP participants and Indigenous unemployed into mainstream employment. The chapter then attempts to estimate the likely effects of the demise of the CDEP scheme using available evidence. The CDEP communities analysed in the case studies are then introduced through a mixture of some rather messy administrative data for CDEP schemes and analyses of some basic census data for remote Indigenous Areas and the Indigenous Location for Wallaga Lake within the far south coast of NSW case study (i.e. the most disaggregated Australian Bureau of Statistics (ABS) geographic levels designed specifically to analyse Indigenous statistics). The final section briefly reflects on this statistical context and the implications for the analysis in the rest of this book.

Charting the decline in the number of participants in the CDEP scheme

In order to provide some statistical context for the recent changes to CDEP, this section analyses administrative data back to 1997. Fig. 3.1 below is an extension of the chart presented in Hunter and Gray (2013) so that it covers the entire period up to the 2011 census. The first thing to note about Fig. 3.1 is that there was a disproportionate number of males employed in the scheme. Some of this gender bias is due to the fact that males are more likely to participate in the labour market (Hunter & Daly 2013). However, this cannot be the sole explanation as males have been at times twice as likely to be employed in CDEP whereas the overall labour force participation rate of Indigenous males is not twice as high as that of Indigenous females (Gray et al. 2014).

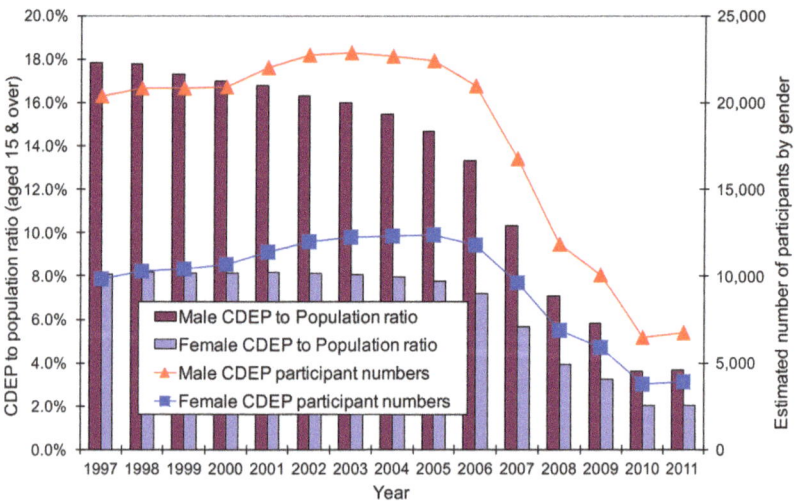

Fig. 3.1 CDEP employment/population ratio, Indigenous males and females aged 15 and over, 1997–2011

Note: There is some CDEP data available before 1997 but it is difficult to compare this information with the most recent data.

Source: Hunter and Gray (2013). The 2011 estimates derived in Gray, Hunter and Howlett (2013).

The information about CDEP participation has become somewhat patchy since 2011, but the limited administrative data that are available show that the downward trend continued unabated. The number of people employed as 'grandfathered' CDEP participants (those who had commenced in the scheme prior to July 2009 and who still received CDEP wages) continued to decline up to 2015 when these transitional arrangements were phased out. In answer to a question on notice to the Senate Finance and Public Administration Legislation Committee by Senator Jan McLucas, the Department of the Prime Minister and Cabinet indicated that, as at 16 March 2015, the total number of recipients grandfathered under the CDEP wages scheme was 2,221. The next section will provide a rough estimate of the loss of around 35,000 CDEP jobs using the analysis provided in Hunter and Gray (2013). However, in order to estimate the effect of the decline of CDEP employment one needs to make an assumption about what happens to the people who are no longer employed in the CDEP scheme.

It is not unreasonable to assume that the vast majority of former CDEP-employed have moved to welfare payments akin to what is commonly called Newstart (or simply unemployment benefits). Forrest (2014: Chapter 4) claimed that there were about 35,000 jobseekers registered in the Remote Jobs and Communities Program (RJCP)—the scheme that had largely replaced CDEP by that time—with only about 3,000 of that number registered as receiving income through the grandfathered CDEP wages arrangement. The remaining jobseekers were in receipt of other forms of income support (e.g. Newstart Allowance and Youth Allowance). It is a remarkable coincidence that the number of people registered in the RJCP was roughly equivalent to the total number of CDEP scheme jobs administered at the height of the scheme in 2002–03. In view of the population growth that has occurred since 2002, the positions in the scheme would have had to expand to maintain the situation that existed 13 years ago. I will consider three possibilities about the movement of former CDEP workers in the next section—that they moved into non-CDEP scheme employment, became unemployed, or exited the labour force.

While the administrative data are relatively consistent, it is important to reflect on the inadequacies of various statistical data sets on Indigenous labour force status, especially with respect to people employed through the CDEP scheme. According to ABS (2013a), and consistent with the numbers presented in Fig. 3.1, there was a total decline of almost 22,000 CDEP participants across Australia between the previous two censuses collected in 2006 and 2011 (i.e. derived by adding the change in male and female participation). However, the total number of people in CDEP scheme employment identified in the census was much lower. The 2006 census counted 14,497 employed in CDEP and the 2011 census counted 5,005 in the same category. Given that there should be a one-to-one correspondence between CDEP employment and participation, this represents a decline of 9,492 CDEP-employed in the census—less than half of the actual decline in CDEP participation measured in administrative data between 2006 and 2011. There are two major reasons for the under-reporting of CDEP in census collections: CDEP information was only being collected by an interviewer in some remote areas (entirely overlooking participant numbers in regional and urban areas); and there is considerable uncertainty about how remote CDEP participants may have reported their CDEP and employment status in the census.

Labour force comparisons between the 2006 and 2011 censuses may also be affected by the recent changes to CDEP. To the extent that some remote CDEP participants were recorded in the census in 2006 and were no longer CDEP participants in 2011, they may be recorded as either unemployed or not in the labour force in the most recent census depending on the respondents' understanding of their circumstances. Similarly, those still participating in CDEP in 2011 may not have understood or reported themselves as such if they were no longer in receipt of CDEP wages. The ABS were certainly aware of such issues. Even though CDEP information for 2011 was collected and processed by the ABS in the same way it was for the 2006 census, the ABS (2013a) recommend care should be taken when comparing 2006 and 2011 census CDEP counts because the recent reforms 'may have an impact on the numbers of people reporting that they are CDEP participants'.

There appear to be some subtle differences in statements in the ABS monthly Labour Force Survey (LFS) about CDEP (ABS 2011a, 2012a, 2013b). In ABS (2011a), participants who joined after July 2009 received unemployment benefits instead of CDEP wages, and were considered by the ABS to be undertaking unpaid work in a similar manner to those in the Work for the Dole scheme. The basis of this decision was a presumption that the relationship between employer/

employee changed with the CDEP policy reforms. In ABS (2012a), the situation was clarified (with a different arrangement of words that avoided any analogy with the Work for the Dole scheme):

> In remote communities, participants who joined CDEP prior to July 2009 will continue receiving wages ... under the new Remote Jobs and Communities Program (RJCP) and continue to be classified as employed. New participants will receive income support benefits instead of CDEP wages, and are therefore not considered to be in an employer/employee relationship and will not be classed as employed.

Another more recent ABS statement indicates that, in order to accommodate the introduction of RJCP (in July 2013), the shorter version of the LFS questionnaire was modified slightly (ABS 2013b):

> to differentiate between those working under CDEP (wages) and those working under RJCP/CDEP (income support payments). Those employed under CDEP (wages) will be classified as employed because they have an employer/employee relationship, while those under RJCP/CDEP (income support payments) will be classified as unemployed or not in the labour force, depending on whether or not they are looking for work.

It is difficult not to sympathise with the ABS who have obviously struggled to make statistical sense of labour force concepts in a time of complex policy reform. However, it also must be incredibly difficult for the participants and the interviewers to interpret and classify people as having CDEP (wages) or CDEP (income support payments). Perhaps the most telling admission on the relevant issues was in ABS (2012a):

> [T]here are practical difficulties with applying these standard LFS concepts and definitions in Indigenous communities, particularly in remote regions. When interviewers encounter significant cultural, language or operational difficulties in remote communities, a 'short form' is used to collect the minimum data required to derive basic labour force characteristics, and this does not always capture the complex issues that are involved in defining CDEP participation.

Since a person in the RJCP was expected to work for their welfare payment, the experience of some former CDEP participants may not have been that different under the RJCP. Alternatively, CDEP participants who were still in receipt of wages in 2011 may have been aware of the policy shift, but may not have believed that their experience was any different to that of the RJCP participants who they knew to be classified as unemployed.

This section has demonstrated that it was very difficult to statistically measure the labour force status of CDEP participants and former participants using surveys and even censuses. Following ABS (2011b), I will not attempt to directly compare the CDEP statistics in the 2006 and 2011 censuses. Nonetheless, it is clear that by July 2015 the 35,000 former CDEP positions no longer existed.

It is important to explore the implications of the loss of these positions, but it is necessary to make some assumptions about what has happened to the former CDEP participants in terms of labour force status. While RJCP (or, at the time of writing, the Community Development Programme (CDP)) participants nominally 'work for the dole', they are arguably closer to being unemployed than CDEP scheme workers in terms of the experience of participants (see Chapter 2). There is some anecdotal evidence that many CDP providers are having trouble providing work-like activities for participants. In the context of the broader policy debate, there have been doubts cast about the value of the mainstream Work for the Dole, which unlike CDEP does not seem to offer different outcomes compared to other unemployed (Borland & Tseng 2011). In attempting to estimate the effect of the loss of CDEP positions, the next section assumes that CDP participation is equivalent to being unemployed for the person in question.

Given that Forrest (2014) reports that there were 35,000 participants in the new scheme, it might be reasonable to assume that many of the 35,000 former CDEP positions have resulted in the participants becoming unemployed. However, it is the explicit intention of the policy reform that former CDEP participants should find mainstream employment. It is difficult to gauge from available data exactly what has happened, but the following section reports some unique data from the 1990s to provide a foundation for the estimation of the impact of the demise of the CDEP scheme.

Evidence on transitions from CDEP from the Indigenous Job Seeker Survey

In order to estimate the extent to which CDEP participants find mainstream jobs, it is necessary to collect longitudinal data. The Australian Census Longitudinal Dataset (ACLD) links data for almost 15,000 Indigenous people identified in the 2006 and 2011 censuses. This new longitudinal data set allows for a representative analysis of some labour force transitions for Indigenous Australians (ABS 2013c). Unfortunately, this analysis cannot document the effect of changes in the CDEP scheme as the ACLD does not include information on it. Therefore, in order to estimate labour force transitions of former CDEP participants one has to consider other non-representative longitudinal data.

In the 1990s, the only large-scale longitudinal data on Indigenous Australians was the Indigenous Job Seeker Survey (IJSS). Gray and Hunter (2005) use the IJSS to show that Indigenous unemployed were around half as likely to move to employment over a 15-month period as were the non-Indigenous unemployed. However, the IJSS also allows analysts to distinguish between CDEP participation, unemployment and non-CDEP employment and hence it provides potentially unique insights.

Hunter, Gray and Jones (2000) provide a detailed introduction to the survey methodology. The survey was conducted using face-to-face interviewing, predominantly involving Indigenous interviewers. Interviews were conducted by Roy Morgan Research who worked collaboratively with Indigenous organisations in each region. One important feature of the IJSS was that jobseekers were eligible for inclusion if they resided within reasonable travelling distance from a mainstream labour market, with the aim of excluding jobseekers who would be limited to CDEP scheme employment. Postcode areas that fell more than 100 km from the city or town centre were excluded to limit interviewer travel costs.

The IJSS is not entirely satisfactory data to estimate what might happen to former CDEP participants as many of the 35,000 former CDEP participants lived in areas that were more than 100 km away from a town. Another limitation for this evidence is that it is based on relatively few observations (65 males and 25 females). Nonetheless, the IJSS provided some evidence that CDEP participation was associated with some transitions into mainstream employment if opportunities for such employment existed (a condition that is implicitly assumed by the designers of the policy). Despite the limitations of the IJSS data, it arguably provides an optimistic estimate of the labour market possibilities of former participants that can be contrasted to the more pessimistic scenario that none of the former participants find employment.

Table 3.1 reports disaggregated labour force transitions for Indigenous males and females over a 15-month period between 1996 and 1997 (Gray & Hunter 2005). In general, CDEP scheme participants had slightly better transitions to full-time and part-time employment than Indigenous persons identified in the IJSS as unemployed. This is consistent with the claim that CDEP prepared participants by providing experience that is useful in mainstream jobs.

The transitions from CDEP into employment are much closer to the average transitions into employment for the Australian unemployed (Gray & Hunter 2005: Table 4) than Indigenous unemployed measured in the IJSS (Table 3.1). While this provides an optimistic assessment of the possible transitions for former CDEP participants, it is consistent with what is observed for non-Indigenous unemployed (at least, as measured in the second half of the 1990s).

In order to operationalise these data, I average the approximate transitions by constructing a weighted average of the male and female data. In the IJSS about 31 per cent of former CDEP participants found mainstream jobs (i.e. including both full-time and part-time jobs), while around 29 per cent stayed in CDEP and just over 24 per cent became unemployed jobseekers. The residual 16 per cent moved out of the workforce altogether and were then classified as not in the labour force (NILF).

Clearly, most CDEP participants did not live close to urban areas, and even where they did the labour force outcomes in the IJSS might not eventuate (see Chapter 4). Nonetheless, while I acknowledge the limitations of these data, they provide some basis for an estimate of the optimistic scenario of what might happen to former CDEP participants.

Table 3.1 Transition probabilities (15-month) between labour force states, Indigenous males and females (percentage)

Labour force status at wave 1	Labour force status at wave 3					
	Full-time employment	Part-time employment	CDEP	Unemployment	NILF	Number of respondents
Males						
Full-time employment	48.8	6.8	5.3	29.0	10.1	207
Part-time employment	22.7	26.7	4.0	33.3	13.3	75
CDEP	27.7	4.6	26.2	26.2	15.4	65
Unemployment	16.2	5.8	3.7	55.2	19.0	431
NILF	6.9	3.4	4.3	37.1	48.3	116
Females						
Full-time employment	49.1	12.7	3.6	12.7	21.8	110
Part-time employment	28.8	28.8	2.4	16.0	24.0	125
CDEP	16.0	12.0	36.0	20.0	16.0	25
Unemployment	8.9	8.9	2.7	39.3	40.1	257
NILF	5.3	9.5	1.8	13.6	69.8	169

Note: The population in this table is respondents who completed the questionnaires for all three waves of the IJSS. The transition probabilities represent the probability of being in a particular labour force state at the wave 3 interview given labour force status at wave 1. The bold entries represent the probability that CDEP participants in wave 1 are in various labour force states in wave 3 (e.g. 27.7 per cent of male CDEP participants found full-time employment by the time that the wave 3 survey was collected). The transition probabilities in each row add to 100 (i.e. excluding the number of respondents in the last column).

Source: Gray & Hunter (2005: Table 2), from IJSS.

Estimating the potential effect of the demise of CDEP

While longitudinal data on labour force status is scarce for Indigenous Australians, there is a substantial amount of cross-sectional evidence available about outcomes for CDEP participants and other labour force states. Hunter and Gray (2013) described the nature of CDEP employment in 2008 and the extent to which it changed between 1994 and 2008. They concluded that CDEP work had remained largely unchanged over that period with virtually no change in the number of hours worked or the income of people employed through CDEP (adjusted to take into account changes in the consumer price index).

Other important evidence from the cross-sectional data presented in Hunter and Gray (2013) is that CDEP appeared to give some support for Indigenous language and customary practice by providing economic activity that allowed participants to live on or near their traditional country. However, the evidence that participation in CDEP improved community development through reducing discrimination or enhancing a sense of personal efficacy in important community issues is weak. Indeed, having a job is probably more important for enhancing the sense of personal efficacy in the community rather than whether or not one's job is associated with the CDEP scheme.

More important in the context of this volume, Hunter and Gray (2013) also compared a selection of economic outcomes of CDEP participants with those of Indigenous people who were non-CDEP employed, unemployed or NILF. While the incomes of CDEP participants had not increased substantially between 1994 and 2008, their incomes were higher than those of both the unemployed and NILF at both points in time. However, over this period the income of the non-CDEP employed increased rapidly and hence the incomes of CDEP participants fell relative to the incomes of the non-CDEP employed. There are several reasons for these findings. First, CDEP participants qualified for additional income above their income support entitlement in the form of a CDEP 'participant supplement'. In 2008, this was $20.80 per fortnight. Second, historically, the income test applied to CDEP payments was more generous than the income test applied to income support payments (e.g. Parenting Payment, Newstart), and CDEP wages were not subject to the same 'taper' as unemployment benefits.

(That is, CDEP participants could earn substantially more additional income over and above their base payment than social security recipients, without that base payment being reduced.)[2]

It is very difficult (or impossible) to identify the causal impacts of participation in CDEP on the well-being of participants compared with other Indigenous people. This is because we do not know what their well-being would have been were they not participating in the scheme (i.e. the counterfactual). The approach taken in this chapter is to compare the outcomes of CDEP participants with people in other labour force states.

Hunter and Gray (2013) estimate the association of labour force status (CDEP, non-CDEP employed, unemployed and NILF) with selected well-being measures using multivariate regression models. The regression models allow the associations between labour force status and well-being to be estimated while holding constant the effects of other variables that might impact upon well-being independent of labour force status. That analysis updates similar estimates by Hunter (2009) of the associations between labour force status and well-being using the 2002 National Aboriginal and Torres Strait Islander Social Survey (NATSISS). The only differences in the measures of well-being analysed here to those analysed by Hunter (2009) are that the earlier study examined substance use, which is not available from the 2008 NATSISS data; and Hunter and Gray (2013) include a measure of living in a low-income household—a measure not examined in the 2009 study.

Three main sets of outcomes are analysed in Hunter and Gray (2013) and reported in Table 3.2 below. The first set relates to crime and safety: whether respondents have been arrested, whether they live in a violent neighbourhood, and whether they have been a victim/survivor of crime. The second set of variables comprises financial measures: whether respondents have experienced financial stress and have a low household income. The third variable relates to health: whether respondents have fair or poor health. Another outcome that was analysed in the Hunter and Gray regressions was whether

---

2   From July 2009 the rules changed so that while new CDEP participants could still work part-time (in addition to their CDEP commitments), their CDEP payment was reduced in line with the standard 'taper' for income support payments. However, it is not entirely clear how these rule changes were implemented in practice.

a person was studying.[3] However, it is not reported here as there was no difference in the probability of studying from either those who were employed through CDEP or those who were NILF.

Table 3.2 Marginal effect of CDEP and other labour force categories on selected social and economic outcomes, 2008

	Marginal effect (difference from unemployed)			
	CDEP (%)	Non-CDEP employed (%)	NILF (%)	Base probability for unemployed (%)
Arrested	-5.8**	-13.1***	-5.6***	21.1
Violent neighbourhood	-3.7	-6.1***	-7.2***	40.0
Victim of crime	-5.5*	-6.9**	-2.3	29.0
Financial stress	-6.3*	-25.1***	1.0	59.5
Low household income	-26.6***	-56.0***	-4.8*	65.5
Fair or poor health	-6.8**	-12.0***	8.5***	25.0

Note: The asterisks indicate statistically significant differences in the outcome variable for each labour force state compared to the unemployed. *** indicates a difference at 1 per cent level, ** a difference at the 5 per cent level and * a difference at the 10 per cent level.
Source: Hunter and Gray (2013: Table 6).

There were statistically significant differences in the social and economic outcomes of CDEP participants compared to the unemployed and those NILF. The CDEP-employed were 5.8 percentage points less likely to have been arrested than the unemployed, 5.5 percentage points less likely to have been a victim of actual or threatened physical violence, 6.3 percentage points less likely to have experienced financial stress, 26.6 percentage points less likely to live in a low-income household and 6.8 percentage points less likely to report having fair or poor health status. While CDEP participants had better outcomes on a range of economic and social measures than the unemployed, CDEP participants had much worse outcomes than the non-CDEP employed for all of the social and economic outcomes analysed.

3   Disability was also included in Hunter and Gray (2013), but is not reported here because the disability rates are not significantly different for CDEP and unemployed in 2008. Also, it is difficult to maintain that it is an outcome of labour force status, as disabilities tend to be long-term health conditions.

Although the data presented in this chapter are consistent with the hypothesis that CDEP participation had some small positive socioeconomic and health impacts, it could equally be the case that the slightly better outcomes for CDEP participants compared to the unemployed are because those who participate in CDEP have better outcomes prior to commencing on CDEP (i.e. there may be 'selection effects' on unobservable characteristics of individuals). While it is not possible to disentangle these alternative hypotheses using the available data, it is the case that the CDEP-employed have slightly better outcomes for most measures than the unemployed, and generally substantially worse outcomes than those for the non-CDEP employed. The estimates in Table 3.2 control for the main sociodemographic, geographic and educational factors measured in the survey.

In order to estimate the effect of the loss of 35,000 CDEP jobs, we need to make an assumption about the participants' effective labour force status after they leave the scheme. Table 3.3 is based on two scenarios: a realistic scenario based on what appears to be happening and an optimistic scenario based on labour force transitions described in the IJSS. The first scenario is based on the 35,000 former CDEP participants eventually all taking up the option of the new CDP scheme, which is ostensibly equivalent to the standard labour force category 'unemployment'. The second 'optimistic' scenario is that a substantial proportion of these former participants either secure mainstream employment or move out of the labour force altogether. One reason why it could be characterised as being excessively optimistic is that most remote labour markets are likely to have relatively few jobs available. This second scenario is based on the IJSS labour force transitions, which are the only Indigenous-specific longitudinal data that could be used. The eventual outcome may lie somewhere between the two scenarios, but probably closest to the realistic scenario.

Table 3.3 Hypothetical simulations of the 'effect' of loss of 35,000 CDEP jobs

	Realistic scenario (albeit pessimistic)	Optimistic scenario
	CDEP participants become unemployed	CDEP participants experience labour force transitions consistent with IJSS
Arrested	2,030	295
Violent neighbourhood	1,295	230
Victim of crime	1,925	1,048
Financial stress	2,205	-462
Low household income	9,310	2,965
Fair or poor health	2,380	1,554

Notes: The probability of each labour force state having a particular outcome is derived from Table 3.2. The estimated number of additional people experiencing the particular outcomes as a result of the loss of 35,000 CDEP jobs is calculated based on the respective scenarios.
Source: Prepared by the author.

Given that CDEP employment has been associated with positive outcomes, we should expect that converting those jobs into income support payments and unemployment will lead to considerable socioeconomic dislocation and stress. In all three domains represented in Table 3.3—interactions with the criminal justice system, income estimates and health estimates—at least 2,000 extra people are adversely affected in the conversion of those places into unemployment. The largest impact of the demise of CDEP appears to be increasing the number of people living in low-income households. The *additional* number of people living in such households represents over one-quarter of the former participants (i.e. 27 per cent).

The optimistic scenario involves substantially less socioeconomic dislocation and stress. Indeed, the assumption that a substantial number of former participants find mainstream work could lead to a situation where there are actually fewer households experiencing financial stress. However, even this optimistic scenario is associated with substantially higher rates of arrest, violence and crime, more people living in low-income households and greater numbers of Indigenous people experiencing fair or poor health. Note that there is no contradiction between the estimated effect for financial stress and low-income households in that the substantially higher wages of those who are assumed to secure mainstream jobs are offset by the larger group who are assumed to be either classified as unemployed or leave the labour force altogether. Therefore, even in the most optimistic scenario, the demise of the CDEP scheme will have had substantial economic and social effects on the communities affected.

Introducing the CDEP schemes analysed

This section identifies and analyses organisations associated with CDEP schemes in the case study areas using data from the 2006 and 2011 censuses. During this period, changes to the scheme were profound in terms of the drop in the number of program participants and rule changes for both the program participants and the organisations providing the scheme. With respect to the organisations running the scheme, there was also considerable rationalisation around 2007, such that community-based schemes were now usually run at a more regionalised level. This regional model evolved out of the Department of Employment and Workplace Relations' contracting process, but presumably this decision was also made in anticipation of cost savings on relatively fixed administration expenses and other 'economies of scale' (Martin 2001).

Table 3.4 reports the names of the case study CDEP organisations in 2006 and 2011 and their numbers of participants, based on administrative data provided by the Department of Families, Housing, Community Services and Indigenous Affairs (FaHCSIA).

The first case study focuses on Anangu Pitjantjatjara communities where there were 10 discrete schemes participating in 2006. By 2011, those schemes were amalgamated and delivered by one organisation (Bungala Aboriginal Corporation) rather than the separate local community councils. In 2011, Bungala was also delivering CDEP to additional regions, such that interpreting the administrative data becomes difficult—that is, a judgement needs to be made about the proportion of Bungala's participants who were in the Anangu Pitjantjatjara region. Bungala advised that the number of participants in 2011 covered by the 10 communities in those original 2006 schemes was 400. Therefore the drop in the overall number of CDEP participants in Anangu Pitjantjatjara communities between 2006 and 2011 was almost 30 per cent (i.e. a drop from 568 to 400).

The Anmatjere case study focuses on the scheme run by the Anmatjere Community Government Council at the time of the 2006 census. By 2011, that scheme had been amalgamated with two other schemes, Yuendumu Community Government Council and the Yuelamu Community schemes, to form a larger CDEP organisation run by the Central Desert Shire Council. If the number of participants in the three 2006 schemes are aggregated, there are 272 people involved, but by 2011 the Central Desert Shire scheme had 316. This is a modest increase of 15 per cent, especially when one takes into account the likely population growth in the area. If the 2011 data are assumed to be based on geographic patterns from the 2006 administrative data, the estimated increase in number of participants in the area covered by Anmatjere Community Government Council CDEP in 2006 is around 16 per cent (i.e. from 120 to 139).[4] Of course, even this aggregate change in CDEP participation could mask some localised changes in CDEP participation.

The Maningrida case study is relatively straightforward in terms of the administrative data in that its CDEP scheme was run by the Bawinanga Aboriginal Corporation in both census years. Between 2006 and 2011, the number of participants fell by 23 per cent from 564 to 437. In terms of sheer numbers this is a noteworthy drop, especially after the likely growth in the resident population is taken into account.

The administrative data for the far south coast of NSW case study are somewhat problematic, in that the number of CDEP participants appears to have changed substantially around August 2006 (i.e. the official census date for that year). From 1 July 2006, Wallaga Lake CDEP Inc., which had historically delivered CDEP in the region, was dissolved and its CDEP activities taken over by OPEN Inc. When Wallaga Lake CDEP Inc. closed it had around 80 participants.[5] The numbers dropped substantially when the program was transferred to OPEN Inc., with administrative data recording 41 participants (see further discussion of this change in Chapter 4).

---

4   That is, the three communities with 2006 schemes were treated more or less equally in terms of the allocation of participants. Therefore the 316 places in the Central Desert Shire scheme in 2011 are distributed in proportion to the number of participants observed in the three 2006 organisations (i.e. (120/272) x 316 = 139).

5   Pers. comm. Richard Barcham, former manager at Wallaga Lake CDEP Inc.

Table 3.4 Administrative data on local CDEP schemes at time of 2006 and 2011 census (8 August)

2006 CDEP organisation	2006 participants	2011 CDEP organisation	2011 participants Raw 2011	Comparable with case study estimates
Anangu Pitjantjatjara case study				
Bungala Aboriginal Corp.	N/A	Bungala Aboriginal Corp.	628	
Amata Community Inc.	114			
Anilalya Council (Aboriginal Corp.)	107			
Mimili Community Inc.	62			
Watinuma Community Inc.	49			
Kaltjiti Community Aboriginal Corp.	48			
Pipalyatjara Community Inc.	47			
Iwantja Community Inc.	45			
Murputja Homelands Council (Aboriginal Corp.)	32			
Pitjantjatjara Homelands Council Aboriginal Corp.	32			
Watarru Community Aboriginal Corp.	32			
Total Anangu Pitjantjatjara case study	568			400
Anmatjere case study				
Anmatjere Community Government Council	120	Central Desert Shire Council	316	139
Yuendumu Community Government Council	113			
Yuelamu Community Inc.	39			

2006 CDEP organisation	2006 participants	2011 CDEP organisation	2011 participants	
			Raw 2011	Comparable with case study estimates
Maningrida case study				
Bawinanga Aboriginal Corp.	**564**	Bawinanga Aboriginal Corp.	437	**437**
Far south coast NSW case study				
Oasis Pre-Employment Network (OPEN) Inc.	**41**	NA	0	**0**

Note: In this table, Incorporated and Corporation are abbreviated to Inc. and Corp., respectively. All the data in this table refer to the number of participants as at early August in either 2006 or 2011 (i.e. on the respective census dates). The 2006 CDEP numbers in bold are those that are comparable to corresponding data for 2011.

Source: Participant data 2006 and 2011 from FaHCSIA.

Whichever number is emphasised for the far south coast of NSW, it is clear that no CDEP scheme operated there in 2011. Hence, the effect of CDEP reforms in 2007 on this regional area is likely to be more pronounced in 2011 than the effect in remote areas because there was in effect an almost 100 per cent loss of employment and services provided by former 2006 participants. The Wallaga Lake CDEP scheme had included participants from the broader region, especially Bega and Eden. However, given data limitations, this chapter focuses on the Wallaga Lake area itself. Wallaga Lake Koori Village is a relatively small and discrete community in the far south coast region so we would expect, all else being equal, that the effect of the loss of CDEP was relatively pronounced there.

Remote CDEP case studies

The administrative data for CDEP provide only limited insights into the effect of CDEP's decline in the case study areas examined in this volume. With the possible exception of Bawinanga, it is difficult to know how much the geographic scope of the organisation changed as a result of the reorganisation of the scheme from around 2007. Accordingly, I now turn to the census counts for 2006 and 2011 to describe what happened to the local populations in the case study areas relative to other remote areas. All 119 remote Indigenous Areas (IAREs) in Australia are included in the following analysis and I use the geographic boundaries for the areas used at the time of the 2011 census. Geographic concordance data is used to ensure that the 2006 census results reported refer to the statistics for the people who lived in those boundaries in 2006.

One advantage of using census data is to construct broad comparable results. The following analysis takes into account the extent of CDEP participation in 2006, well before the major changes to the scheme (especially the regionalisation of providers from 2007 and the shift away from CDEP wages from 2009). Table 3.5 reports the basic census counts of the working-age population (aged between 15 and 64) for the IAREs that contain the three remote case studies. In most of these areas, the census also records information on the number of CDEP-employed. Note that in 11 remote IAREs, no CDEP-employed were recorded in the census. This could indicate one of two things: first, and most probably, there was no CDEP scheme operating in the IARE, and second that CDEP-employed were not identified because that census information was not collected by interviewers in those areas.

It is somewhat reassuring that the counts of CDEP-employed people in the census are not too different from the number of participants recorded by the organisations administering the scheme (reported in Table 3.4). If we express the counts of CDEP-employed in the 2006 census as a percentage of participants recorded in FaHCSIA databases at a similar time (6 August 2006), then over 60 per cent of participants in the respective remote case study areas were counted in the 2006 census. Sometimes the coverage of CDEP participants is even higher, with almost nine-tenths of Anmatjere Community Government Council CDEP participants being counted in the 2006 census (88 per cent). This is remarkably close given that the counts do not take into account the significant tendency for census data to under-enumerate the Indigenous population (ABS 2012b). We can be reasonably confident that the coverage of CDEP participants is reasonably good in the three remote case study areas, at least in 2006.

In order to construct valid analysis of the case study areas with broadly comparable areas, I have divided the IAREs with some CDEP employment into those areas with less than 20 per cent of the working-age population employed in the scheme and those areas with 20 per cent or more of their population so employed. All three case studies fall in the latter category where CDEP employment is relatively prominent among the potentially economically active population. This allows us to make some rudimentary comparisons of the outcomes in the case study areas with other remote areas depending on the intensity of their initial participation in the CDEP scheme. Before examining the facts, we expect the case studies to be most like those IAREs with relatively high participation in CDEP schemes. Conversely, we expect the case studies to be least like the IAREs without any CDEP employment in 2006. That is, if an area had a substantial labour market then there would be less pressure to set up a CDEP scheme in the first place. The comparator groups for the case studies are listed in the first three columns of numbers. The CDEP comparator groups are evenly split into the less intense CDEP scheme areas where the effect of CDEP is likely to be relatively weak and the areas where the effect of CDEP is more likely to be pronounced.

Table 3.5 Working-age population (aged 15–64 years) and major mining investment in remote IAREs by 2006 CDEP employment rates in 2006

	No CDEP	CDEP areas		Case study areas		
		<20% CDEP in 2006	>20% CDEP in 2006	Anangu Pitjantjatjara	Anmatjere	Maningrida
Indigenous counts						
2006	401	458	511	1,168	483	1,232
2011	445	507	573	1,320	475	1,444
Non-Indigenous counts						
2006	4,251	1,874	294	262	82	129
2011	4,171	2,126	431	249	88	184
Proportion of IAREs with a major mining investment in 2012	36.4	20.8	9.6	0.0	0.0	0.0
Number of IAREs	11	53	52	1	1	1

Note: In order to make valid geographic comparisons over time, population concordances provided by the ABS are used to ensure that all data effectively refer to the residents in the area defined by the respective 2006 IARE boundaries. Earlier versions of this table included detailed breakdowns of labour force status and related outcomes. However, reservations about the reliability of census data on labour force status in remote areas (see above), means that it is more prudent to focus on the basic population counts. Notwithstanding, Altman and Hunter (1996) demonstrate using 1991 census data that CDEP communities tend to have substantially higher employment and labour force participation rates than non-CDEP communities.

Source: Census Tablebuilder. Data on major mining investments taken from Figure 1 in Hunter, Howlett and Gray (2014).

Table 3.5 is also useful for identifying distinctive features of the case study IAREs, which may make them atypical communities. Anangu Pitjantjatjara and Maningrida both have relatively large Indigenous populations with well in excess of 1,100 Indigenous working-aged residents in 2006. However, the IARE that includes the Anmatjere case study has similar counts of Indigenous residents to that reported in our three groups of comparator IAREs (listed in the first three columns). All three case study regions are strongly Indigenous and all have relatively few non-Indigenous residents in the working-age range. In terms of the comparator groups, only the 'CDEP intense areas' have a relatively small non-Indigenous presence.

When the 2006 census counts of CDEP-employed are expressed as a proportion of the working-age population (Fig. 3.2), the Anangu Pitjantjatjara case study was the most CDEP intense case study, with well over a third of the relevant population recorded as working in the scheme (35.3 per cent). All else being equal we would expect that any effect of CDEP reforms would be felt most keenly in this IARE. Given that the average proportion of the remote Indigenous working-age population employed in CDEP in the 2006 Census is around 24 per cent (i.e. excluding areas without any CDEP scheme), the participation in CDEP is reasonably typical in both Anmatjere and Maningrida (21.7 per cent and 28.1 per cent respectively).

Fig. 3.2 presents the relative frequency of IAREs with some CDEP jobs identified in the 2006 census. Note that the frequency distributions exclude the three IAREs being studied. All three of the case studies are in the range of distribution where CDEP employment is relatively prominent. Hence the case studies are well chosen, in that if we are to expect the changes in the CDEP scheme to affect anywhere, it will be those three areas.

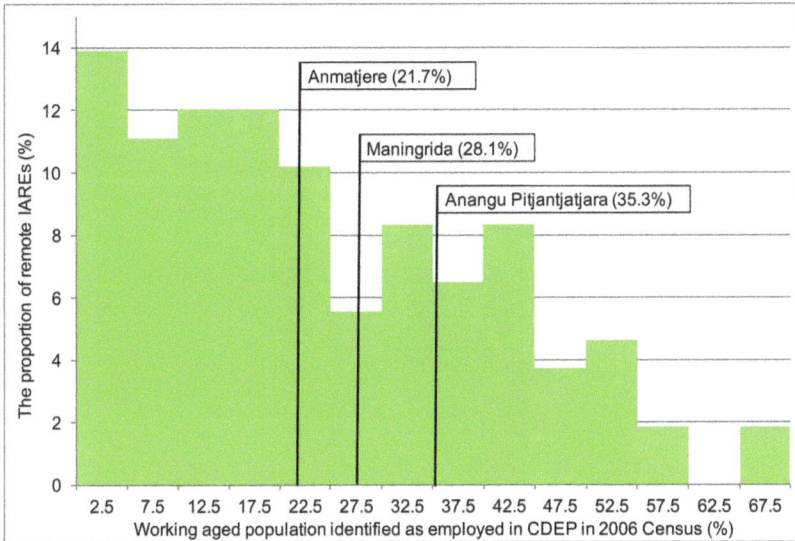

Fig. 3.2 The proportion of remote IAREs by per cent in CDEP employment in the 2006 census (%)

Note: This figure excludes remote areas without any CDEP employment.

Source: Tablebuilder cross-tabulations from the 2006 census.

The reduction in the number of places available in the scheme nationwide manifested itself in Fig. 3.3, which reports the analogous relative frequency of incidence of CDEP employment among the working-age population in remote IAREs in 2011 (again excluding the three case studies). The first thing that is evident in Fig. 3.3 is that over two-thirds of remote IAREs have less than 10 per cent of the relevant populations working in the scheme in 2011. In 2006, only around one-quarter of IAREs had a similar prevalence of CDEP employment. Clearly there was a substantial contraction in CDEP employment in remote areas between 2006 and 2011. By the time of the 2011 census, the Anangu Pitjantjatjara and Anmatjere IAREs had around 10 per cent of the working-age population working in the scheme (9.8 per cent and 12.8 per cent respectively), according to the census. The CDEP scheme in Maningrida appeared to be relatively successful in retaining its places as almost one-fifth of the census working-age population still indicated they were working in the scheme in 2011. Accordingly, we might expect to see less impact of the CDEP reform, at least in terms of the effect of the loss of CDEP scheme jobs to 2011, in the Maningrida IARE.

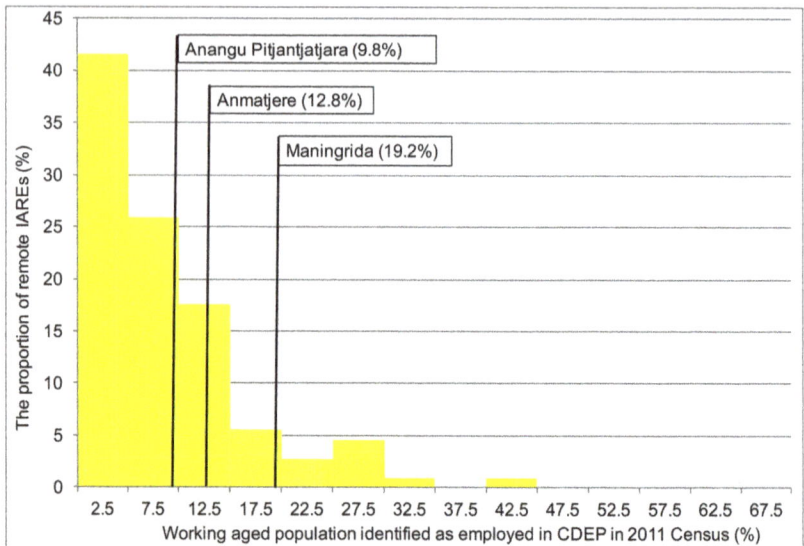

Fig. 3.3 The proportion of remote IAREs by per cent in CDEP employment in the 2011 census (%)

Note: This figure excludes remote areas without any CDEP employment.

Source: Tablebuilder cross-tabulations from the 2011 census.

Figs 3.2 and 3.3 are based on census data on the level of CDEP scheme employment, which proved difficult to reconcile with the number of CDEP scheme participants in the administrative data provided in Table 3.4. The issue was especially pronounced in the 2011 census data for Anangu Pitjantjatjara areas, which may partially explain the apparently large fall in the CDEP/population ratio for that case study between 2006 and 2011. As documented above, the possible confusion about the treatment of CDEP in ABS collections around the time of the 2011 census means that the measured change in reported labour force status could be unreliable. Notwithstanding, the CDEP scheme is prominent in both censuses and the three remote case study areas will reflect the issues for CDEP intense areas.

As speculated above, CDEP may be more likely to be found in areas where there is little alternative employment. One of the major employers of Indigenous people in remote areas has been the mining sector. Hunter, Howlett and Gray (2014) demonstrated that areas with relatively high levels of mining were likely to have relatively positive outcomes for Indigenous people in both the labour and housing markets (although there was some evidence of housing stress among low-income renters). The level of mining activity in our case studies is negligible compared to other remote IAREs. Table 3.5 reports the percentage of areas with major mining investments in 2012 valued at over $50 million. There appears to be a consistent tendency for the labour demand associated with mining to be higher in IAREs with less reliance on CDEP schemes. That is, there may have been an implicit trade-off between the number of jobs available outside the CDEP scheme and need to establish CDEP schemes in the first place. Certainly, the three remote case studies analysed in this volume have little access to major mines and hence the labour market alternatives to CDEP employment are likely to be rather limited.[6]

Case study in the far south coast of NSW

The far south coast case study is different from the remote case studies in several crucial ways. First, being located in 'outer regional' NSW it is more accessible to adjacent areas and towns.[7] There is more scope for short-run mobility or even commuting to nearby areas with substantial labour markets (as long as one has access to affordable transport). Also, it may be easier to maintain social connections in the home community if a person migrates to a nearby town for work. The IARE geography used for the remote case study is not appropriate for setting the statistical context for this non-remote case study, in that there are two larger IAREs nearby and the data will be dominated by the large numbers of residents in the more populous areas. The number of jobs in the IAREs near Wallaga Lake is substantial with around 66 per cent of all working-age residents in the Bega Valley and Eurobodalla areas recorded as employed in the 2006 Census. The employment ratios declined by just over 5 percentage points in these areas. While the labour market is substantial in the far south coast, any changes in Indigenous employment outcomes must be viewed in the context of declines in the local labour market.

---

6   This observation is consistent with earlier evidence in Altman and Hunter (1996) that non-CDEP communities tended to have higher rates of private sector employment than CDEP communities. Table 3.5 shows that at least some of this employment differential is likely to be in the mining sector in more recent censuses. One caveat on the observation about mining employment is that Jordan (2011) identifies a mine that employed eight local people in the Aṉangu Pitjantjatjara region.

7   As classified by the ABS (2011c) remoteness classification.

Rather than use an inadequate geographic level to analyse the local context, the following analysis uses the next level down in the ABS Indigenous geography, Indigenous Locations (abbreviated to ILOCs, as in ABS publications). While the population in ILOCs are more geographically homogenous, the number of residents tend to be very small and hence the capacity for detailed analysis is circumscribed.

The previous section compared the case study areas to all other remote areas by taking into account the level of CDEP employment identified in the 2006 census. However, it is not possible to take into account the level of CDEP employment in non-remote areas, because no such information is identified in the census. Accordingly, there is no natural comparator for the far south coast of NSW case study and hence this section focuses only on the Wallaga Lake ILOC in this region. The boundaries of the Wallaga Lake ILOC changed significantly between 2006 and 2011. In order to make valid geographic comparisons over time we again use population concordances provided by the ABS to ensure that all data effectively refer to the residents in the area defined by the 2006 Wallaga Lake ILOC boundaries.

Wallaga Lake community, unlike all the surrounding ILOCs, is a predominantly Indigenous community with relatively few non-Indigenous residents. Indeed, in 2011 there was no non-Indigenous person employed full-time in the community. Given the small populations involved, Table 3.6 focuses on basic count data and a few estimates of labour force status.

Table 3.6 Labour market outcomes for 15–64-year-olds by Indigenous status, Wallaga Lake, 2006 and 2011

	Indigenous		Non-Indigenous	
	2006	2011	2006	2011
Counts aged 15–64	70	59	28	15
Employment/population ratios (%)	31.4	8.5	39.3	33.3
Unemployment/population ratios (%)	15.7	16.9	10.7	20.8
Labour force participation rates (%)	47.1	25.4	50.0	54.1

Note: Apart from the counts, all statistics in this table are measured as a proportion of the working-age population counts. The labour force participation rate is equal to the sum of the employment/population ratio and the unemployment/population ratios. The reference to labour force participation rates, but not employment and unemployment rates, is intentional. In the standard labour economics literature, the terms employment and unemployment rates are usually expressed as a proportion of the labour force and not as a proportion of the working-age population. The unemployment/population ratios are based on relatively small cell sizes, that may be affected by the ABS practice of confidentialising small area data, especially the non-Indigenous unemployment data in Wallaga Lake. This data should be treated with caution.

Source: ABS Tablebuilder for the 2006 and 2011 censuses.

The first thing evident in Table 3.6 is that Wallaga Lake was a small community that appeared to become smaller, at least in terms of the working-age population. Population level data often adjust for the undercount or the propensity to not count certain groups in the population. Indigenous people have historically been identified as a group with a high undercount, but population adjustments to correct for this tendency are not available for ILOC or even IARE levels, hence it is impossible to calculate the local Estimated Residential Population. Unless the undercount rate increased dramatically over time, the Wallaga Lake population fell substantially between 2006 and 2011.[8] The population decline is most marked in the non-Indigenous census counts, falling by almost half in this period (i.e. from 28 to 15).

One possible reason for population decline is an economic shock such as the closure of the local CDEP scheme. Another explanation might be the rise of community conflict in the community that encouraged some residents to leave. The census estimates indicate that the employment rate collapsed after 2006, and by 2011 only 8.5 per cent of the Indigenous working-age population were employed. The employment ratio for the non-Indigenous population appeared to hold up somewhat better, but the population leakage means that the effective number of employed halved in that five-year period.

One possible response to the loss of CDEP jobs among Indigenous residents who remained in Wallaga Lake was to leave the labour force altogether. The labour force participation rate of the working-age Indigenous population was cut almost in half, from 47 per cent to 25 per cent. The Indigenous unemployment ratios have stayed largely unchanged with around one in six of the working-age population being unemployed in both 2006 and 2011. Wallaga Lake was a disadvantaged community in 2006 and remained so in 2011. While it is not reported in Table 3.6 to save space, all households in

---

8   It is also possible that the local population fluctuates naturally in coastal communities in the short term, but the census data is consistent with a substantial population decline in this period.

the community (both Indigenous and non-Indigenous households) were in the lowest category of (equivalised) household income in both census years.

In summary, like the remote case studies, Wallaga Lake community was heavily dependent on CDEP for providing jobs. All the case studies in this volume will provide substantial insights into the significant loss of CDEP employment on the local communities.

Concluding comments

Overall, the above evidence indicates that the remote case studies are broadly representative of communities with substantial concentrations of CDEP employment. Furthermore, there is sufficient CDEP engagement and changes in the numbers of CDEP participants over time (after taking into account population growth rates) to reasonably expect some socioeconomic change resulting from the changes in the rules and organisation of the schemes. In a sense, the above analysis provides a rationale for and a validation of the choice of organisations and areas covered in the case studies. The administrative data also illustrate the dynamic nature of the organisations that managed CDEP and provide an indication of the challenges that are faced in comparing organisations whose nature and scope changed at regular intervals.

One might expect the far south coast of NSW case study to be more affected by the changes to CDEP than the remote case studies in the intercensal period, in that CDEP schemes retained a significant presence in the latter but disappeared completely in the former. Outcomes there may provide some indication of what might happen in remote areas now those schemes have been closed down completely.

CDEP or similar programs can have substantial effects of boosting the local economy. Mouda (2001) argued that it was essential for CDEP organisations to exploit any economies of scale so that their activities could contribute to the local economy (also see Nalliah 2001). While the rationalisation and amalgamations of CDEP organisations that took place around 2006–07 make it difficult to analyse administrative data, it would be a mistake to completely ignore the potentially lower costs associated with the economies of scale of larger organisations, and associated trade-offs, if those savings were to be realised. However, consideration of such matters is left to the case studies whose in-depth analysis is better suited to providing the context necessary to understand the trade-offs involved than the statistical context presented in this chapter.

References

ABS (Australian Bureau of Statistics) (2011a). *Labour force characteristics of Aboriginal and Torres Strait Islander Australians, estimates from the Labour Force Survey*, 2010, cat. no. 6287.0, ABS, Canberra.

ABS (Australian Bureau of Statistics) (2011b). *Census dictionary, Australia, 2011*, cat. no. 2901.0, ABS, Canberra.

ABS (Australian Bureau of Statistics) (2011c). *Australian Standard Geographical Classification*, cat. no. 1216.0, ABS, Canberra.

ABS (Australian Bureau of Statistics) (2012a). *Labour force characteristics of Aboriginal and Torres Strait Islander Australians, estimates from the Labour Force Survey*, 2011, cat. no. 6287.0, ABS, Canberra.

ABS (Australian Bureau of Statistics) (2012b). *2011 Census of population and housing – details of undercount, Australia*, cat. no. 2940.0, ABS, Canberra.

ABS (Australian Bureau of Statistics) (2013a). *Australian social trends*, Nov 2013, cat. no. 4102.0, ABS, Canberra.

ABS (Australian Bureau of Statistics) (2013b). *Labour force, Australia*, Jun 2013, cat. no. 6202.0, ABS, Canberra.

ABS (Australian Bureau of Statistics) (2013c). *Information paper: Australian Census longitudinal dataset, methodology and quality assessment, 2006-2011*, cat. no. 2080.5, ABS, Canberra.

Altman JC, Gray MC & Sanders W (2000). Indigenous Australians working for welfare: what difference does it make? *Australian Economic Review* 33 (4), 355–62.

Altman JC & Hunter B (1996). *The comparative economic status of CDEP and non-CDEP community residents in the Northern Territory in 1991*, CAEPR Discussion Paper No. 107, Centre for Aboriginal Economic Policy Research, The Australian National University, Canberra.

Borland J & Tseng Y (2011). Does 'Work for the Dole' work?: an Australian perspective on work experience programmes. *Applied Economics* 43 (28): 4353–68, DOI: 10.1080/00036846.2010.491457.

Forrest A (2014). *The Forrest review: creating parity*, Commonwealth of Australia, Canberra.

Gray M, Howlett M & Hunter B (2014). Labour market outcomes for Indigenous Australians. *The Economic and Labour Relations review*, 25(3): 497–517 DOI: 10.1177/1035304614545943.

Gray M & Hunter B (2005). The labour market dynamics of Indigenous Australians. *Journal of Sociology*, 41(4): 389–408.

Gray M, Hunter B & Howlett M (2013). Indigenous employment: a story of continuing growth. *Topical Issue 2/2013,* Centre for Aboriginal Economic Policy Research, The Australian National University, Canberra.

Hunter B (2009). A half-hearted defence of CDEP scheme. *Family Matters* 81: 43–54. aifs.gov.au/publications/family-matters/issue-81/half-hearted-defence-cdep-scheme.

Hunter B & Daly A (2013). The labour supply of Indigenous Australian females: the effects of fertility and interactions with the justice system. *Journal of Population Research,* 30(1): 1–18.

Hunter B & Gray M (2013). Continuity and change in the CDEP scheme. *Australian Journal of Social Issues*, 48(1): 35–56.

Hunter B, Gray M & Jones R (2000). *An analysis of data from the longitudinal survey of ATSI job seekers, topic 1: labour market participation patterns and pathways to employment*, Report to the Department of Employment, Workplace Relations and Small Business, Centre for Aboriginal Economic Policy Research, The Australian National University, Canberra (archived at pandora.nla.gov.au/tep/39721).

Hunter B, Howlett M & Gray M (2014). *The mining boom and Indigenous socio-economic status*, Working Paper 93, Centre for Aboriginal Economic Policy Research, The Australian National University, Canberra.

Jordan K (2011). *Work, welfare and CDEP on the Anangu Pitjantjatjara Yankunytjatjara Lands: first stage assessment*, Working Paper No. 78, Centre for Aboriginal Economic Policy Research, The Australian National University, Canberra.

Martin D (2001). Community development in the context of welfare dependence. In Morphy F & Sanders W (eds), The Indgineous Welfare Economy and the CDEP Scheme, CAEPR Research Monograph No. 20, ANU E Press, Canberra.

Mouda R (2001). A part of the local economy: Junjuwa Community/ Bunuba Inc., Western Australia. In Morphy F & Sanders W (eds), The Indgineous Welfare Economy and the CDEP Scheme, CAEPR Research Monograph No. 20, ANU E Press, Canberra.

Nalliah S (2001). Adequate funding as a question of equity: Lake Tyers Aboriginal Trust CDEP, Victoria. In Morphy F & Sanders W (eds), The Indgineous Welfare Economy and the CDEP Scheme, CAEPR Research Monograph No. 20, ANU E Press, Canberra.

Sanders W (2012). Coombs' bastard child: the troubled life of the CDEP scheme. *Australian Journal of Public Administration,* 71 (4): 371-9.

4

Just a jobs program? CDEP employment and community development on the NSW far south coast

Kirrily Jordan

Introduction

Discussions about Indigenous public policy often focus on remote areas. However, the role and influence of Commonwealth-funded programs like the Community Development Employment Projects (CDEP) in more densely settled Australia is no less profound. The far south coast of NSW was one of many regional areas where CDEP was closed in 2007. For some observers, the justification for this was sound: CDEP had never been intended for regional or urban locations and was not warranted because Indigenous residents of these areas lived within reach of mainstream labour markets. If CDEP was simply an employment program, it was argued, participants would do better without CDEP wages, getting support instead from mainstream employment services to find alternative jobs. It was this kind of reasoning that was used to justify many of the program changes outlined in Chapters 1 and 2.

The story on the far south coast, however, is much more complicated than this reasoning allows. Since CDEP closed there have been some gains in mainstream employment, but they are small. The reasons why more non-CDEP employment has not eventuated are complex and warrant further investigation if policymakers are serious about wanting to improve outcomes there. Moreover, the closure of CDEP has had other consequences for Koori communities that demonstrate the much broader role that CDEP played in the region. Local residents implicate CDEP's closure in a range of ongoing concerns, including lost assets and services, closed businesses, reduced institutional capacity, fractured relationships and an enduring loss of morale. For these reasons, many Aboriginal people on the far south coast still see their communities as worse off since CDEP's decline.

This chapter investigates these concerns and the implications for future livelihoods of Aboriginal people in this region. It first briefly documents the history of CDEP in urban and regional Australia, identifying the factors that led to its expansion from 1987 and eventual decline to 2007. It focuses specifically on how CDEP was used on the NSW far south coast in this period, and the evidence of outcomes since the program's closure. The analysis suggests that defining CDEP as 'just a jobs program' was too narrow and that the social, community and economic development functions it could provide have never been adequately replaced. Moreover, the case is made that these social and community development functions were not peripheral to job outcomes but central to addressing some of the significant barriers to mainstream work.

One of the immediate consequences of closing CDEP on the far south coast was that its administering organisation, Wallaga Lake CDEP Inc., was dissolved. This is significant in itself because, as in many locations, the CDEP organisation had become much more than the provider of publicly funded services and taken on a broader role as a social and institutional actor in the region (see Rowse 2001; and Altman, this volume, for an institutional analysis of CDEP). It is also significant from a research perspective in that, unfortunately, very few written records from Wallaga Lake CDEP Inc. remain. Material for this chapter is therefore drawn from relevant secondary sources as well as a series of interviews and discussions undertaken during several visits between 2012 and 2015; these were with former CDEP participants, other Aboriginal residents in the region, and staff of Local Aboriginal Land Councils and mainstream employment services. While individuals are quoted here, no names or identifying characteristics have been included. This is to protect the anonymity of research participants who live in relatively small communities and where tensions surrounding the closure of CDEP are, for some, still felt deeply.

Social policy is always complex, and while many Aboriginal people on the far south coast want to see increased employment within their communities, some do now believe that CDEP was relied on too heavily, or for too long. Equally, however, they are unsatisfied with the current alternative, which sees many people unemployed long-term and finding little benefit from their interactions with mainstream employment services. This chapter suggests that rather than relying on an overly simplistic distinction between the needs of 'urban' and 'remote' Aboriginal people, policy settings for places like the NSW far south coast should be reconsidered in light of unique local challenges and opportunities. New strategies—based on genuine consultation and perhaps drawing on old ideas like a Community Employment and Enterprise Development scheme—are needed to support both increased employment and improved livelihoods for many Koori residents of the region.

CDEP in urban and regional Australia

Although CDEP was originally envisaged as a program for remote areas, from 1987 it expanded into regional and urban locations. This followed the 1985 Miller Review that highlighted what the review committee saw as successes of the program and recommended an exploration of 'its potential beyond the distinctive remote community context' (Miller 1985: 407; also see Appendix 1, this volume).

The Hawke Government's response to the Miller Review was the 1987 Aboriginal Employment Development Policy (AEDP). A key feature was the expansion of CDEP into non-remote areas with the aim of achieving employment equity between Indigenous and non-Indigenous people by the year 2000. Policymakers at that time saw participation in CDEP as a legitimate form of publicly funded employment and justified the program's expansion on several bases. First, they argued that in and around small country towns employment prospects for Aboriginal people were bleak because the agricultural employment base had virtually disappeared, and because common recruitment methods put Aboriginal people at a disadvantage:

> most job vacancies in such areas are either filled through personal contact with the employer (noting that there are few Aboriginal employers) or by the recruitment of staff from outside the local area (Australian Government 1987a: 5).

Further, they listed a number of reasons why 'some Aboriginal people living in urban and rural areas' were 'not able to compete for jobs in the open labour market', including 'the desire to work in an Aboriginal working environment, a lack of marketable job skills and discouragement due to entrenched long-term unemployment' (Australian Government 1987a: 5).

The AEDP was clearly framed around the notion that Indigenous people have a right to self-determination, and the policy approach—including the expansion of CDEP—was seen as supporting that right by ensuring efforts to attain employment equity were 'consistent with Aboriginal social and cultural values' and circumstances (Australian Government 1987a: 3). This again reflected a strong sentiment in the Miller Review that Aboriginal control over delivery of CDEP was one of the program's principal strengths. The review committee reflected positively on the control that Aboriginal people were able to exercise over CDEP, with 'the role of government officers being to facilitate decisions, rather than to dictate the options available'. They cautioned against governments 'using programs as a means to interfere and coerce people into action they believe to be appropriate' (Miller 1985: 363). Implicit in the review's recommendations was the notion that self-management would be equally productive in remote and more densely settled areas.

With CDEP's expansion following the introduction of the AEDP, the program operated in many non-remote areas for close to 20 years. As in remote locations, the non-remote CDEPs had a variety of functions including income support, enterprise development, employment creation, cultural production, institutional and financial support for self-management and investment in community infrastructure and equipment (see, for example, Australian Government 1987b; Altman & Sanders 1991; Altman & Smith 1993; Rowse 2002: 67; Smith 1995). However, as Chapter 2 identified, characterisations of the scheme changed dramatically during those 20 years, from a focus on supporting these multiple aspects of Indigenous social and economic development to a principal focus on transitioning participants into non-CDEP jobs. Briefly reflecting on those changes helps put the closure of CDEP on the NSW far south coast into this much broader, and highly contentious, context.

Praise for CDEP, and a growing focus on non-CDEP jobs

Major reviews in the early 1990s were largely favourable towards CDEP, including its operation in rural and urban areas (some of these reviews are further documented in Appendix 1). The 1991 Royal Commission into Aboriginal Deaths in Custody (RCIADIC) suggested that 'despite its shortcomings and considerable room for improvement, [CDEP] is one of the most successful programs presently operated by the government' (RCIADIC 1991: 437). It noted examples of 'successful' CDEP schemes supporting enterprise development, the construction of community infrastructure and a lessening of problems like alcohol abuse, violence and criminal behaviour. The Commission's recommendations for CDEP included that the government consider further expanding it '(or some similar program) to rural towns with large Aboriginal population and limited mainstream employment opportunities for Aboriginal people' (RCIADIC 1991: 439). This led the Australian Government to substantially increase the number of CDEP participant places.

In 1992, a parliamentary review into the specific needs of urban dwelling Indigenous Australians ('Mainly Urban') found CDEP 'proving of great value in rural towns' where there was intractable and structural Aboriginal unemployment (HRSCATSIA 1992: 114). In these and other non-remote areas there was evidence that it engaged participants in a wide range of productive activities as well as providing 'valuable social effects', including improved self-esteem within Aboriginal communities, increased school attendance among children, improved relations with non-Aboriginal people in country towns and a lessening of social problems associated with unemployment (HRSCATSIA 1992: 116). Like the Royal Commission it recommended increasing the coverage of CDEP, here suggesting a substantial expansion particularly into urban areas (HRSCATSIA 1992: 120).

Despite these mostly favourable reviews, concerns were raised relatively early on that CDEP could function to create a 'second' labour market in CDEP jobs while potentially institutionalising exclusion from mainstream employment (see, for example, Altman & Sanders 1991; Altman & Smith 1993). This was seen as problematic because, it was argued, jobs in the conventional labour market could better provide opportunities for higher wages and overcoming material poverty (Smith 1993). The Royal Commission, too, suggested there should be a clearer distinction between the aims of CDEP in different locations, with CDEP able to provide ongoing income support for 'subsistence' communities but focusing on mainstream employment, or establishing profitable enterprises, in other areas:

> It is especially important that means be devised to ensure that (unless the scheme is being used primarily as income support for a subsistence community) the CDEP scheme operates as a means to achieve a greater degree of self sufficiency, through the generation of employment in the public or private sector, or through the development of profitable enterprises (RCIADIC 1991: 439).

Ultimately, the Commission argued, CDEP should 'serve as a springboard to less artificial and more independent ways of improving the economic position of community members', with projects being 'a means to enhanced economic independence for Aboriginal people rather than simply becoming institutionalised as another form of welfare dependency' (RCIADIC 1991: 428). For these reasons, both the Royal Commission and 'Mainly Urban' reviews recommended sunset targets for CDEP—the former advocating for a sunset clause 'where enterprise development is the aim of a project' (RCIADIC 1991: 428) and the latter where the scheme 'is operating as a labour market program' (HRSCATSIA 1992: 120). In principle, these would have put a time limit on CDEP funding for some individuals.[1]

---

1   A one-year time limit was much later introduced for non-remote participants in July 2006 but, by the end of the 12 months, those non-remote schemes had been closed entirely in any case.

By the late 1990s, the argument that CDEP was institutionalising exclusion from mainstream employment was becoming increasingly influential, perhaps in spite of evidence that many CDEPs were by now effectively transitioning people into non-CDEP jobs. An assessment by the Aboriginal and Torres Strait Islander Commission (ATSIC) Office of Evaluation and Audit (1997)—focused especially on the outcomes of urban CDEP programs—found that individuals who had participated in urban CDEPs had better mainstream employment outcomes than a comparison group of non-Indigenous jobseekers registered with the then Commonwealth Employment Service. This indicated 'a positive impact of the urban CDEP on employment outcomes for its participants' (ATSIC Office of Evaluation and Audit 1997: i). However, the release of the so-called 'Spicer Review' of CDEP in the same year is sometimes seen as a turning point in the prevailing political attitudes towards the scheme. Overall it was supportive of CDEP and highlighted the wide range of personal, social, cultural and economic benefits that could flow from it. Nonetheless, it placed special emphasis on the need to equip participants for non-CDEP employment, and while it found 'many examples' where CDEP had enabled participants to move into mainstream jobs, it argued that:

> The overriding challenge is to ensure that, where possible, CDEP does not become a life time destination for all participants but provides a conduit to other employment options. While work that facilitates community development must remain an important part of CDEP, greater attention in the future must be given to meeting the needs of the individual participants in order that they acquire new skills to access new employment opportunities, where they exist (Spicer 1997: 4–5).

A 'dead end' for employment? The curtain call for non-remote CDEPs

The policy response following the Spicer Review included placing increasing emphasis on performance measurement of CDEPs, especially in relation to non-CDEP employment outcomes and the facilitation of skill acquisition suited to mainstream jobs (see Sanders 2001; Whitby 2001). These outcomes, after all, seemed the most easily measurable. From 2002, CDEPs in some regional and urban areas were also encouraged to become 'Indigenous Employment Centres'; these were to be focused specifically on transitioning CDEP participants into other jobs or employment assistance (Champion 2002). As noted in Chapter 2, this focus on mainstream employment outcomes became even more dominant after the dismantling of ATSIC in 2004, when CDEP was moved into the Department of Employment and Workplace Relations (DEWR).

The 'fit' between CDEP and the employment department may well have been uncomfortable; the former with its original list of broad, often intangible goals and the latter with a clear focus on getting more Australians into paid work. Nonetheless, Kevin Andrews, the minister then responsible for the employment portfolio, did publicly express support for CDEP even if only on the basis of job outcomes. As late as July 2006, he praised the scheme for substantially increasing the number of participants transitioned into mainstream employment, with over 3,500 people moving into non-CDEP jobs in the previous 12 months. This, he announced, represented a 135 per cent increase on the preceding year (Andrews 2006a). Again in October 2006, Andrews announced the scheme was 'performing strongly' on mainstream employment outcomes, including in urban areas, and while he was 'delighted with this result' he looked forward 'to even better results in the future' (Andrews 2006b).

Within a few weeks, however, the government's public pronouncements about CDEP had changed. Mal Brough, then Minister for Indigenous Affairs, declared that the scheme needed to be further overhauled 'so that it does not continue to be a dead end for people where there are jobs available' (Brough 2006). On 6 November 2006, Kevin Andrews released the *Indigenous Potential meets Economic Opportunity* Discussion Paper in which he announced the government's intention to close CDEP in urban areas and major regional centres. Replacing CDEP with the Structured Training and Employment Projects (STEP) brokerage service would 'increase the focus on placement directly into jobs taking advantage of the strong employment opportunities provided in these areas' (Andrews 2006c).

This approach may seem contradictory given Andrews' earlier reflections on CDEP's employment success. According to DEWR, however, by replacing CDEP with the new STEP services job outcomes would be further improved.[2] Along with the closure of ATSIC, this new direction dovetailed neatly with the Howard Government's explicit rejection of self-determination as an appropriate policy framework for Indigenous affairs. Some government ministers argued that existing policies had encouraged separatism and entrenched the prolonged exclusion of Indigenous Australians from the market economy and 'normal' Australian life (see, for example, Brough 2006). Despite its move from ATSIC into DEWR, CDEP had remained a unique institution premised on the notion of Aboriginal and Torres Strait Islander people having distinct needs and, as such, was a clear target for 'mainstreaming' in line with the government's broader ideological approach.

In mid-2007, only three years after DEWR had taken responsibility for CDEP, around 60 urban and regional CDEPs were closed (Hunt 2008: 36). These were deemed to be in areas with strong labour markets, corresponding to unemployment rates of below 7 per cent. The closures directly affected around 6,000 people (Altman 2007: 1). Unfortunately, a government review of the impacts of closing CDEPs in urban areas in 2007 was terminated very shortly after it commenced, and no results have been publicly released (Steering Committee for the Review of Government Service Provision 2009: 4.71). Some evidence of the effects of closing non-remote CDEPs—garnered from questions put to a federal Senate committee—suggested that by March 2009, 40 per cent of former participants were receiving unemployment benefits. It was not known how many had moved into alternative employment or how many had exited the labour force. In the absence of more evidence at the national level, the remainder of this chapter focuses on local evidence from the closure of CDEP on the NSW far south coast.

---

2   STEP provided funding and assistance to employers to take on Indigenous staff. Assistance could include, for example, pre-employment training services, the development of Indigenous recruitment strategies, and post-placement mentoring services for Indigenous employees. It was envisaged that STEP could also provide 'community work activities', which would be similar to CDEP activities, for clients who were 'not ready for training or job placement' (DEWR 2006: 8).

CDEP on the NSW far south coast

In this chapter the far south coast of NSW is defined as the region from Eden in the south to Wallaga Lake, around 100 km to the north. The region therefore includes small coastal towns such as Bermagui as well as the larger inland centre of Bega. This definition reflects the way CDEP was organised in that, until 30 June 2006, CDEP in Wallaga Lake, Bega and Eden was run by a single organisation—Wallaga Lake CDEP Inc.—which provided central administration for work crews in each of the three locations.

The NSW far south coast

The 2011 census shows the Aboriginal and Torres Strait Islander proportion of the population of the far south coast to be slightly higher than the nationwide figure at the time (around 3.3 per cent compared to 2.7 per cent).[3] There are a number of locations where this figure increases substantially, including Bega (where, in 2011, 6 per cent of the population were Aboriginal or Torres Strait Islander), Eden (8 per cent) and Wallaga Lake (92 per cent).[4]

The very high proportion of people in Wallaga Lake who are Indigenous reflects the significant history of the area as an Aboriginal reserve. Established in 1891 by the NSW Aborigines Protection Board, the formation of the reserve at Wallaga Lake meant that Aboriginal people from coastal areas and inland through the Monaro Plain were brought together under the control of a state-appointed manager[5] (see Goulding & Waters 2005; Midlam 2011; White 2010). Almost 100 years after the Wallaga Lake Reserve was established, the 1983 passage of the NSW Aboriginal Land Rights Act paved the way for an end to

---

3   Census data for the whole far south coast region are here derived by adding the population counts for the Wallaga Lake Indigenous Location and Bega Valley Local Government Area. The data refer to place of usual residence; this is likely to count fewer Indigenous people than reflected in the Estimated Resident Population (ERP), but ERP also shows a higher-than-average proportion of the far south coast population who are Indigenous.

4   Indigenous Locations (ILOCs), place of usual residence.

5   The land for the Wallaga Lake reserve was set aside by the Aborigines Protection Board in 1891; in 1909 the passing of the *Aborigines Protection Act* allowed the board to segregate the Aboriginal population (White 2010).

the reserve system in that state: in 1984 the title deeds for the Wallaga Lake Reserve lands were transferred to the local Koori community (Midlam 2011).

Now known as the Wallaga Lake Koori Village the area is home to a fluctuating population usually between around 100 and 150 people. The village is managed by Merrimans Local Aboriginal Land Council, who act for Aboriginal people across a much larger geographic area; this includes Wallaga Lake and nearby coastal locations but also stretches over 100 km inland (Merrimans Local Aboriginal Land Council 2014: 8). The Koori communities in and around Bega and Eden are larger than at Wallaga Lake: in 2011 each of these two locations was home to around 230 Aboriginal people (ABS 2011). Both Bega and Eden have separate Aboriginal land councils. Along with Merrimans, the three land council regions comprise the traditional country of several Aboriginal groups; these include the Yuin in the coastal areas and the inland country of the Ngarigo-speaking people of the Monaro region.[6] Historically, the Monaro and Yuin moved across the region at various times, with coastal people travelling to the alpine areas during summer, and some tribes travelling to the coast during winter (Cruse et al. 2005; Hunt 2013: 8; White 2015). Throughout the region—and as far as Sydney, the north coast of NSW and parts of Victoria—strong kinship networks between Aboriginal communities remain, and there is significant mobility between these locations.

The relatively high Aboriginal proportion of the population in the far south coast region likely reflects, in part, a more general trend along the NSW coast in which European settlement tended to alienate inland areas before coastal ones (with the former initially deemed more economically productive because of a priority on agriculture, forestry and mining). This meant that land along the coasts was 'largely seen as not useful' and 'for a long time left vacant by settlers, enabling Aboriginal people to live or camp by the sea while remaining out of sight, and working in local industries' (NSW Office of Environment and Heritage 2012: 1).

---

6   For more information about the Aboriginal heritage of the region there is a significant published literature. See, for example, Chittick and Fox 1997; Donaldson 2006, 2008; Egloff, Peterson and Wesson 2005; Wesson 2000; White 2015.

For many years, Aboriginal people in this area worked seasonally as agricultural labourers, especially picking beans and peas (White 2010; see also Egloff et al. 2005; McKenna 2002). They were also heavily involved in fishing and maritime industries, both for consumption and commercial purposes, with Aboriginal involvement in commercial fishing dating back to at least the early 19th century (Egloff et al. 2005; NSW Office of Environment and Heritage 2012: 22; see also Cruse et al. 2005). By the early 20th century, many south coast Kooris were working for wages in these industries, or in commercial forestry operations (such as at saw mills) or as domestic workers (Feary & Donaldson 2011: 9).

It is often said that industries like agriculture, fishing and forestry suited Aboriginal people on the south coast well, allowing them to maintain access to country and continue to utilise and pass on traditional knowledge, as well as providing flexibility and supporting the maintenance of social and cultural relationships (see, for example, Cruse et al. 2005; Donaldson 2006; White 2010). For example, much of the work was seasonal and allowed families to work together and travel up and down the coast where they could camp on country and meet with other families travelling the same routes. Sue Donaldson (2006: 121) has argued that, for these reasons, work like seasonal farming jobs 'remained in keeping with the traditional transient, family oriented lifestyle maintained by many Aboriginal families' and 'encouraged the maintenance of kinship links and ensured cultural links to the land were maintained'.

Aboriginal employment in agriculture, forestry and fishing declined very substantially in the late 20th century. Demand for Aboriginal labour fell as these industries themselves went into decline, coupled with increasing mechanisation (Donaldson 2006; Hunt 2013; White 2010). At the same time, increased access to town housing and social security payments may have reduced the supply of Aboriginal workers for these jobs (White 2010). The implications of these changes are ongoing: apart from employment in CDEP, Aboriginal employment on the far south coast has remained low, with consequences not only for peoples' financial position but also for opportunities to maintain social and cultural relationships and connections to some parts of their country (see Hunt 2013; NSW Office of Environment and Heritage 2012: 31).

CDEP on the NSW far south coast

CDEP was introduced to the NSW far south coast around 1989 when the Wallaga Lake Koori Village opted into the scheme. This was only five years after the title deeds for the Wallaga Lake Reserve lands had been transferred to Aboriginal ownership and, interestingly, around the same time that CDEP arrived in the much more remote Maningrida region, as detailed in Chapter 7.

Setting up a CDEP scheme at Wallaga Lake also meant establishing an administering organisation there—this initially comprised just a CDEP manager and was first run from the manager's home. An administering organisation with an Aboriginal board was subsequently incorporated as Wallaga Lake CDEP Inc. In the context of CDEP rolling out into urban and regional areas, the Wallaga Lake scheme came relatively early, with the program opened to non-remote locations only from 1987. By that time, local industries—especially those that had a history of employing Aboriginal people—had started to decline and unemployment in the region was rising.

According to those involved at the time, when the Wallaga Lake CDEP was established it had around 30 participants, but this grew to around 50 participants within the first six months. Other communities on the far south coast had initially been sceptical about the scheme, but by the early 1990s they were also keen to come on board. By 1995 new schemes in Bega and Eden were amalgamated with Wallaga, with a work shed and work crew in all three areas. The combined total of up to around 120 people was initially administered centrally from Wallaga Lake (and later from Bega).

Those working for CDEP were employed in a range of work projects, many of which incorporated formal training and some of which brought a commercial return. The scheme was used to support several enterprises including the Umbarra Cultural Centre (just outside Wallaga Lake community), which sold locally produced arts and crafts, maintained a small museum for visitors, ran boat tours on Wallaga Lake and 4WD tours on nearby Gulaga mountain. CDEP was also used to establish a number of additional small enterprises, including commercial cardboard recycling, lawn mowing and a firewood scheme that serviced both Aboriginal and non-Indigenous residents of the south coast. The firewood enterprise, for example, meant negotiating a contract with Forests NSW to harvest firewood from State Forests and on-sell it to retailers. It required CDEP participants to be formally trained in first aid and licensed to use chainsaws for tree falling. As well as generating significant commercial returns, this enterprise facilitated the free delivery of firewood to elderly Aboriginal residents of the region. Firewood and lawn mowing crews operated from Bega, Eden and Wallaga Lake, with cardboard recycling run from Eden. The self-generated funds allowed industrious workers to earn top-up over and above their standard CDEP wages, as well as giving some workers the opportunity for promotion to supervisor.

Other activities provided essential services for the Wallaga Lake Koori Village—such as rubbish collection, burial services and yard maintenance. Still others at Wallaga Lake were centred on exploring the commercial potential of possible enterprises in oyster farming and furniture making, as well as projects geared towards self-sufficiency (with CDEP running a substantial market garden including two paddocks and a purpose-built dam).

In Bega, Eden and Wallaga Lake, activities also included opportunities for on-the-job training (such as through housing construction projects), subsidised work placements and the completion of formal qualifications and licensing requirements—the latter usually for driving vehicles or operating machinery. Subsidised work placements were made in Local Aboriginal Land Councils and Shire councils (e.g. providing administrative support) and as Aboriginal Education Officers in public schools. From 1999 women began participating in CDEP activities, sometimes in tailored programs (such as sewing and catering or subsidised work placements like office administration) and sometimes in the male-dominated activities like firewood harvesting and building construction. Several participants moved off CDEP into other paid jobs (including with Shire councils and Forests NSW); this will be returned to later in this chapter.

In creating economic development opportunities and supporting a range of community services, the scheme also invested in substantial capital and equipment that could be used for community benefit. This included tractors, trucks, a boat, chainsaws and log splitters, as well as land that was intended for development to bring a commercial return.

The way CDEP was managed sought to match local realities on the far south coast, reflecting one of the original aims of CDEP as supporting self-management. For example, participants were rostered on for two days per week but flexibility allowed them to split those hours over four days, swap to a different two days, or add an extra two days for top-up. Work crews were allocated to each of the various CDEP activities, with participants rotating through the different jobs over time to multiskill. Where one work crew needed assistance for a particularly large job, another could travel from a satellite location to provide support.

This flexibility was an important element of the scheme, differentiating it from more 'mainstream' employment in several ways. For example, it allowed a changing balance of work and other commitments as peoples' needs and family responsibilities fluctuated. This often sat more comfortably with local availability for paid work than the requirements of a full-time job, and formed somewhat of a continuum with the way Aboriginal people had engaged seasonally and flexibly in fishing, agricultural labour and cultural activities in earlier generations. Some local people point to the opportunity for communal types of work and training as particularly beneficial for Aboriginal jobseekers. According to one Aboriginal resident of the region:

> The grandparents could all work together as a community, so they could still do cultural stuff together. But [before CDEP] the next generation couldn't do that—they had to find individual work. Some did, but not the majority.
>
> (local Aboriginal resident)

Significantly, CDEP was also an Aboriginal workplace where supervisors were better able to understand the needs of their workers than many non-Aboriginal employers. In addition, it allowed participants to earn an income without exposing themselves to what has long been perceived as widespread racism towards Aboriginal people in the region. Training was often conducted 'on the job' rather than in classrooms, with many participants having had negative experiences of classroom learning in the past. A number of people on the far south coast remember CDEP as providing an opportunity to work together in an environment of understanding and peer support:

> With CDEP the manager was always well known in the community. So they knew peoples' issues and could work with them.
>
> (former CDEP participant)

> People got a lot of training out of it [CDEP]. Now, even if a course is offered, people have to go on their own. It used to be a big group of them would go, so they could help each other if they couldn't read or write.
>
> (local Aboriginal resident)

In these ways CDEP allowed what has previously been called an 'Aboriginalisation' of work (Altman & Smith 1993: 7; Smith 1995: 6). On some accounts it was the 'most radical aspect' of the scheme (Altman & Smith 1993: 7), but on the far south coast the nature of the CDEP workplace as a 'self-determined space' became an attraction in itself for participants to turn up. By and large, it meant that CDEP was much better placed than many mainstream employers to engage Aboriginal people in work and training, given the particular economic and cultural characteristics of the region.

Many people involved in CDEP recall that as well as delivering the formal elements of the program in training and employment, the far south coast scheme had significant benefits for individual and community well-being. For example, it is a common recollection that CDEP helped to bring the Koori communities of the south coast together in a way that had not happened for some time before, easing tensions in relationships between families and providing opportunities for shared goals and activities. Many people also argue that encouragement to engage in CDEP, within a supportive and productive environment, created a sense of pride and enthusiasm among participants and helped some people 'get off the grog', stop using drugs and—for those previously engaged with the criminal justice system—avoid a return to jail. Because it could offer guaranteed work, CDEP could also support supervised prisoner release.

> It was deadly with CDEP, beautiful. Before that people were getting the dole, drinking and partying. But then [with CDEP] people started getting paid, working, and that was good. It was good times for the kids … there was jobs everywhere.
>
> (former CDEP participant)

Such recollections of CDEP among former participants are remarkably similar to the views documented in several reviews of the scheme discussed earlier in this chapter, as well as in previous case study research. Diane Smith's research in urban Redfern in the mid-1990s found that CDEP was not only an 'economic endeavour' but also 'part of a social process which is pre-eminently Aboriginal' and an important part of the Aboriginal community's social fabric (Smith 1995: 6). The ATSIC Office of Evaluation and Audit review that focused especially on urban CDEPs found that the program brought 'a strong sense of pride and hope' to the community, partly because services were delivered 'within a self-governing framework' (ATSIC Office of Evaluation and Audit 1997: ii). It also found that 'tangible and objective benefits' of the scheme included 'significantly higher incomes, lower alcohol consumption, lower number of police arrests, and higher cultural identification' among CDEP participants as compared to unemployed Indigenous people, and argued this had important implications for addressing the increasing incarceration rates and 'cultural alienation' of Indigenous people in urban Australia (ATSIC Office of Evaluation and Audit 1997: ii).

Winding up Wallaga Lake CDEP Inc.

After more than 15 years of CDEP on the far south coast, the mid-2000s saw it draw to a close. On 1 July 2006, administration was transferred from Wallaga Lake CDEP Inc.—a local Aboriginal organisation with an Aboriginal board—to Campbell Page, which was a not-for-profit company tasked with delivering the Australian Government's Job Network and other employment services.[7]

Although it was generating a significant amount of its own income, Wallaga Lake CDEP Inc. was informed by DEWR that it would not be able to trade beyond 30 June 2006, and that it would be wound up as a corporation. A liquidator was appointed to sell off the corporation's assets and finalise its liabilities. The announced closure of Wallaga Lake CDEP Inc.—well before DEWR announced the intended closure

---

7   Trading then as Oasis Pre-Employment Network (OPEN) Inc.

of other non-remote CDEPs—took CDEP supervisors and participants on the far south coast by surprise. They were given only 15 days' notice of the change.

Campbell Page continued running the CDEP scheme until late 2007, when it became one of the 60 or so programs in non-remote locations that were closed—apparently because they were in regions with strong local labour markets.[8] In the year leading up to the closure, the directive from DEWR was that Campbell Page should prioritise moving CDEP participants into non-CDEP jobs wherever possible, and get CDEP activities that were generating a commercial return to a point where they could be sustainable without CDEP wages. Under Campbell Page all CDEP participants were placed with host employers, including with Local Aboriginal Land Councils. In mid-2007, a performance review criticised the lack of conversion from hosted placements to non-CDEP jobs, and advised the scheme would be closed. Although there is still confusion among local residents about why CDEP was transferred to Campbell Page and then terminated, some believe that giving it to Campbell Page was principally a way for the government to 'contract out' the scheme's closure and the inevitable contestation it generated. The next sections explore what happened when CDEP closed on the far south coast of NSW, and the ongoing implications for Aboriginal people in the region.

The employment implications of closing CDEP on the far south coast

When Wallaga Lake CDEP Inc. closed it had around 80 participants; around 40 to 50 of these were transferred to Campbell Page in July 2006.[9] Although this figure is not directly comparable to the census data collected in August 2006, it does indicate that a significant proportion of the paid employment of Aboriginal people in the region was in CDEP. That is, the census recorded 77 Aboriginal people

8   Few records from this time have survived and recollections about the exact date CDEP closed diverge. There is some evidence though, in the form of employment separation certificates, that CDEP employment was terminated for all participants by January 2008.

9   The figure of 80 participants is based on the recollections of the then manager of Wallaga Lake CDEP Inc., Richard Barcham. Unfortunately, administrative records from this time have not survived. Some participants exited voluntarily after the scheme changed hands, and a significant number of listed participants never turned up to work for Campbell Page. The government's administrative data for August 2006 record 41 participants registered with Campbell Page (see Chapter 3), but those involved in the scheme at the time recall that there were closer to 50.

resident in Bega, Eden or Wallaga Lake who were employed.[10] Hence it is reasonable to assume that a very large proportion of paid Koori workers at that time were employed in the CDEP scheme.

The closure of Wallaga Lake CDEP Inc. was experienced by many local people as sudden and unexpected, even if it had been decided in government circles for some time. And although DEWR asked Campbell Page to subsequently move as many participants as possible into non-CDEP jobs, no participants had found alternative work during the period of Campbell Page's management. This meant that when the Campbell Page scheme closed in late 2007 the immediate impact on employment was profound: almost all of the remaining 40 to 50 CDEP workers found themselves unemployed. The few exceptions to this included three men based in Eden who were able to retain a truck to keep the cardboard recycling enterprise going, and a skeleton staff of three people at Umbarra who kept the centre open for around 18 months without CDEP wages until available non-CDEP funds were exhausted. The cardboard recycling operation continued until around 2012, but was never able to employ more than three people in the absence of CDEP wages; under CDEP it had employed eight. Other programs, like land management crews that were subsidised via CDEP wages, became defunct (see Hunt 2013: 20).

The government's approach in closing CDEP on the far south coast seemed to be based on several assumptions. First, that transferring delivery of CDEP to Campbell Page would assist in transitioning participants into non-CDEP employment (in effect suggesting that the management of Wallaga Lake CDEP Inc. were responsible for low mainstream employment outcomes). With this first apparent assumption quickly proving false, the second was that employment outcomes would improve in the absence of the CDEP scheme. An immediate increase in unemployment was to be expected when the Campbell Page CDEP closed, but the policy intent was that mainstream job services would subsequently move those affected into other jobs.

In the absence of appropriate data tracking the outcomes for individuals, the census is the best statistical indicator of how Aboriginal employment rates in the region changed after CDEP's

10 Data from Community Profiles for Bega, Eden and Wallaga Lake Indigenous Locations, usual place of residence. It should be noted that, unlike in remote areas, the census in non-remote locations did not record CDEP employment separately.

closure. It should be noted, though, that the use of census data for this purpose should be treated with caution. There are introduced random errors to ensure confidentiality that can have a significant impact when the census count is small.[11] Nonetheless, the census does give an indication of broad trends in Aboriginal employment in the areas likely to have been most affected by the change.

Comparing census data for 2006 and 2011 in Bega, Eden and Wallaga Lake suggests there was an increase in the unemployment rate for Aboriginal people in the region (with data from the 'Community Profiles' publications showing an increase from 21 per cent to 36 per cent over the period). Breaking it down further to each of these three locations, Table 4.1 suggests that outcomes may have deteriorated least in Bega, and probably most in Wallaga Lake.

Table 4.1 Labour force characteristics for Bega, Eden and Wallaga Lake Indigenous Locations, Indigenous people aged 15–64 years, 2006 and 2011

	Unemployment rate (%)		Labour force participation rate (%)		Employment/ population ratio (%)	
	2006	2011	2006	2011	2006	2011
Bega	19	24	44	41	35	31
Eden	11	41	41	41	37	24
Wallaga Lake	35	60	54	25	35	10

Note: Data presented here are not adjusted for geographic correspondences.[12]

Source: ABS Census of Population and Housing, Community Profiles, place of usual residence.

---

11   For example, using the same census data sourced from two different ABS products—Tablebuilder and Community Profiles—varies the apparent 2006 unemployment rate for Eden ILOC by 12 percentage points, from 11 per cent (Community Profiles) to 23 per cent (Tablebuilder). This was the largest difference observed on any of the measures in Table 4.1, and is very likely due to the introduction of random errors. This means the data should be treated with caution and is indicative of broad trends rather than absolute measures.

12   Adjusting for correspondences is usually understood to improve the accuracy of intercensal data comparisons by accounting for changes in the geographic boundaries of statistical regions. The only significant difference this makes to data in Table 4.1 is for Wallaga Lake. The area included in the Wallaga Lake ILOC in 2006 was significantly smaller than the area included in the Wallaga Lake ILOC in 2011 (i.e. 14 per cent of what was the 'Eurobodalla remainder' ILOC in 2006 was added to the 'Wallaga Lake' ILOC in 2011; this was the area at the southern boundary of the Eurobodalla Remainder ILOC immediately adjoining Wallaga Lake). However, the 2006 Eurobodalla Remainder ILOC was a very large area extending as far north as Batemans Bay; the demographic profile of the Aboriginal residents in almost all of this region would bear little relevance to the closure of CDEP in Wallaga Lake. As such, including 14 per cent of the whole Eurobodalla ILOC in the 2006 Wallaga Lake ILOC is not likely to provide a clearer indication of the outcomes of Wallaga Lake CDEP's closure.

Of course, it is not possible to conclude that changes in labour force status are entirely due to the closure of CDEP. Other factors in the region include the continued decline of industries such as forestry and fishing that had been employers of Aboriginal people (most jobs in the region are now in service industries, especially health care and social assistance, retail and tourism). It is pertinent to note that non-Indigenous unemployment is also high, though according to the census the overall unemployment rate in the region declined slightly over the period from 7 per cent in 2006 to 6 per cent in 2011 (ABS 2006, 2011).[13]

Discussions with local residents suggest that most people who had been employed in CDEP on the far south coast have not since found stable employment. This is most obvious in Wallaga Lake, where the 2011 census shows only 10 per cent of Indigenous people aged between 15 and 64 years with paid jobs, and over two-thirds of people in this age group outside the labour force. This compares to the average of around one-third of the working-age population who had been employed in Wallaga Lake through CDEP at any one time.

Unemployment for younger Indigenous people on the far south coast remains especially high, at 52 per cent of 15- to 24-year-olds at the 2011 census, compared to 11 per cent for non-Indigenous people in the same age group (ABS 2011).[14] However, there are some recent employment programs that have been notable for employing young Aboriginal people, including 12 people trained, and six employed, at Woolworths, and 20 people accepted for 12-month construction-based traineeships with Brookfield Multiplex.[15] Increasing rates of high school completion bode well for further improvements in Aboriginal employment over time, as do additional planned initiatives such as Aboriginal owned and operated tourism services associated with the development of the Bundian Way near Eden (see Hunt 2013: 14).

---

13   These figures are for the Bega Valley LGA. Wallaga Lake ILOC is excluded due to data limitations, but given its small size this should not significantly affect the results. Correspondences are not necessary for LGAs unless local government boundaries change.

14   The geographic areas considered here are slightly different. The figures for Indigenous young people are derived from the Bega Valley LGA plus the Wallaga Lake ILOC, whereas the figures for non-Indigenous young people are derived from only the Bega Valley LGA. However, given the small size and demographic makeup of Wallaga Lake ILOC (92 per cent Indigenous), it can be assumed the two data sets are comparable.

15   Some of the participants in the traineeship program are from further afield, including Cooma and Batemans Bay.

Nonetheless, substantial challenges in improving Aboriginal employment outcomes on the far south coast remain. None of these challenges are easily resolved, but their presence well beyond the closure of CDEP shows that limited mainstream employment outcomes under the scheme cannot sensibly be attributed exclusively to its failings. Perhaps most fundamentally, major structural barriers have continued to frustrate employment outcomes, including the very seasonal labour market and the high unemployment rate that creates strong competition for limited local jobs.

Many in the Koori community point to continued discrimination from local employers as another significant problem. Although some believe this is slowly changing, it is often seen as an enduring barrier. Several participants in this study raised it as a concern.

> The majority of people who were on CDEP haven't got jobs. The main reason is that there are no jobs. The second reason is that if there are two people going for a job, and one is white and one is black, the white one gets the job.
>
> (former CDEP participant)

> Business owners make decisions based on stereotypes, and some family names have reputations, so those people find it hard. The business owner might have had one bad experience but then rely on stereotypes.
>
> (local Aboriginal resident)

> The older generations did bean picking. There was less racism then, good relationships with farmers ... There were restrictions then— they had to sit separately in the picture theatre, couldn't enter pubs, the kids couldn't go to the same school. So there were rules but at least they were known, overt. Now, the racism's covert ... it's much harder to deal with.
>
> (former CDEP participant)

This effect of discrimination on employment is summed up simply by one former CDEP participant:

> Being black has been a barrier to getting a job.

This view is strongly supported by some local job service providers. One provider, for example, has gone to the length of testing employer responses by asking an Aboriginal and non-Aboriginal person to approach the same employer on the same day and ask if they had any job vacancies. While the Aboriginal person was told there were no vacancies, the non-Aboriginal person was told there were three. According to a senior staff member at that job service provider:

> Racism's a fact. If we're going to be successful in placing people into employment, we need to acknowledge it.

Where job vacancies exist, access can also be limited for Aboriginal people in other ways. It is relatively common, for example, not to have a driver's licence or access to a reliable car. This is a particular problem for people at Wallaga Lake because the community is geographically separate from surrounding population centres and—since the CDEP bus stopped running—there is no public transport to local towns for job interviews or indeed for regular attendance at work.

> There's not much public transport to get to a job. You've got to have a car or you're stuffed.
>
> (local Aboriginal resident)

Research reported by the Australian Government's Department of Employment also suggests that a relatively high proportion of vacancies on the south coast are filled via informal methods—that is, they are filled through informal networks or direct approaches from jobseekers rather than public advertising to solicit applications (Neville 2014).[16] Interestingly, this is the same concern about recruitment methods in regional areas that the Hawke Government noted in 1987 in its AEDP. It is still the case that disadvantaged jobseekers are less likely to have the appropriate networks to be aware of these vacancies, and less likely to make successful direct approaches to employers where there is real or perceived discrimination.

Apart from the limited demand for labour and access to available positions, some people in far south coast Aboriginal communities can face additional challenges in securing paid work. While these factors are by no means universal, they can include limited experience of the requirements of formal employment, a discomfort in working in

---

16 Neville defines the far south coast more broadly to include the Shoalhaven, Eurobodalla and Bega Valley Shires. Data on recruitment methods are for the Illawarra Priority Employment Area for February 2014.

predominantly non-Aboriginal workplaces, a prioritising of family obligations and caring responsibilities and the implications of physical and mental health problems including substance abuse.

With such complex and multiple barriers to paid work being relatively common, an important question is whether CDEP helped or hindered mainstream employment participation. As noted at the outset of this chapter, over time notions of the 'success' or otherwise of the program were eventually reduced to this singular issue. On this subject there are differences of opinion among local Aboriginal people. Some argue that while CDEP was helpful to a point—particularly in providing training and work experience—it had become too much of a destination and did not do enough to try to move people into other jobs.

> The original aim of CDEP was great—to get them trained in CDEP and do small business (that was also about training), and we could have funded the best ones as permanent and used it to train others to move on to other jobs. But it became too much of a destination. We need to be self-sufficient and not rely on government funding.
>
> (local Aboriginal resident)

Others point out that CDEP helped people prepare for employment by getting necessary licences, and emphasise that some participants did move into mainstream jobs. Among people interviewed for this project, it was commonly argued that the participants who transitioned into alternative employment were the individuals with the right aptitude for non-CDEP work. The rest tend to be seen within two broad groups: those not suited to mainstream jobs because of major and enduring barriers to regular employment, or those who were best able to help their peers by remaining on CDEP as supervisors and role models for other participants.

> People got licences. Forklift, chainsaw, tree fallers, drivers' licences, plus upgrading them to light rigid and heavy rigid. That could help people get other jobs.
>
> (former CDEP participant)

> CDEP prepared the ones who were going to make it in other jobs well. Then there are the ones who were never going to get other jobs regardless. And you can see that many of them are still unemployed.
>
> (former CDEP supervisor)

On CDEP the ones that were able to would move into other work. But the ones not able to – there was nothing else for them. The best place for them was CDEP. Now they're just Stream 4 clients sitting at home doing drugs.[17]

(former CDEP participant)

Some of the older ones stayed on CDEP because they had the experience, they could show the younger ones what to do. The aim was to help young ones build respect and move onto other things. Respect their elders, watch what we do, get licences.

(former CDEP participant)

Making sense of divergent views about CDEP's effectiveness in assisting people into mainstream jobs can be difficult. However, some of the above quotes raise what is perhaps the most pertinent question in this debate: has the closure of CDEP improved the employment prospects of participants who had been in CDEP long-term (or other jobseekers with similar circumstances)? Most Aboriginal people consulted on the far south coast argue that such people are worse off now. For example, several believe that CDEP was more effective at engaging people in productive activity than the current system, which relies on Centrelink payments and job search assistance from mainstream employment services. It is commonly held that most people were eager to do their CDEP work, that 'no work no pay' was usually enforced, and that participants were able to model the benefits of active paid work to their children.

With CDEP we could work four days. And if we didn't turn up we got no money.

(former CDEP participant)

Wallaga Lake participants had to do their minimum hours. If they didn't turn up they got docked. It was unheard of in other places prior to those days, in the mid-'90s. We always stood by that and the participants accepted it. Because we said to them if you go out in the real world this is what will happen.

(former CDEP supervisor)

---

17   Under the mainstream employment service known as 'Job Services Australia', Stream 4 clients were those who had been assessed as being the most difficult to place into paid work.

> People saw CDEP as a job and wanted to go … It showed the kids there were opportunities.
>
> (former CDEP participant)

> Those two days [when they were rostered on], people were on the side of the street waiting for the bus to pick them up. And they were keen for extra days when they could get it.
>
> (former CDEP participant)

> People were really keen to be involved in CDEP, it was amazing.
>
> (former CDEP participant)

In contrast, there is a widespread concern that appointments with employment services (until 1 July 2015 called JSAs, or 'Job Services Australia') bring little benefit and that, post-CDEP, an increased proportion of people are now disengaged from productive activity or paid work altogether.

> You have to go in for your appointment [with the JSA] or you get docked, but they do nothing for you … CDEP got people off their butts and working better than the JSA does.
>
> (former CDEP participant)

> Critics said people were 'parked' on CDEP. But now they're parked nowhere.
>
> (local Aboriginal resident)

Many people consulted for this chapter argue that one of the reasons job outcomes have remained so challenging post-CDEP is that the scheme's closure exacerbated a suite of other problems that have made increasing employment participation much harder. Some of these— including reduced morale, increased lateral violence and a loss of local services—are discussed in the next section. To the extent that any deterioration on these measures has reduced peoples' capacity for mainstream work, the Australian Government's determination to separate the 'employment' goals of CDEP from its other community development functions was misguided.

The broader implications of closing CDEP in the region

Some of the most common concerns people have about the closure of CDEP on the far south coast are the broader effects on individual and community well-being. It is widely agreed that closing CDEP had a profound effect on the prevailing mood—while many people saw CDEP as a job and were usually keen to participate, they were enormously disheartened by the decision to close CDEP with no consultation and little explanation. Faced first with the forced removal of the program from community control and then the loss of employment, closure of enterprises, and pressure to return assets that were seen as belonging to the community, people felt both angry and disempowered.

> We got a call from DEWR Narooma ... He said let's meet tomorrow at Wallaga Lake. We walked into the hall with all these suits—they said 'We're closing CDEP as of now'—like within a week or two ... They had the JN [Job Network] and RTOs [Registered Training Organisations] there signing everybody up.
>
> People were dumbfounded. A few screamed out, 'What are we going to do?!' ... I was bitter.
>
> (former CDEP participant)
>
> On CDEP people had a purpose to get up and come into work. And they were looked up to in the community.
>
> (former CDEP participant)
>
> When people lost CDEP, they lost a lot of morale ... All across the state people have lost morale.
>
> (local Aboriginal resident)

Many people perceive that relationships have also deteriorated, both within Koori communities and between Aboriginal people and others on the far south coast. CDEP provided a forum for different families—and communities—to work together, as well as physical spaces for people to meet and talk in CDEP offices and sheds. There were clear work rules that any conflicts between individuals or families should stay outside work.

> We had to work together, so it kept the community together. We had to get to know each other. Now we don't see people from the other communities.
>
> (former CDEP participant)

Enterprises like lawn mowing and firewood delivery, as well as subsidised work placements with external employers, also provided opportunities for Aboriginal and non-Aboriginal people to interact in positive ways, which went some way towards challenging negative stereotypes.

It is a common perception that in the absence of CDEP—and with nothing to replace its role in mediating relationships—lateral violence among Aboriginal people on the far south coast has substantially increased. Lateral violence is sometimes referred to as 'internalised colonialism' and can include:

> [T]he organised, harmful behaviours that we do to each other collectively as part of an oppressed group: within our families; within our organisations and; within our communities. When we are consistently oppressed we live with great fear and great anger and we often turn on those who are closest to us (Frankland & Lewis, in Aboriginal and Torres Strait Islander Social Justice Commissioner 2011: 52).

As well as physical violence, lateral violence can involve bullying, shaming, family feuding and social exclusion (Aboriginal and Torres Strait Islander Social Justice Commissioner 2011: 54). While disputes between Aboriginal families and individuals did exist under CDEP, including disputes about whether particular families were benefiting more from the scheme, it is a common concern on the far south coast that all of these forms of lateral violence have increased since CDEP closed.

> The government stuffed everything up, divided us all. We were going to work, going shopping, it was going good. Now a big piece of the pie is missing.
>
> (former CDEP participant)

> We had riots here in 2011 [post-CDEP], partly because CDEP was the only thing that brought people together.
>
> (former CDEP participant)

Associated with reduced morale and increased lateral violence, many people suggest that after the closure of CDEP problems of substance abuse have also been exacerbated. Under CDEP there were strict work rules about not being under the influence of alcohol or other drugs on the job, which may have put a 'brake' on substance abuse. Now, it is a common perception among those consulted on the south coast that there has been an increase in reliance on drugs and alcohol. Some people also identify this as having increased the barriers to paid work:

> CDEP was creating jobs for the young ones—it was getting them off the grog.
>
> (former CDEP participant)

> People [who had been on CDEP] just went back to the dole, drink, drugs.
>
> (former CDEP participant)

> The young ones are getting into drugs and alcohol more now, where CDEP might have stopped it.
>
> (former CDEP participant)

> When CDEP closed people were angry and upset. The crime rate went up, alcohol. People had looked forward to work on CDEP, but then everyone went on Centrelink ... Now a lot of people don't want to work, there's too much grog and drugs.
>
> (former CDEP participant)

In addition to these personal and social implications, local people also point to the very significant effects of CDEP's closure on organisational capacity and service delivery. As already noted, when CDEP was transferred to Campbell Page, Wallaga Lake CDEP Inc. and its Aboriginal board were dissolved. Further, because the Local Aboriginal Land Councils in the region had all relied on CDEP labour to fulfil some of their functions, their capacity was substantially reduced. By hosting CDEP participants they had been able to access much-needed administrative support, employ cleaners for their offices and facilities, and provide local services like maintaining common areas and community assets. When CDEP closed there was no immediate alternative funding stream to continue many of these services, and some of the services have never been re-funded or revived. For example, although Merrimans land council has been able to employ a part-time administrative assistant, both Bega and Eden land councils have often had to fulfil their very wide-ranging functions as peak Aboriginal organisations with only one paid member of staff.[18] Eden land council has had long periods without a cleaner, and Merrimans has had very little funding to maintain common areas in Wallaga Lake Koori Village. As one staff member of an Aboriginal organisation describes:

> CDEP was good because we could bring people in for admin support and training for two days a week. We'd love to have it back. It also supported other Aboriginal organisations the same way.

The impacts of the closure of CDEP also extend to the loss of some other essential services. When CDEP stopped so too did the only regular bus service and individual rubbish collection for Wallaga Lake Koori Village. The CDEP bus that had taken residents shopping or to appointments could no longer operate. And for six months residents of the village were without individual rubbish collection as the local shire council would not send its trucks onto the privately owned roads. This meant that rubbish continued to pile up at the 35 houses until a resident with a vehicle could drive it the one kilometre out to the public road.

At the same time, not only did almost all of the CDEP enterprises close, but most of the CDEP equipment—including trucks and machinery— became unavailable for community purposes. Although many assets had been purchased, in part, with funds self-generated through the work of employees in CDEP enterprises, DEWR deemed that these were CDEP assets and should therefore be transferred to Campbell Page to continue running CDEP.

There are different recollections among those consulted for this study about which assets were transferred to Campbell Page. However, there is general agreement that the only large assets retained by Aboriginal organisations were the boat used for tours at Umbarra Cultural Centre and the truck used for the recycling enterprise at Eden. Proceeds from the sale of other large assets—including a land holding in Bega that was intended for development for community benefit—were withheld by the Australian Government. A portion of these proceeds paid off a

---

18   Eden Local Aboriginal Land Council has been able to employ project officers with special funding for the Bundian Way project, but they have no responsibility for assisting with normal land council functions.

tax debt Wallaga Lake CDEP Inc. had incurred, but there was a well-developed plan to pay off this debt through self-generated funds had the scheme not closed, and it remains unclear how much, if any, additional revenue the government retained after the sale.

> We had the car yard in Bega—half from self-generated funds, we'd bought the block. But they came and took the lot. We had approval for a subdivision and a buyer to recapitalise. But DEWR wouldn't let it happen.
>
> (former CDEP supervisor)

Some CDEP participants recall that DEWR requested all other items be returned—including lawn mowers, whipper snippers, chainsaws, metal-working equipment and even the diesel pump in the dam at Wallaga Lake that had helped irrigate the market garden. Many remain deeply disappointed that the vehicles, equipment and land they helped purchase through their own labour in CDEP enterprises were effectively lost to the community. Some describe the ongoing bitterness they feel when they see trucks that they worked hard to buy through CDEP now being driven by non-Indigenous people who purchased them at government auction. It is a common concern that many of the productive activities undertaken through CDEP cannot be done without new funding for equipment, even though there are willing workers.

> All the equipment—we needed it badly to keep businesses going. We had several trucks ... Some were from self-generated funds, but we couldn't touch them. No rights whatsoever.
>
> (former CDEP participant)

> With CDEP we used to do funerals ... but now we need a backhoe to dig graves. At the moment a contractor does it but it's expensive and unreliable.
>
> (former CDEP participant)

> The yard maintenance, lawn mowing, wood sales all stopped ... We wanted to keep the tractor, plough and slasher for the veggie garden, and for the old people, doing their yards and getting wood. But now these services are all gone. The cemetery's not mown. They should have left the equipment.
>
> (former CDEP participant)

Many of the issues canvassed here—including increased substance abuse, lateral violence and disengagement from productive activity—should properly be of concern in their own right. However, they also suggest that in helping to address these enormously complex issues, CDEP was likely assisting people to become more employable, even if the outcomes of this were slow and hard to measure and resulted in non-CDEP jobs for only a few.

Implications

This chapter shows that CDEP on the far south coast of NSW was never 'just a jobs program'. Defining it in this way, the government of the day overlooked the broader social, community and enterprise development functions of the scheme, as well as the intrinsic connection between improved social outcomes and individual capacities to participate in mainstream work.

The evidence presented here focuses on just one region where CDEP was closed. It is certainly possible there are other locations where the scheme's closure was experienced as an improvement. This is most likely in areas where CDEP had not been working well. Nonetheless, the far south coast of NSW is not the only regional location where the demise of CDEP has been implicated in deteriorating outcomes. Media reporting on the closure of CDEP in Toomelah in western NSW, for example, suggests that the aims of increased employment have not been met and the broad social and economic benefits of the scheme have been undermined. This appears to have had devastating results for local residents, who were not only faced with the loss of jobs but also the loss of essential services and increased material poverty, violence and crime (see Graham 2012).

There are other notable comparisons between Toomelah and the experience on the NSW far south coast. These include the problem of racism among potential employers in the surrounding region that limited job opportunities once CDEP closed, as well as the increased pressure on an overstretched local Aboriginal land council in the absence of the services CDEP had provided. Two cases can never be considered representative of the whole, but it is certainly reasonable to assume that along with Toomelah and the far south coast of NSW, there would be other regional and urban areas that have faced similar challenges with the loss of CDEP.

None of this should come as a surprise. Indeed, there was substantial opposition in the lead-up to the closure of urban and regional CDEPs from a wide range of stakeholders. Community organisations expressed concern that it would lead to 'disappointment, anger, lowering of morale, and disempowerment' (Redfern Residents for Reconciliation 2006; see also Graham 2012). Demonstrating the fickle nature of politics in Indigenous affairs, members of the Australian Labor Party (who would later oversee the closure of CDEP in remote areas) argued strongly against the change. Closing CDEP in urban and regional locations was, they maintained, ignoring 'the essential job it does for community development' (Snowdon 2006), and overlooking the way that CDEP's broader functions could target the causes of lower economic participation among Indigenous Australians (Evans 2006). For those reasons, Warren Snowdon (then Shadow Parliamentary Secretary for Indigenous Affairs) argued that treating CDEP as simply an employment program was a mistake (Snowdon 2006).

Nonetheless, the many challenges faced by CDEPs in transitioning participants into mainstream jobs apparently sealed their fate. How effective the far south coast scheme was on this measure is difficult to discern. Certainly, it directly helped some individuals find non-CDEP work. By offering training, work experience and support to get relevant licences—as well as more intangible functions like peer support, role modelling, and encouragement to stay 'off the grog'—it also ensured others were as well-equipped as possible to find alternative jobs. That said, many participants saw themselves as productively employed in CDEP and were content to stay in the scheme, and some faced such substantial barriers to employment that other options were not available. For most former participants, closing CDEP in favour of mainstream employment services has not led to sustainable non-CDEP jobs. They remain unemployed or outside the labour force, and on the far south coast it is widely believed that the welfare and livelihoods of those individuals—as well as their communities—have substantially deteriorated.

This suggests that the mainstream services currently on offer are inadequate for the needs of many Indigenous people, even in this densely settled area of the NSW coast. In the strong push for 'mainstreaming' of services, important elements of what CDEP was originally designed for—particularly its community and enterprise development functions—have been lost. If there are lessons here, they must surely include caution in choosing ideology over evidence, and a warning against seeking simple solutions to complex and multifaceted problems. But they also suggest that to improve the livelihoods of Aboriginal people in this region something beyond the current 'mainstream' is required.

This may necessitate a rejection of the overly simplistic division of Indigenous policy into 'urban/regional' and 'remote'. Policy decisions have too often been made on the assumption that there is a clear distinction between the needs and opportunities of Indigenous people in urban and regional areas from those in more remote locations. However, as Diane Smith argued more than 20 years ago, urban Aboriginal populations are diverse, and some may share characteristics 'more akin to remote communities' (Smith 1995: 13–14). This can be maintained for the far south coast of NSW where there is significant labour market segregation and a range of enduring demand- and supply-side barriers to mainstream employment. Indeed, many of the challenges facing urban and regional Aboriginal populations that were identified in reviews in the 1980s—including barriers to equal competition in the open labour market, the desire to work in a more 'Aboriginalised' work environment, and discouragement due to long-term unemployment—can equally be said for parts of the NSW far south coast in 2016. In the 1980s, recognition of these challenges encouraged the expansion of CDEP into urban areas; today, the persistence of these issues suggests that a specialised service approach is still required.

The need for tailored services is now compounded by discouragement from the last decade of 'top down' policymaking that has actively undermined local community institutions and initiatives. A scheme that many local people perceived as working well has been closed, and what were seen as community resources and equipment have been alienated. Among the people consulted for this study there is a pervasive belief that this is to the ongoing detriment of the Koori community. It is reasonable to assume that the reduced morale and enduring anger and frustration commonly identified have had flow-on effects for peoples' motivation to engage with mainstream institutions. Addressing these concerns will require a recommitment of governments to genuinely consult with Koori residents about their needs and priorities, and a renewed targeting of resources to support ground-up and community-based initiatives.

Many local people have a vision for their communities, and while they are actively seeking to improve outcomes, they are limited by a lack of support and resources. At Wallaga Lake, for example, a men's group has recently been established to voluntarily fulfil some of the functions of the old CDEP. With no regular source of funding, they successfully secured finances from the visiting drug and alcohol service to resurrect the badly dilapidated CDEP shed. Before work commences, however, they need to find funding for basic work gear like gloves and boots. According to one participant:

> The men's group's gonna be like CDEP but without funding and equipment.
>
> (former CDEP participant)

The community vision at Wallaga Lake also includes re-establishing Umbarra as an art and cultural centre, hopefully with a commercial return. Progress is stalled, though, because enterprise development now falls to the already overstretched land council, which has neither the resources nor the staffing to develop a business plan. At Eden, the land council has successfully secured support to develop a major cultural tourism project through development of the Bundian Way. There, too, however, progress has been slowed by limited resources. According to project officer Les Kosez, closing CDEP has made it more difficult to get development projects off the ground and create employment opportunity:

> If we had that [CDEP] program right now the development of the Bundian Way would be far more progressed ... Realistically we would have been in a position now where we could probably be moving boys completely off CDEP into sustainable employment with us where we are paying them from the generated income that we [would] have (in Brown 2015).

One option might include reviving something like the Community Employment and Enterprise Development scheme that, under the Hawke Government, provided capital grants to establish small community enterprises (which tend to be overlooked by Indigenous Business Australia), as well as the Enterprise Support Units that provided management support and technical advice. Such a grants scheme might also offer support to community development activities and social enterprises that are not likely to generate significant income, such as for capital equipment and recurrent non-wage costs. Grants would need to be multiyear to ensure sustainability. With this approach, mainstream employment service providers could contribute a portion of their existing funding (allocated to assist jobseekers find work) to link these projects to formal training.

An appropriate policy response would necessitate much further consultation with local Koori communities, who are best placed to identify local needs. But if governments are serious about improving outcomes for Aboriginal people on the far south coast of NSW, this may go some way to redressing what remains an ongoing policy failure.

References

Aboriginal and Torres Strait Islander Social Justice Commissioner (2011). *Social justice report 2011*, Australian Human Rights Commission, Sydney.

ABS (Australian Bureau of Statistics) (2006). *Census of population and housing*, Australian Bureau of Statistics, Canberra.

ABS (Australian Bureau of Statistics) (2011). *Census of population and housing*, Australian Bureau of Statistics, Canberra.

Altman J (2007). Neo-paternalism and the destruction of CDEP, *CAEPR Topical Issue No. 14/2007*, caepr.anu.edu.au/sites/default/files/Publications/topical/Altman_Paternalism.pdf.

Altman J & Sanders W (1991). The CDEP scheme: administrative and policy issues. *Australian Journal of Public Administration*, 50(4), 515–25.

Altman J & Smith DE (1993). *Compensating Australian 'losers': a community-oriented approach from the Aboriginal social policy arena*, CAEPR Discussion Paper No. 47, Centre for Aboriginal Economic Policy Research, The Australian National University, Canberra.

Andrews K (2006a). *CDEP 2006–07 to build on success*, media release, 1 July.

Andrews K (2006b). *Twice as many CDEP participants get jobs*, media release, 20 October.

Andrews K (2006c). *Indigenous employment discussion paper released*, media release, 6 November.

ATSIC Office of Evaluation and Audit (Aboriginal and Torres Strait Islander Commission) (1997). *Evaluation of the Community Development Employment Projects (CDEP) program: final report*, ATSIC Office of Evaluation and Audit, Canberra.

Australian Government (1987a). *Aboriginal employment development policy statement: policy paper no. 1*, Australian Government Publishing Service, Canberra.

Australian Government (1987b). *Aboriginal employment development policy: policy paper no. 3: community-based employment, enterprise and development strategies*, Australian Government Publishing Service, Canberra.

Brough M (2006). *Blueprint for action in Indigenous Affairs*, speech by The Hon. Mal Brough MP, 5 December, Canberra.

Brown B (2015). South East Aboriginal communities are falling through the disadvantage gap, *ABC South East NSW* [online], 24 February, www.abc.net.au/local/stories/2015/02/24/4186054.htm.

Champion M (2002). *Urban CDEPs as Indigenous employment centres: policy and community implications*, CAEPR Discussion Paper No. 228, Centre for Aboriginal Economic Policy Research, The Australian National University, Canberra.

Chittick L & Fox T (1997). *Travelling with Percy: a south coast journey*, Aboriginal Studies Press, Canberra.

Cruse B, Stewart L & Norman S (2005). *Mutton fish: the surviving culture of Aboriginal people and abalone on the south coast of New South Wales*, Aboriginal Studies Press, Canberra.

DEWR (Department of Employment and Workplace Relations) (2006). *Indigenous potential meets economic opportunity*, Discussion paper, Department of Employment and Workplace Relations, Canberra.

Donaldson SD (2006). *Stories about the Eurobodalla by Aboriginal people: public report, stage two Eurobodalla Aboriginal cultural heritage study*, Eurobodalla Shire Council, Moruya NSW.

Donaldson SD (2008). *Aboriginal men & women's heritage: Eurobodalla*, Eurobodalla Shire Council, Moruya NSW.

Egloff B, Peterson N & Wesson S (2005). *Biamanga and Gulaga: Aboriginal cultural association with the Biamanga and Gulaga National Parks*, Office of the Registrar, Aboriginal Land Rights Act 1983 (NSW), Sydney.

Evans C (2006). *Cut to Indigenous employment services a backward step*, media release, 6 November.

Feary S & Donaldson S (2011). *Connecting with Country in the Eurobodalla, south coast, New South Wales: exploring the connections between Aboriginal people, places and cultural practises*, report prepared for Eurobodalla Shire Council and the Aboriginal community, www.esc.nsw.gov.au/living-in/about/culture-and-heritage/heritage-items-and-places/Connecting_with_Country_Part_A.pdf.

Goulding M & Waters K (2005). *Eurobodalla Aboriginal cultural heritage study south coast New South Wales*, Eurobodalla Shire Council, Moruya NSW.

Graham C (2012) 'White trash mixed with black blood': The truth about Toomelah, *Chris Graham at large*, chrisgrahamatlarge.com/2012/07/04/white-trash-mixed-with-black-blood-the-truth-about-toomelah/.

HRSCATSIA (House of Representatives Standing Committee on Aboriginal and Torres Strait Islander Affairs) (1992). *Mainly urban: report of the inquiry into the needs of urban dwelling Aboriginal and Torres Strait Islander people*. Australian Government Publishing Service, Canberra.

Hunt J (2008). Between a rock and a hard place: self-determination, mainstreaming and Indigenous community governance. In Hunt J, Smith DE, Garling S & Sanders W (eds), *Contested governance: culture, power and institutions in Indigenous Australia*, CAEPR Research Monograph No. 29, ANU E Press, Canberra.

Hunt J (2013). *Looking after Country in New South Wales: implementing a Land & Sea Country Plan on the far south coast*, CAEPR Working Paper No. 90/2013, Centre for Aboriginal Economic Policy Research, The Australian National University, Canberra.

McKenna M (2002). *Looking for Blackfella's Point: an Australian history of place*, UNSW Press, Sydney.

Merrimans Local Aboriginal Land Council (2014). *Merrimans Local Aboriginal Land Council Community Land and Business Plan 2014 – 2019*, Merrimans Local Aboriginal Land Council, Wallaga Lake.

Midlam A (2011). A tale of three Missions, *Online Opinion*, 27 May, www.onlineopinion.com.au/view.asp?article=12098&page=0.

Miller M (Chairman) (1985). *Report of the Committee of Review of Aboriginal Employment and Training Programs*, Australian Government Publishing Service, Canberra.

Neville I (2014). *Labour market overview of the Far South Coast (Shoalhaven, Eurobodalla and Bega Valley Shire)*, Australian Government Department of Employment.

NSW Office of Environment and Heritage (2012). *Aboriginal people living and working on the NSW coast: A historical review*, NSW Office of Environment and Heritage, Sydney.

Redfern Residents for Reconciliation (2006). *Submission to the 'Indigenous potential meets economic opportunity' discussion paper*, www.redwatch.org.au/redw/cdep/061215rrr.

RCIADIC (Royal Commission into Aboriginal Deaths in Custody) (1991). *Royal Commission into Aboriginal Deaths in Custody: National report volume 4*. Australian Government Publishing Service, Canberra.

Rowse T (2001). The political dimensions of community development. In Morphy F & Sanders W (eds), *The Indigenous welfare economy and the CDEP scheme*, CAEPR Research Monograph No. 20, ANU E Press, Canberra, 39–46.

Rowse T (2002). *Indigenous futures: choice and development for Aboriginal and Islander Australia*, UNSW Press, Sydney.

Sanders W (2001). Adjusting balances: reshaping the CDEP scheme after 20 good years. In Morphy F & Sanders W (eds), *The Indigenous welfare economy and the CDEP scheme*, ANU E Press, Canberra.

Smith B (1993). Unemployment income support, the active society and AEDP. *Family Matters* (35), 22–24.

Smith DE (1995). *Redfern works: the policy and community challenges of an urban CDEP scheme*, CAEPR Discussion Paper No. 99, Centre for Aboriginal Economic Policy Research, The Australian National University, Canberra.

Snowdon W (2006). *CDEP changes: gutless approach, missed chances*, media release, 6 November.

Spicer I (1997). *Independent review of the Community Development Employment Projects (CDEP) scheme*, Aboriginal and Torres Strait Islander Commission, Canberra.

Steering Committee for the Review of Government Service Provision (2009). *Overcoming Indigenous disadvantage: key indicators 2009*. Productivity Commission, Canberra.

Wesson S (2000). *An historical atlas of the Aborigines of Eastern Victoria and Far South-Eastern New South Wales*, Monash Publications in Geography and Environmental Science No. 53, Monash University, Melbourne.

Whitby T (2001). Reforming the CDEP scheme. In Morphy F & Sanders W (eds), *The Indigenous welfare economy and the CDEP scheme*, ANU E Press, Canberra.

White J (2010). Peas, beans and riverbanks: seasonal picking and dependence in the Tuross Valley. In Keen I (ed.), *Indigenous participation in Australian economies: historical and anthropological perspectives*, ANU E Press, Canberra.

White J (2015). Reconstructing Aboriginal economy and society: The New South Wales South Coast at the threshold of colonisation. In Toner PG (ed.), *Strings of connectedness: essays in honour of Ian Keen*, ANU Press, Canberra.

5

Looking for 'real jobs' on the APY Lands: Intermittent and steady employment in CDEP and other paid work

Kirrily Jordan

Introduction

The principal justification for restructuring the Community Development Employment Projects (CDEP) scheme over the last 10 years, and eventually abandoning it, has been an argument that the availability of CDEP work has prevented the take-up of more favourable 'real jobs'. This chapter draws on evidence from the remote Anangu Pitjantjatjara Yankunytjatjara (APY) Lands in the far north of South Australia to argue that a binary distinction between CDEP and 'real jobs' is a fiction. This has important implications not just as a critique of past policy decisions, but also for designing future strategies to sustainably improve livelihoods for remote-living Anangu where recent policy directions are falling short.

Some of the concerns raised by Aboriginal residents of the far south coast of New South Wales (Chapter 4) have been evident in the APY Lands too, with rates of participation in CDEP activities falling as wages were removed from 2009, and Anangu worried that declining engagement in productive activity would see an increase in 'sit-down money' and attendant social problems. While these issues have been documented elsewhere (Jordan 2011), the analysis presented in this chapter moves beyond a focus on outcomes to explore why the dominant policy logic might have failed.

The exact features of 'real jobs' have never been clearly defined. However, commentators have contrasted them to a construction of CDEP as 'pretend jobs' that had no clear career path and perpetuated meaningless 'make work' activities (see, for example, Hughes & Hughes 2010; Pearson 2007, 2011). Implicit in this binary was the idea that instead of participation in CDEP that led nowhere and condemned Aboriginal participants to ongoing poverty and economic exclusion, 'real jobs' would engage Aboriginal people in the broader economy in a way that would substantially improve their well-being in both the short and long term.

Pitting conceptual notions of CDEP and 'real jobs' against each other in this way was a failure of logic for several reasons, which can be demonstrated for the APY Lands. Firstly, CDEP did facilitate the movement of some participants through the scheme and into other paid work. Secondly, while the number of participants exiting into regular salaried jobs was relatively small and retention rates were often low, insisting that this was due to a supposed disincentive effect of CDEP wages—in which the bulk of participants were discouraged from seeking out other employment because CDEP was a more comfortable option—overlooks the complex and intractable structural barriers to regular paid work across the APY Lands. Most of these barriers persist regardless of the name, design and rules of any employment program, such that the idealised notion of large numbers of Aṉangu participating in regular work routines for anything other than intermittent and casual wages remains elusive and is likely to do so into the future. This is still true despite the move away from CDEP and regardless of the kinds of employment services the government offers. Thirdly, and perhaps even more tellingly, the same intractable structural issues mean that many so-called 'real jobs' on the APY Lands end up looking much like the jobs that existed under CDEP.

The next section introduces CDEP on the APY Lands by summarising key events in its local history. The chapter then turns to an evaluation of the supposed binary distinction between CDEP and 'real jobs', arguing that such a distinction misrepresents and dramatically oversimplifies reality for the three reasons outlined above. The final sections seek to draw out lessons for future employment policy for the APY Lands, arguing that effective policy must be based on much clearer policy aims that emphasise improved livelihoods for Anangu rather than simply increased rates of non-CDEP employment. In addition, achieving better outcomes for Anangu requires more careful consideration of what motivates participation in different kinds of paid work and—fundamentally—a more genuine and sustained consultation with Anangu about what is required. Many Anangu hope that consistent, regular employment for Aboriginal people will increase across the APY Lands, and some have a vision of Anangu eventually running the services now almost universally delivered by outsiders. However, rather than blaming CDEP for slow progress, a more productive approach is to recognise the enormous complexity of the task at hand and listen, at the community level, to ideas about what works.

Putting CDEP on the APY Lands in context

When CDEP was first piloted in 1977, two of the earliest communities to receive it were Ernabella (Pukatja) and Fregon (Kaltjiti) in the remote far north of South Australia.

From these small beginnings, CDEP expanded to become by far the regions' biggest employer, extending into 16 communities and homelands on what are now known as the APY Lands.[1] By the early 1990s, CDEP in the APY Lands included more than 850 participants (O'Connor 2013: 140) out of a total estimated population of roughly 2,200 (South Australian Centre for Economic Studies 1994: 15). All of the larger communities and some small homelands had their own CDEP scheme, each administered separately through a local community council.

---

1   The APY Lands are Aboriginal-owned under inalienable freehold title under the *Anangu Pitjantjatjara Yankunytjatjara Land Rights Act 1981* (SA). The traditional owners of the APY Lands are Pitjantjatjara, Yankunytjatjara and Ngaanyatjarra peoples, often collectively referred to as Anangu. More than 2,000 Anangu live on the APY Lands in a number of dispersed communities and small homelands.

As elsewhere across Australia, CDEP on the APY Lands was subject to significant changes in its administration, delivery and expected outcomes, especially from the late 1990s. From around this time the government increasingly emphasised the need to transition CDEP participants into non-CDEP jobs. After 2004, when the administration of CDEP was transferred from the Aboriginal and Torres Strait Islander Commission to the Department of Employment and Workplace Relations, the pace of change increased. New rules included the introduction of a lower CDEP youth wage[2] and new job targets, a tightening up of payments (such as restrictions on 'top up') and a reorientation of the kinds of work people could do under the scheme to focus more on mainstream job readiness. On the APY Lands the number of CDEP providers was also reduced, from 16 in 2004 to only 10 in 2006. The number of participants declined from around 750 in 2004 to around 600 by 2007 (Paper Tracker 2011).

While APY communities were still adjusting to these substantial alterations to program delivery, another major change occurred when, in June 2007, the separate community-based programs were replaced by one single regional CDEP scheme for the whole of the APY Lands. The new regional contract was awarded to Bungala Aboriginal Corporation, a decision that was highly controversial at the time. Based in Port Augusta, Bungala had a long history of delivering CDEP elsewhere in the state, but no established formal connections with the APY region prior to 2007. The government's decision to remove control of the CDEP scheme from local community councils came at the same time as a significant defunding of those councils. Some people experienced the combination of these changes as a deliberate attack on Anangu self-determination. This was particularly so because a local organisation—Anangu Pitjantjatjara Services (now Regional Anangu Services Aboriginal Corporation)—had also bid for the regional CDEP contract.

Despite initial local resistance, over the next five years Bungala became a highly visible presence across the APY Lands. By 2011 it directly employed 24 non-CDEP staff in seven APY communities, including

---

2   The lower youth wage, introduced in 2006, was designed to reduce any disincentive effect for Indigenous youth in the hope that—if not offered the full adult CDEP wage—they might choose further education or low-paid non-CDEP jobs like apprenticeships or traineeships over CDEP participation.

on-site managers, CDEP work supervisors and mentors (only one of these staff was Aṉangu—this substantial underrepresentation of Aṉangu in permanent service provider positions is a common feature throughout the region). While policy changes during this period saw CDEP participant numbers continue to decline (detailed later in this chapter), Bungala remained the largest employer on the APY Lands, delivering CDEP to more than 400 participants across 11 communities and associated homelands.

Bungala's period of administering CDEP on the APY Lands corresponds to the most significant period under study in this book: the ultimate demise of CDEP after its 36 years in the region. For this reason, the chapter focuses on CDEP under Bungala's management, as well as reflections on the situation now that CDEP has gone. It draws on fieldwork undertaken between 2011 and 2015, including interviews and discussions with Aṉangu, as well as staff from Bungala Aboriginal Corporation, employment service providers, relevant government departments and several of the major employers of Aboriginal people on the APY Lands. It also utilises available administrative data.

Does the distinction between CDEP and 'real jobs' stack up?

The changes to CDEP over the last 10 years have been heavily influenced by arguments that contrasted work on CDEP to 'real jobs'. Among the most prominent commentators taking this position has been Noel Pearson, whose rhetoric singling out CDEP as distinct from the 'real economy' became very influential in subsequent critiques of the program as well as informing the dominant policy approach (see, for example, Cape York Institute for Policy and Leadership 2007; Hughes 2007; Pearson 2007; Hudson 2008; Stone 2008; Hughes & Hughes 2010).

Summing up his criticism in 2007, Pearson argued that CDEP had become part of a welfare economy that removed the incentive to work in return for financial reward, and that rather than being a 'stepping stone to a real job' in reality CDEP had 'become a permanent destination' (Pearson 2007). Although Pearson's comments lent moral authority to this position, here he was reflecting what had become an increasingly common argument from politicians and bureaucrats: that CDEP had become a 'dead end' (see, for example, Shergold 2001; Andrews in Yaxley 2005; Brough 2006). According to Pearson, reducing the rate and availability of CDEP payments and introducing mainstream employment services would shift a 'large group of people to work-readiness training that is more likely to lead to employment than the present CDEP' (Pearson 2007). While this became one of the most persistent and influential critiques of the program, this section outlines three reasons why such a categorical distinction between CDEP and other paid work was never appropriate and led to misguided policy decisions.

First, CDEP was, in fact, a pathway to other employment for some participants. Second, just like on the far south coast of NSW (Chapter 4), structural constraints that limited non-CDEP employment outcomes on the APY Lands persist well beyond CDEP, such that casting the program as a principal barrier to mainstream employment was too simplistic. And third, the notion of 'real jobs' was always idealised. That is, in important ways, many of the 'real jobs' on the APY Lands actually look very much like CDEP.

CDEP as a pathway to other employment

The original aims of CDEP had included direct publicly funded job creation in situ in remote communities, with the rationale being to accommodate the livelihood choices of remote-living Aboriginal people while minimising reliance on welfare. When CDEP was recast towards moving participants into unsubsidised employment from the late 1990s, some CDEP providers were criticised as 'backward-looking' and hanging on to the past in their reluctance to adopt the new performance measures. However, Bungala management made a conscious effort to embrace the new focus of CDEP.

The organisation had a long history of running CDEP programs elsewhere in South Australia and had been recognised as highly successful in placing CDEP participants into non-CDEP employment in Port Augusta. Bungala management described this as based in their 'philosophical belief' that the CDEP program should 'facilitate employment and training opportunities that articulate to economic independence for Aboriginal people' (Bungala 2010). Based on their operations in Port Augusta, they believed this could be achieved 'when CDEP is used as a vehicle to expose participants to the replication of a real employment situation' (Bungala 2010). For example, although CDEP had a set weekly base wage, Bungala encouraged active engagement in CDEP work by offering industrious workers additional hours or responsibilities so they could earn extra 'top up' pay. They also adopted the principle of 'no work no pay' with the aim of reinforcing commitment to a work culture. While there was some flexibility in how this was implemented (e.g. to allow for cultural leave and attendance at sorry camps), Bungala could and did penalise people financially for unexplained and unapproved absences.

Bungala's strategy also focused on the transition of CDEP participants into mainstream employment wherever possible. For example, between July 2008 and March 2011, Bungala assisted 217 CDEP participants across the APY Lands into non-CDEP employment, and another 38 into subsidised work experience placements (16 of which led to unsubsidised jobs). Organisations taking on CDEP participants for paid jobs or subsidised placements included community art centres and stores, schools, private building contractors, a major mining company, TAFE and state government agencies. Interpreting these figures requires some care because the period in question was an unusual one in which governments provided specific funding to create additional non-CDEP jobs for Anangu on the APY Lands. Of the 217 participants placed in non-CDEP jobs, 89 secured these CDEP 'conversion' positions created by the state or federal government to transition CDEP participants formerly engaged in delivering municipal and essential services into fully funded jobs.

During the period under study, Bungala's CDEP operations were integral to many of the employment placements of Anangu both on and off the APY Lands. For example, apart from the 89 conversion positions, Bungala also sought out employment opportunities by liaising with potential employers and tailoring training to their needs. Such projects included the placement of 41 Anangu in housing maintenance and construction jobs on the APY Lands. This was the culmination of negotiations to separate non-time-critical tasks out of Housing SA construction contracts so that they could be carried out by CDEP participants (who also undertook formal training in Certificate I in Construction through TAFE). In a similar approach, Bungala also helped facilitate the employment of eight Anangu as full-time trainees at Oz Minerals' Prominent Hill mine, the first significant mining employment program for the APY Lands. Individuals recruited for both projects were those who had been regularly attending CDEP, and hence had proved their commitment to a formal work routine.

This role of CDEP as a 'testing ground' for recruiters should not be understated. Regular participation in CDEP did not guarantee long-term retention in non-CDEP work. However, it could assist employers to direct training and mentoring to participants with the most enthusiasm for consistent employment and the best prospects for staying in the job. For this reason, some employers on the APY Lands had decided to only employ Anangu who had proved their commitment to regular employment through consistent participation in CDEP (and subsequently through the Remote Jobs and Communities Program (RJCP) and the Community Development Programme (CDP)).

By the same token, the APY Lands shows that CDEP could assist those individuals most aligned to regular participation in paid work into other employment where appropriate vacancies were available—even if these individuals were a minority of the CDEP caseload. It should also be noted that while CDEP supervisors actively supported this transition of the most reliable workers off CDEP and into salaried jobs, it was a common source of frustration that their program was then judged on the attendance of the remaining caseload who were, almost by definition, the hardest to engage and place into regular paid work.

The use of CDEP to facilitate movement into non-CDEP employment, as well as the reliance on the scheme by some employers to help assess the suitability of potential recruits, suggest that rather than creating a binary distinction with 'real jobs', CDEP could in fact be part of a continuum of different types of paid work with relatively flexible boundaries. This becomes even more apparent when considering that the structural constraints faced by CDEP providers persist well beyond the demise of the program and equally extend to non-CDEP work.

Structural constraints are persistent beyond CDEP

The 217 job placements achieved under Bungala over the three years of study may seem a little less impressive when one considers that although retention rates were initially quite high (74 per cent at 13 weeks) they fell away substantially over six months (44 per cent at 26 weeks), after which they were not measured (Jordan 2011: 43).

However, the challenges that any employment service provider faces in securing large numbers of sustainable Anangu jobs can hardly be overstated. These challenges are well known, but worth documenting briefly here because they help to explain key and persistent features of the employment landscape for both CDEP and other employers on the APY Lands.

Across the Lands, literacy and numeracy are often well below the standard needed for regular employment, even among recent school leavers. Low school attendance rates and high dropout rates from secondary schooling persist. Rates of physical and mental illness are very high, with many individuals of working age facing such significant personal barriers to employment that they may never be able to accommodate regular work. (As an example, recent estimates from just one APY community put the number of working-age men profoundly and permanently impaired by previous petrol sniffing at around 30; this roughly approximates 20 per cent of the community's working-age population.) There is also evidence of serious social pathologies in some APY communities, including high rates of domestic and sexual violence and regular drug abuse (see, for example, Mullighan 2008: xii–xiv). In those communities, family conflict and interpersonal violence can have very real implications not only for peoples' safety and well-being but, unsurprisingly, also for attendance at school and work. At the same time, it is important to note the diversity of Anangu experience, with many people across the APY Lands being highly skilled, knowledgeable and adaptable, and frustrated at the common portrayal of their lives as dysfunctional.

The limited availability and inflexible administration of some government services also create barriers to employment on the APY Lands. For example, in many communities there is a lack of childcare services where mothers can leave their children and go to work.[3] Some service providers also have inflexible administrative arrangements such as the common requirement for prospective employees to undergo official clearances. Service providers regularly complain that some clearances—such as those from the South Australian Department for Communities and Social Inclusion—can take up to six months, by which time the immediate enthusiasm of an

---

3   There are a number of playgroups, but mothers or carers must stay in attendance while the children are there.

applicant for the job has almost always waned. With governments ostensibly focused on removing obstacles to increased employment, problems like these should be priorities to resolve.

Adding even more complexity to this mix are very different patterns of socialisation from a young age, such that there is often a mismatch between the day-to-day demands of regular employment and local Anangu priorities. As in other parts of remote Australia, dominant notions of what constitutes a competent and successful person can be very different to those of the non-Indigenous population (in which 'success' largely corresponds to career progression and personal wealth), and Aboriginal patterns of social obligation mean that the ongoing negotiation and maintenance of relationships is often prioritised over employment commitments (see Vickery & Greive 2007; and for other parts of Australia, Austin-Broos 2006; Gibson 2010; McRae-Williams & Gerritsen 2010).

This can work both ways in that Anangu may be required at a moment's notice to leave work to attend to a family need or, on the other hand, may refuse to attend a workplace or participate in work activities if their participation may bring them into contact with someone with whom they are in an avoidance relationship or current conflict (see also McRae-Williams & Gerritsen 2010). There are many examples of this on the APY Lands, including situations where longstanding family conflicts have meant that entire workplaces are effectively 'out of bounds' for members of opposing family groups. Perhaps even more significantly, many Anangu are highly motivated by immediate need rather than projected future needs, and to the extent that they participate in paid employment, some do so in the form of what Peterson (2005) has called 'target working' (that is, turning up when there is an immediate need for money and not turning up when there is not).

The complex interaction of so many factors can often make the obstacles to regular and sustained employment seem insurmountable. They constitute major structural barriers to increased employment and retention rates that will undoubtedly persist well beyond the demise of CDEP. In taking stock of these 'on the ground' complexities, it is clear the notion that removing CDEP wages would be key to moving more Anangu into mainstream jobs was misguided. Unfortunately, this has also been evidenced by the rising unemployment rate as CDEP has been phased out, with RJCP and now CDP unable to move large numbers of Anangu into paid work. Indeed, as noted in Chapter 1, Minister for Indigenous Affairs Nigel Scullion recently suggested that in the absence of CDEP many remote-living Aboriginal people may now face long-term Work for the Dole, perhaps over many decades (in Martin 2015).

The next section argues that in considering these persistent barriers to employment, any sharp distinction between CDEP and 'real jobs' becomes blurred. That is, such complex and overlapping challenges not only shaped participation in CDEP but also influence the nature of most non-CDEP employment. This obvious point seems to have been overlooked by most proponents of dismantling CDEP who suggested that non-CDEP jobs were somehow more 'real' than the activities carried out for CDEP wages.

The idealised notion of 'real jobs'

While the supposed dichotomy between CDEP and 'real jobs' came to dominate policy discussions during the last 10 years of CDEP, exactly what such jobs constituted was never clearly defined. Nonetheless, some features of the so-called 'real jobs' can be gleaned either from absolute statements about their supposed benefits (such as that they have 'proper wages and conditions'), or relative statements about how they would compare to CDEP (e.g. they would require a commitment of more hours, lead to a more regular career, or constitute more serious work). Presumably, the ultimate aim of getting more people into 'real jobs' was to improve the income, working conditions and well-being of workers, as well as increasing their engagement with the market economy.

A common suggestion was that 'real jobs' would ensure people received 'proper wages and conditions' (see, for example, Australian Government 2013: 1). One of the basic principles of CDEP was that all participants would be offered the opportunity to earn at least as much as they would otherwise have been entitled to through unemployment payments. However, there was no formal minimum weekly wage because individuals who did not complete all of their work hours could face a reduction in their pay (see Race Discrimination

Commissioner 1997: 13, 17).[4] Criticisms that even the full CDEP wage could constitute underpayment as against the relevant awards were made as early as 1977 (Sanders 1988: 37). Later criticisms about the rights of CDEP participants concerned access to superannuation, termination payments and leave conditions—with CDEP originally having no specific provisions for parental leave, bereavement or long service leave (see, for example, Altman & Hawke 1993: 10–12).

Some of these concerns were addressed over the years. For example, while CDEP was never covered by an award, by the mid-1980s a determination was made that CDEP participants should be paid 'part-time pro-rata equivalents of award rates of pay' (Sanders 1988: 37). In effect, this meant that the base rate of pay (while fixed as notionally equivalent to unemployment benefits) determined how many work hours could be required of CDEP participants. Provisions were also made for parental, bereavement and long service leave for CDEP participants, as well as sick leave and relatively flexible cultural leave.

Superannuation remained a concern, with super payable on 'top up' wages (where these were generated from profits) since 1992, but not on base CDEP wages. It should be noted that a similar situation has been faced by some low-income casual workers, who are not entitled to superannuation contributions from their employers if their monthly income falls below a certain threshold. In CDEP's case, however, the limited entitlement to superannuation reflected the contradictory ways in which CDEP payments were considered by different government authorities. (Some considered them income support, while others taxable wages.) Critics of the limited availability of superannuation for CDEP participants therefore tended to fall into two camps—those who argued that the solution was abolishing CDEP, and those who argued that CDEP should be considered as waged public sector employment with all the rights to superannuation that entails.

'Award wage' and leave provisions show that changes to CDEP rules were able to address some shortfalls in payment conditions where there was the political will to do so. With superannuation, however,

---

4   It should also be noted that a number of reviews in the early 1990s found CDEP providers sometimes failed to offer sufficient work to participants to allow them to earn a wage equivalent to unemployment benefits (see Race Discrimination Commissioner 1997: 17).

governments became increasingly committed to the notion that the best way to improve provisions for CDEP workers was to wind back CDEP wages and, eventually, to replace CDEP with RJCP (and subsequently CDP) Work for the Dole (see, for example, Macklin et al. 2010). This, it was anticipated, would help people transition into real jobs with 'proper wages and conditions' including superannuation (Macklin et al. 2013). Unfortunately, this has not eventuated for the significant numbers of former CDEP participants who now remain in CDP.

There is some irony here because CDP participants accrue no superannuation on their CDP payments (which are clearly defined as welfare). In addition, the longstanding principle that CDEP hours should be limited to reflect award rates of pay has been abandoned in CDP rules. Participants are now required to work more hours for roughly the same income—up to 25 hours per week rather than the usual 15 hours under CDEP (Scullion 2014). This reduces participants' hourly income to well below the award rate for equivalent paid work. Despite initially proposing that participation in these activities would be required for 52 weeks of the year, the Minister for Indigenous Affairs has backed down and agreed to include some allowances for annual and cultural leave (Martin 2015). Notably, though, these were challenges addressed many years ago under CDEP. For those CDP participants who do not move quickly into mainstream employment, it is difficult to see how this could be construed as an improvement in working conditions.

As well as contrasting CDEP to properly paid real jobs, critics of the scheme also suggested that non-CDEP jobs would be better because they would entail longer hours, a more developed career path and more meaningful work. Longer hours were presented as a better option because they would require workers to conform to the demands of most employers and hence become more disciplined workers. This would also make it possible to develop 'careers' rather than simply participate in CDEP activities (see Pearson 2007). Such arguments were also evident in claims that non-CDEP jobs would provide more meaningful work, not the 'pretend' work or 'make work' activities argued to be prevalent under CDEP (Hughes 2007; Hudson 2008; Hughes & Hughes 2010).

According to some commentators, CDEP created a fiction around work activity, either deliberately paying people to waste their time (such as by 'painting rocks white', e.g. see Yanner 2013),[5] or paying them for such basic activities that no payment should be due (such as housework, mowing the lawn or attending funerals, see Hudson 2008: vii). From this perspective, even the most mainstream 'job-like' CDEP activities (such as working as teachers' aides or the equivalent of park rangers) were sometimes seen as 'pretend jobs' because they were believed to require fewer qualifications than comparable jobs elsewhere and did not mandate English language literacy and numeracy (Hughes & Hughes 2010). In Sarah Hudson's (2008: vii) words, 'CDEP participants do not need to know how to read and write, and CDEP training does not qualify them for mainstream jobs'.

By casting CDEP as 'pretend' work without any of the demands or disciplines of regular employment, those arguing for the scheme's closure could portray it as a principal barrier to participants taking on other paid jobs. As Helen Hughes (2007) argued, it is 'difficult for men and women to contemplate mainstream work standards when they know they will receive "sit-down" CDEP money for doing very little or nothing at all'. The vision, although not clearly spelled out, was that without the supposed disincentive effect of CDEP and its overly permissive payments, 'work' in remote Aboriginal communities would begin to look much more like an urban employment market. That is, CDEP participants would tend to become employees in mainstream jobs where they would have to adopt 'mainstream work standards' (turning up on time, staying all day, and leaving personal issues at the door) and be motivated to build career paths.

A key argument in this chapter is that this vision of 'real jobs' did not match the reality even for many Anangu who participated in mainstream employment. On the APY Lands the complex, overlapping and persistent structural issues outlined in the previous section have equally shaped CDEP and other work. Just like the experience of CDEP—in which a small but significant number of participants embraced the particular disciplines of consistent work

---

5   Note that this was such a common claim that it could seem almost apocryphal. However, in some communities CDEP participants did indeed paint rocks white as part of landscaping works in public areas. Large painted rocks were positioned, for example, to clearly delineate public parking zones.

and training—a proportion of non-CDEP workers have done the same. For example, there are some service providers with small work teams who attend work reliably and work fixed hours five days per week. At the same time, there are many Aṉangu who work in non-CDEP jobs irregularly, receiving casual wages for a day, a week or even a month's work until another priority takes precedence.[6]

The prevalence of this irregular or casual commitment to paid employment is one reason why some service providers are unable, or unwilling, to employ Aṉangu in key responsible roles. It means that some services relying on Aṉangu staff regularly open late (or occasionally not at all). It also contributes significantly to low retention rates of Aṉangu staff across many employers (e.g. one service provider in an APY community employed 22 staff in three years, with the longest period of employment for any staff member being six months). While to outsiders such intermittent working may look like ill-discipline or dysfunction, it is arguably strategic. It may involve 'target working' (i.e. for just long enough to raise money for a specific purpose), or a deliberate rejection of work environments that are perceived as ill-suited to people's needs. Importantly, it may also represent repeated attempts to negotiate the competing demands of paid work and other pressing concerns—such as poor health or cultural and familial responsibilities—as described earlier in this chapter. Because an irregular commitment to paid employment can often be influenced by non-monetary factors, for the rest of this chapter I use the term 'intermittent working' to broaden the scope beyond Peterson's conceptualisation of 'target working'.

In their bid to present a dichotomy between the 'illegitimate' CDEP and 'legitimate' real jobs, commentators who pressed for CDEP's closure failed entirely to acknowledge the widespread reality of intermittent working in non-CDEP employment. But the prevalence of intermittent work means that most of the criticisms of CDEP canvassed here— including its part-time hours, the common lack of career progression, irregular engagement among participants, lack of clarity about leave conditions and in some cases even eligibility for superannuation— can equally apply to many of the 'real jobs' on the APY Lands. This raises serious questions about the reasoning behind many of the most

---

6   Patterns of intermittent working have also been noted in case study research from other regions. See, for example, Austin-Broos 2006; Smith 1991.

strident critiques of CDEP. It also suggests that policymakers need to more carefully consider the ultimate aims of remote employment policy to better account for the complexities of intermittent work.

What is the policy aim?

Perhaps the most critical issue for developing any public policy is a clear understanding of what it is that policymakers are trying to achieve. The Council of Australian Governments' 'Closing the Gap' targets set out to halve the gap in employment outcomes between Indigenous and other Australians by 2018. This focus on statistical equality has been criticised elsewhere (e.g. Altman 2009), and indeed the emphasis on measurable targets has tended to obscure or even displace the stated intention to improve Indigenous well-being (see the references to well-being in the National Indigenous Reform Agreement, COAG 2009).

The same can be argued of the government's approach to remote employment services: if the aim is simply to improve statistical employment outcomes (such as the employment/population ratio) then a focus not only on employment participation, but also on consistent employment over time, is warranted. It is reasonable to assume that policymakers also see this as necessary to improve Indigenous peoples' lives. If, however, the principal aim is actually to advance Indigenous livelihoods and well-being then it may be possible that intermittent working is a valid prospect also worthy of state support, if it affords Indigenous people both raised incomes and the ability to effectively combine paid work with other priorities.

A key argument, then, is that the focus on 'non-CDEP work' has obscured a more productive concern with the kinds of work, and work practices, that would best improve the livelihoods and well-being of remote Indigenous people. Looking again to the APY Lands, this chapter suggests that there are at least two broad types of working practices: intermittent working; and what could be called 'steady employment', which includes a commitment to consistent work hours over relatively long periods of time. To reiterate, imagining that these categories correspond neatly to CDEP participation is inappropriate because both intermittent working and steady employment have been patterns played out across the spectrum of CDEP and non-CDEP jobs.

Determining whether intermittent working, steady employment or some combination of both can best improve livelihoods for Anangu will necessarily entail informed and sustained discussion between Anangu, policymakers and the relevant stakeholders (such as local employers). At present, the approach is at best confused. The Australian Government is seemingly intent on trying to force Anangu to become steady employees through a system of penalties for non-participation in CDP activities or non-attendance at appointments. At the same time, several employers support intermittent working practices, and while many Anangu desire skill development and career progression, intermittent working is very widely accepted.

A useful discussion with Anangu would ask what visions people hold for their future and what kind of working practices could help make progress towards those goals. If, for example, the priority is temporal flexibility to pursue commitments outside of paid work combined with periodic increases in cash income, then intermittent working could continue to be supported (without any stigma that periodic workers were somehow failed employees). However, the discussion should also include consideration of the trade-offs of this approach. That is, for some people there may be a continuum between intermittent work and steady employment, in that participation in the former can sometimes help to generate the commitment and confidence for the latter. For others, though, intermittent work will remain insufficient to lead to career progression, and may limit the ability to find jobs off the APY Lands, gain the skills required for business development or replace non-Indigenous contractors and staff in APY communities. If these are all features of Anangu visions for their futures, then assisting more people to become steady employees should be a shared priority. The next section considers some of the ways in which such assistance might be provided, particularly by re-examining the factors that motivate people to engage in paid work.

What motivates people to do paid work?

Apart from CDEP wages and the associated ability to offer 'top up' payments for additional work, the principal approach the Australian Government has used to encourage people into employment has been a punitive one. That is, it is assumed that disengagement from regular work can be effectively addressed by 'breaching' recipients of unemployment payments who do not meet compulsory participation requirements. Research by Sanders (1999, 2004) shows that the degree to which governments have subscribed to this punitive approach in administering social security payments to Aboriginal and Torres Strait Islander Australians has changed over time. In this context, the current period can be seen as an 'upswing' in the emphasis on breaching, with consecutive Labor and Liberal governments introducing a series of bills into federal parliament intended to 'strengthen' compliance measures for social security recipients.[7] At the same time, compulsory participation requirements have been ramped up (see Fowkes & Sanders 2016).

This system is designed to discipline Anangu into regularly attending CDP activities and appointments in the hope that they will subsequently move into steady employment. Assuming this kind of transition will become 'normalised' ignores the deeply embedded nature of intermittent work as described above. Just as importantly, however, it also overlooks the more complex factors involved in what motivates people to engage in productive activity. Central to the current policy approach is the belief that the practice of paying 'sit-down money'—providing social security payments to able-bodied, working-age people without requiring them to undertake productive activity in return—is one of the principal barriers to remote-living Indigenous people taking up paid work (and especially steady employment). This is an argument strongly advocated by Pearson. In his words, people will be discouraged from taking up paid jobs when 'it's easier to remain on the handout' (Pearson in O'Brien 2007).

There is some reason to support this perspective, but there is also reason to believe that the realities are much more complex. For example, previous research on the APY Lands suggests the availability of 'sit-down money' can indeed be a deterrent to active work (Jordan 2011). Although the Rudd Government tried to sell the removal of CDEP wages as giving people 'the strongest incentives to get a job' (Macklin & O'Connor 2008), in practice the shift away from CDEP

---

7   These include, for example, the Social Security Legislation Amendment (Stronger Penalties for Serious Failures) Bill 2014; Social Security Legislation Amendment (Strengthening the Job Seeker Compliance Framework) Bill 2014; Social Security Legislation Amendment (Job Seeker Compliance) Bill 2011. Recent research by Fowkes and Sanders (2016) suggests that RJCP (and now CDP) participants have faced serious income penalties at much higher rates than those in mainstream job services.

wages to social security payments actually reduced the incentive structures within CDEP to engage in productive activity (see Jordan 2011 for evidence from the APY Lands; also Langton 2014 for reflection on these concerns more broadly).

In short, this is because the monetary incentive structures within CDEP included both a 'carrot' (the ability to offer 'top up' payments for additional work above the required minimum) and a 'stick' (the application of 'no work no pay' to dock wages for non-participation in CDEP activities). However, when new participants were made ineligible for CDEP wages from July 2009 these structures were undermined. Now in receipt of social security payments as their principal source of income, these new participants could no longer receive 'top up' for additional work hours. If they took on part-time or casual employment outside of their CDEP activity they were now subject to the normal income taper on their social security payments, reducing the financial incentive to do additional paid work.[8] In addition, although CDEP participants in receipt of income support payments could theoretically be breached for non-attendance, the CDEP provider no longer had any ability to dock wages directly and it was uncommon for Centrelink to enforce breaches (see Jordan 2011: 47–48).

This meant that 'no work no pay' held little sway over CDEP participants who received income support payments, as they could receive the same income whether they worked their full hours on CDEP or not. On the APY Lands there is evidence that this led to declining engagement. For example, roughly two years after the changes were introduced, participation rates of those still receiving CDEP wages and those receiving income support payments differed markedly,

---

8   Nigel Scullion has recently proposed the introduction of new rules that would allow CDP participants to earn more money over and above their social security payments before the income taper would apply. However, they would still have to participate in required CDP activities of up to 25 hours per week; for any hour of CDP activities they missed due to engagement in paid work their income support payments would be reduced. At the time of writing this chapter, precise details of such proposed penalties have not yet been announced, so it is difficult to assess whether participants would likely be better off (see Australian Government 2016). Some analyses, though, raise significant cause for concern (e.g. Fowkes 2016).

with three-quarters of the former group and only one-quarter of the latter group regularly turning up for CDEP work or training (Jordan 2011: 44).[9]

This suggests that monetary incentives provide some, but not all, of the picture. There has been very little research into what motivates remote-living Indigenous people to engage in paid work, or to become 'steady employees'. Peterson (2005) has provided support to the notion that welfare payments have reduced the incentive to engage in productive activity, with their availability unintentionally contributing to the reproduction of a domestic moral economy. In this economy, circulation (dedicated to the reproduction of social and cultural relationships) is emphasised over material production. This sits somewhat uncomfortably with analyses that present the motivation of remote-living Indigenous people to engage in employment as a simple 'income leisure trade off' (see, for example, Pearson 2007). The latter approach draws from mainstream economic theory in which people are assumed to be rational utility maximisers weighing up the quantity of hours that they are willing to supply as labour (and hence give up as leisure) at different wage rates (Gratton & Taylor 2004). It likely reflects a significant oversimplification given the very complex barriers to employment participation described earlier.

For example, if an individual is constrained from participating in paid work because of caring responsibilities, drug or alcohol dependency or an undiagnosed mental health condition, or they have been socialised from a young age to prioritise family responsibilities as the most important work of day-to-day life, then positing a simple 'income leisure trade off' makes little sense. In this context, apparent 'choices' to skip CDEP or Work for the Dole activities are at best heavily restricted, and approaches that rely too greatly on financial penalties are unlikely to produce the behavioural changes that policymakers desire. Indeed, on the APY Lands many Anangu and service providers suggest that although increased breaches might encourage some Anangu to engage more fully with the new CDP, more likely outcomes include further alienation of those with the greatest

---

9   The influence of age on participation might account for some of this difference but, because both the wages and income support 'streams' of CDEP included participants across the age spectrum, it could not account for it all.

barriers to steady employment, an intensification of existing patterns in which Anangu rely on kinship networks for material needs, and escalating resentment, intracommunity violence, poverty and theft.

In the absence of empirical research in the field, it is instructive here to consider approaches to 'motivation' taken by various employers of Anangu—both on and off the APY Lands. While some employers support intermittent working with casual wages, others use various systems of incentives and penalties to encourage Anangu staff to engage in paid work consistently as steady employees. Penalty arrangements are not unusual, with common features including warnings that staff will lose their jobs if they repeatedly fail to turn up on time or leave early without prior approval. Where employment is casual, pay is docked for non-attendance in the next payment period. However, in workplaces with significant retention rates, penalties are accompanied by a range of non-monetary 'incentives' that give Anangu a sense of ownership over their own professional and personal development and offer a supportive team environment in which to work.

This almost always includes intensive mentoring (usually one-on-one assistance tailored for each individual's needs), facilitation of desired training and development, and a high degree of autonomy for Anangu staff. For example, in one workplace widely regarded as very successful in retaining and upskilling Anangu employees, those staff are included in all significant decisions ranging from the daily division of work tasks, to appropriate penalties for non-attendance, to recruitment of new colleagues. This has encouraged a strong sense of teamwork and ownership among staff. It has also allowed deeply held cultural relationships between different family groups to be sensitively accommodated. Organising work practices in this way has much in common with the 'Aboriginalisation' of the workplace that was a locally valued feature of CDEP on the NSW far south coast, as detailed in Chapter 4. On the APY Lands, it has helped to make paid work with some employers a particularly attractive prospect for their Anangu staff.

This combination of factors—financial penalties for non-attendance, the threat of dismissal for continued poor performance and ensuring that workplaces are attractive to Anangu—has proven effectiveness in supporting steady employment among those individuals most predisposed to it. If more Anangu become role models for this way of working over time, it is quite possible that it will increasingly become a social norm. However, even if many Anangu determined that increased participation in steady employment was in their best interests, it is highly unlikely that attempts to extend this approach would rapidly eliminate intermittent working while so many complex barriers to more consistent employment still exist. That is, at present there is a relatively small pool of Anangu available for steady employment over significant periods of time, and efforts to force others into a similar employment relationship would undermine the sense of agency and teamwork relied upon by effective employers and almost inevitably fail.[10] Equally, although financial incentives and penalties can be important, approaches that simply seek to 'breach' intermittent Work for the Dole participants into becoming steady workers are unlikely to make much headway.

If, as suggested here, the recent experience with removing CDEP wages on the APY Lands had the unintended consequence of reducing rather than increasing participant engagement, it suggests policymakers have much to learn about effective incentive structures for Anangu. In this context there is a clear need to engage with Anangu, not only about their vision for their future, but also how to achieve it—including whether there should be penalties for non-participation in Work for the Dole activities and if so what these should be. While many Anangu are opposed to sit-down money for able-bodied people of working age, they are likely to have more creative ideas about appropriate—and effective—incentives and penalties to encourage compliance.[11]

That kind of discussion might also go some way to relieving the 'resistance and withdrawal' of remote-living Indigenous people that some commentators identify as a response to the 'merry-go-round of changing top-down initiatives' forced upon them over the last decade (Rothwell 2015: 17). Research on the APY Lands lends some

---

10   It should also be noted that some employers on the APY Lands rely on casual, intermittent work by Anangu and the required tasks are not suited to steady employment of the same individual over significant periods of time. This can be the case, for example, where staff are only needed periodically and/or where different staff are needed to work with clients from the different family groups.

11   For example, some suggestions from Anangu include prohibiting those not turning up to their Work for the Dole activities from participating in competition football. This would avoid the possibility of shifting a financial penalty onto family members and, since playing football is highly prized, be keenly felt by those penalised.

support to this thesis—with local responses to the removal of CDEP wages including frustration at yet another rule change implemented with little consultation (Jordan 2011: 42). If the thesis is right then forging ahead with policies designed to force behavioural change through increasingly severe financial penalties runs the risk of further alienating the most disengaged Aṉangu and again leading to outcomes at odds with what policymakers are trying to achieve.

Conclusion

The principal justification for closing CDEP has been the argument that the availability of CDEP work prevented the take-up of more favourable 'real jobs'. CDEP may indeed have been chosen by some participants over other employment, but assuming that the removal of CDEP would therefore improve outcomes for remote-living Indigenous people shows several flaws in logic. For example, experience on the APY Lands demonstrates that CDEP could help those Aṉangu most suited to steady employment to find non-CDEP jobs. At the same time, 'top up' and 'no work no pay' provisions could be utilised to try to encourage more consistency among intermittent workers. Moreover, while participation and retention rates were often low, this reflects much broader structural challenges that will persist well beyond CDEP and that are equally apparent in intermittent working within both Work for the Dole and many non-CDEP jobs.

Ignoring the nature of the so-called 'real jobs' allowed commentators and policymakers alike to overlook the question of whether movement from CDEP into other employment would necessarily improve outcomes. By encouraging a focus on the removal of CDEP wages, it also suited the dominant policy discourse that has assumed not only that the major barrier to increased participation in steady employment is behavioural, but also that behaviour can be changed by the top-down implementation of policies that shift people onto income support payments and increase breach rates to force compliance. This focus has given much too little attention to increasing the availability of non-CDEP work (such as through enterprise development) and has largely ignored the need to remove institutional barriers to employing Aṉangu in existing vacancies (such as unduly lengthy record checks and clearances required by some employers).[12] It has also assumed that governments adequately understand how to appropriately support improved Indigenous well-being, and what incentive structures will encourage behavioural changes in which direction. Like policymakers, many Aṉangu say they want to see an end to sit-down money. However, the recent experience of removing CDEP wages suggests that governments do not have sufficient insight into the way unilateral policy changes are likely to affect Aṉangu, and even the best-intentioned policies can have consequences at odds with their stated goals.

In this context, it is reasonable to conclude that the most suitable policy responses will be determined through appropriate consultation with Aṉangu. Such consultations should first seek to understand how different types of work practices might support or detract from improved well-being. Rather than casting some types of work as 'real' and others as 'pretend', this discussion could sensibly acknowledge both the entrenched nature of intermittent working (even beyond CDEP) and identify its advantages and disadvantages as against steady employment. Significantly, this discussion should also engage with ideas promoted in the Forrest Review that the 'success' of publicly funded employment programs in remote areas should only be judged on the basis of 26-week employment outcomes (see Forrest 2014).

If, in informed negotiations, some Aṉangu do conclude that greater engagement with steady employment is necessary to improve their livelihoods, such discussion should ask Aṉangu how policy changes might best support that aim. Part of this picture might indeed be adjusting policy settings to encourage individual behavioural change, but it might also include a greater emphasis on varied and interesting work that is attractive to Aṉangu as well as ensuring access to appropriate support services (with some health, child care and drug and alcohol services, for example, still too often limited). While social security policy will undoubtedly play a part, if the tougher application of income penalties for social security breaches does increase poverty, theft and resentment as some Aṉangu predict, then

---

12   Inadequate support for small enterprise development is a very common concern raised by Aṉangu and others on the APY Lands. Several people consulted for this study stressed the need to leverage more economic development opportunities from tourism and other industries in surrounding regions, as well the need for investment in infrastructure that would make employment opportunities off the APY Lands more accessible.

ignoring the views and insights of Anangu in making these decisions risks further entrenching many of the problems governments are seeking to resolve. At the same time, if not adequately grounded in a genuine agreement between Anangu and governments then any efforts to reduce intermittent working and force people into steady employment through increased financial pressure may well be interpreted as assimilationist and encourage local resistance. Options for such agreement-making are currently limited, but with remote Indigenous employment outcomes continuing to decline it seems an appropriate time for governments to consult with Anangu about broader livelihood options.

References

Altman JC (2009). *Beyond closing the gap: valuing diversity in Indigenous Australia*, CAEPR Working Paper No. 54, Centre for Aboriginal Economic Policy Research, The Australian National University, Canberra.

Altman JC & Hawke AE (1993). *Indigenous Australians and the labour market: issues for the union movement in the 1990s*, CAEPR Discussion Paper No. 45, Centre for Aboriginal Economic Policy Research, The Australian National University, Canberra.

Austin-Broos D (2006). Working for and working among Western Arrernte, *Oceania* 76: 1–15.

Australian Government (2013). *Remote Jobs and Communities Program: CDEP Provider fact sheet*, Commonwealth of Australia, Canberra.

Australian Government (2015). *Guide to social security law*. Version 1.210—Released 9 February 2015, Commonwealth of Australia, guides.dss.gov.au/guide-social-security-law/3/1/13.

Australian Government (2016). *Consultation paper: changes to the Community Development Programme*, Commonwealth of Australia, Canberra.

Brough M (2006). *Blueprint for action in Indigenous Affairs*, speech to the National Institute of Governance, 5 December.

Bungala (2010). *Bungala Aboriginal Corporation , welcome to Bungala*, [website], www.bungala.com.au.

Cape York Institute for Policy and Leadership (2007). *From hand out to hand up, Cape York Welfare Reform Project Arakun, Coen, Hope Vale, Mossman Gorge, design recommendations*, Cape York Institute for Policy and Leadership, Cairns.

COAG (Council of Australian Governments) (2009). *National Indigenous Reform Agreement (Closing the Gap)*, Council of Australian Governments, Sydney.

Department of Employment and Workplace Relations (2005). *Building on success: CDEP Discussion Paper 2005*, Commonwealth of Australia, Canberra.

Edwards WH (1992). Patterns of Aboriginal residence in the north-west of South Australia. *Journal of the Anthropological Society of South Australia*, 30 (1): 2–33.

Edwards WH (2004). *A Moravian mission in Australia: Ebenezer through Ernabella eyes*, unpublished, The Australian National University, Canberra.

Forrest A (Chair) (2014). *Creating parity—the Forrest review*, Commonwealth of Australia, Canberra.

Fowkes L (2016). Submission to the Senate Finance and Public Administration Legislation Committee Inquiry into the Social Security Legislation Amendment (Community Development Program) Bill 2015, January, www.aph.gov.au/Parliamentary_Business/Committees/Senate/Finance_and_Public_Administration/Social_Security/Submissions.

Fowkes L and Sanders W (2016). *Financial penalties under the Remote Jobs and Communities Program*, CAEPR Working Paper No. 108, Centre for Aboriginal Economic Policy Research, The Australian National University, Canberra.

Gibson L (2010). Making a life: Getting ahead, and getting a living in Aboriginal New South Wales, *Oceania* 80 (2): 143–160.

Gratton C & Taylor P (2004). The economics of work and leisure. In Haworth JT & Veal AJ (eds), *Work and leisure*. Routledge, Sussex.

Hudson S (2008). CDEP: Help or hindrance? The Community Development Employment Program and its impact on Indigenous Australians, *CIS Policy Monograph 86*, The Centre for Independent Studies, Sydney.

Hughes H (2007). *Lands of shame: Aboriginal and Torres Strait Islander 'Homelands' in transition*, The Centre for Independent Studies, Sydney.

Hughes H & Hughes M (2010). Indigenous employment, unemployment and labour force participation: Facts for evidence based policies, *CIS Policy Monograph 107*, The Centre for Independent Studies, Sydney.

Jordan K (2011). *Work, welfare and CDEP on the Anangu Pitjantjatjara Yankunytjatjara Lands: first stage assessment*, CAEPR Working Paper No. 78, Centre for Aboriginal Economic Policy Research, The Australian National University, Canberra, caepr.anu.edu.au/ Publications/WP/2011WP78.php.

Langton M (2014). Remote jobs program all pain, no gain. *The Australian*, 27 October.

Macklin J, Ellis K & Collins J (2013). *Transitioning to the new Remote Jobs and Communities Program*, media release, 18 June, ministers. employment.gov.au/macklin/transitioning-new-remote-jobs-and-communities-program.

Macklin J & O'Connor B (2008). *Strengthening Indigenous employment opportunities*, media release, 19 December, www.formerministers. dss.gov.au/14806/strengthening-indigenous-employment-opportunities/.

Macklin J, Plibersek T & Arbib M (2010). *Increasing employment and participation in remote Indigenous communities*, media release, 10 December, www.nesa.com.au/media/23297/mr_ arbib;macklin;plibersek_increasing%20employment%20 and%20participation%20in%20remote%20indigenous% 20communities%2009.12.10.pdf.

Martin S (2015). 30 years working for dole a reality, *The Australian*, 2 March, www.theaustralian.com.au/national-affairs/indigenous/ years-working-for-dole-a-reality/story-fn9hm1pm-1227243883240.

McRae-Williams E & Gerritsen R (2010). Mutual incomprehension: The cross-cultural domain of work in a remote Australian Aboriginal community, *The International Indigenous Policy Journal* 1 (2): 1–27.

Mullighan E (Commissioner) (2008). *Children on APY Lands: a report into sexual abuse*, Children on APY Lands Commission of Inquiry, Adelaide.

O'Brien K (2007). Pearson explains plan to overhaul Aboriginal welfare. *The 7.30 Report*, Australian Broadcasting Corporation, broadcast 19 June, www.abc.net.au/7.30/content/2007/s1956147.htm.

O'Connor A (2013). Indigenous enterprises and entrepreneurship in remote Aboriginal welfare, PhD thesis, University of South Australia, Adelaide.

Paper Tracker (2011). APY Lands: Community Development Employment Projects (CDEP), *The Anangu Lands Paper Tracker*, www.papertracker.com.au/archived/apy-lands-community-development-employment-projects-cdep/.

Pearson N (2000). *Our right to take responsibility*, Noel Pearson and Associates, Cairns.

Pearson N (2007). Stuck on the welfare pedestal. *The Australian*, 10 February.

Pearson N (2011). Job-service parasites get rich living off the unemployed. *The Weekend Australian*, 3–4 September.

Peterson N (2005). What can the pre-colonial and frontier economies tell us about engagement with the real economy? Indigenous life projects and the conditions for development. In Austin-Broos D & Macdonald G (eds), *Culture, economy and governance in Aboriginal Australia*, Sydney University Press, Sydney.

Race Discrimination Commissioner (1997). *The CDEP Scheme and racial discrimination: a report by the Race Discrimination Commissioner*, Human Rights and Equal Opportunity Commission, Canberra.

Rothwell N (2015). Pathways to indigenous empowerment in remote communities. *The Australian*, 31 January.

Sanders W (1988). The CDEP scheme: bureaucratic politics, remote community politics and the development of an Aboriginal 'workfare' program in times of rising unemployment. *Politics* 23 (1): 32–47.

Sanders W (1999). *Unemployment payments, the activity test and Indigenous Australians: understanding breach rates*, CAEPR Monograph No.15, Centre for Aboriginal Economic Policy Research, The Australian National University, Canberra.

Sanders W (2004). Indigenous Australians and the rules of the social security system: universalism, appropriateness and justice. *Australian Journal of Public Administration* 63 (3): 3–9.

Scullion N (2014). *More opportunities for job seekers in remote communities,* media release, 6 December, minister.indigenous.gov.au/media/2014-12-06/more-opportunities-job-seekers-remote-communities.

Shergold P (2001). The Indigenous employment policy: a preliminary evaluation. In Morphy F & Sanders F (eds), *The Indigenous welfare economy and the CDEP scheme*, CAEPR Research Monograph No. 20, ANU E Press, Canberra.

Smith DE (1991). *Aboriginal unemployment statistics: policy implications of the divergence between official and case study data*, CAEPR Discussion Paper No.13, Centre for Aboriginal Economic Policy Research, The Australian National University, Canberra.

South Australian Centre for Economic Studies (1994). *Economic study of the Anangu Pitjantjatjara lands: a report prepared for the Aboriginal and Torres Strait Islander Commission*, South Australian Centre for Economic Studies, Adelaide.

Stone J (2008). Aboriginal employment and the CDEP. *Quadrant Online*, 52 (9), quadrant.org.au/magazine/2008/09/aboriginal-employment-and-the-cdep/.

Vickery D & Greive C (2007). *Culture of work and community: consultations on the Anangu, Pitjantjatjara Yankunytjatjara Lands of South Australia*, Report prepared for the Department of Education, Employment & Workplace Relations, ETM Perspectives, Brisbane.

Yanner M (2013). A proving ground for proud carers of country. *The Canberra Times*, 13 May.

Yaxley L (2005). Kevin Andrews focuses on education and training to address Indigenous unemployment, *ABC Radio AM*, 22 April, www.abc.net.au/am/content/2005/s1351214.htm.

6

Work habits and localised authority in Anmatjere CDEPs: Losing good practice through policy and program review

Will Sanders

Introduction

In 2004, as part of an Indigenous community governance project, I began attending monthly meetings of the Anmatjere Community Government Council (ACGC) two or three times per year. ACGC was not an Indigenous community organisation. It was a general remote-area local government, but its constituency and elected membership were about 90 per cent Indigenous. ACGC in 2004 did not administer a Community Development Employment Projects (CDEP) scheme, but there were three CDEP providers in its area, two at the southern outlying settlements of Laramba and Engawala and one in the north at Wilora. In the geographic centre of ACGC's operations around Ti Tree there was no CDEP (see Fig. 6.1). The unemployed in this central area received Newstart Allowance from Centrelink, as did the unemployed elsewhere in Anmatjere if positions on CDEP were not available. In 2006, as a result of the Department of Employment and Workplace Relations' (DEWR) contested contractualism (see Chapter 2), these arrangements for the provision of CDEP in the Anmatjere region began to change. ACGC was encouraged to apply to become a new

CDEP provider in Ti Tree, Nturiya, Alyuen and Pmara Jutunta. In this they were successful. However, DEWR also asked ACGC to take on the existing CDEPs in Laramba and Engawala, which DEWR regarded as too small and not well administered. ACGC agreed, somewhat reluctantly, knowing that this would be viewed unfavourably in Laramba and Engawala as a Ti Tree takeover. Thus began my involvement with Anmatjere CDEPs, first assisting a governance consultant over a couple of months and then over the longer term as a researcher who kept turning up at local government meetings.

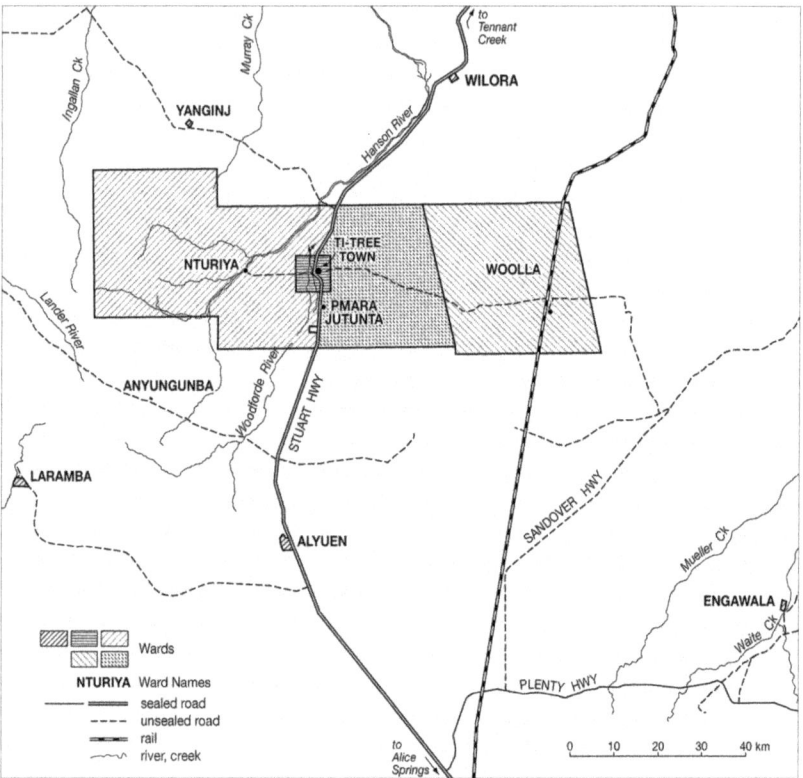

Fig. 6.1 Wards of Anmatjere Community Government Council

Notes: ACGC's main office, works yard and chambers were in Ti Tree town, one of 10 wards that were each allowed two elected council members. Three large surrounding wards covered the Ahakeye Land Trust, Aboriginal-owned land that had previously been the pastoral lease know as Ti Tree Station. The six tiny outlying wards were Aboriginal community living area excisions from surrounding pastoral leases. These pastoral leases and their residents were not included in ACGC. Neither was a small rectangle of horticultural land to the southwest of Pmara Jutunta. ACGC thus combined nine wards based on Aboriginal community living areas and land with one open-town ward.

Source: CartoGIS, College of Asia and the Pacific, The Australian National University.

In the following analysis, I emphasise the highly localised authority structures of Anmatjere CDEPs and the work habits of participants as these developed from 2006 to 2013. This period includes the amalgamation of ACGC in 2008 into the much larger Central Desert Shire. The new Shire became the CDEP provider in five other settlements outside the Anmatjere region. My observation of CDEP in the Shire expanded to one of these settlements to the east, but not to those in Warlpiri country to the west. My analysis also covers the closure of CDEP in 2013 and the transition to the Remote Jobs and Communities Program (RJCP) over the next year or two. It is this latter period that gives this chapter its subtitle and argumentative theme—that good practice was lost through the processes of policy and program review that led to RJCP. This should not be taken as a critique of all policy and program review, but it should alert us to the potential for such processes to have negative, as well as positive, consequences. I will return to this argument about the relationship between policy review and practice in a later section of the chapter, but first I tell the story of Anmatjere CDEPs as I observed them from 2006 to 2013.

Governance work in Laramba and Engawala

When DEWR announced that ACGC was to become the new CDEP provider in Laramba and Engawala in mid-2006, ACGC wisely sought help from a governance consultant to manage the transition process. Rob, from the Alice Springs firm Burdon-Torzillo, convened meetings at Laramba and Engawala and I became his assistant. The purpose of the meetings was to clarify understandings among CDEP participants and community leaders about how the new arrangements for CDEP would work. CDEP participants would have to change to become ACGC employees, but there were many other aspects of the existing CDEP arrangements that ACGC wanted to preserve, such as basic daily work routines and access to local work spaces and equipment. Rob explained, on behalf of ACGC, what needed to change and what existing arrangements in Laramba and Engawala could remain. CDEP teams would still assemble and work under local supervision in local work spaces in the two communities using local equipment. Written agreements to this effect were drawn up and signed, but the process of doing so was of more importance than the later existence of the documents, which quickly faded from view.

Rob was a very experienced operator who handled with skill two very different meeting styles at Laramba and Engawala, one a small meeting of community leaders around a table, and the other an open-air, gender-divided mass community meeting. He also dealt well with ACGC's central administration in Ti Tree, explaining how he thought local autonomy in Laramba and Engawala could be respected while also creating some sense of one regional Anmatjere CDEP. Rob's work, together with my assistance, also reinforced some ideas the ACGC central administration had about how to set up the new CDEP in the area around Ti Tree (see Fig. 6.1). Primary among these ideas was having CDEP offices at Pmara Jutunta and Nturiya within easy walking distance of the houses of participants.

CDEP offices in Pmara Jutunta and Nturiya

Reconditioning an old community office at Pmara Jutunta became the first task for CDEP participants in that community. They assembled there four mornings per week to assist other ACGC staff with the work and the renovated office then became their daily meeting place. There was an equipment enclosure created on the verandah on one side of the building from which the male team of CDEP participants would take out whipper snippers and other equipment to undertake landscape maintenance around the community and adjacent cemetery. Art equipment was also available and often led to small groups of participants working along the verandah, mainly women but sometimes also men. Inside there was office work, such as answering the phone and filling in forms. The Pmara Jutunta CDEP participants seemed proud in 2006 and 2007 to be part of getting their community office up and running again after some years of closure (see Fig. 6.2).

Fig. 6.2 Pmara Jutunta CDEP Office 2008
Source: Photograph taken by author.

At Nturiya, an unoccupied house was identified for conversion to a CDEP office. This never had quite the sense of being a community office, as in Pmara Jutunta, but it was the place where CDEP participants in Nturiya were expected to turn up four mornings per week. A produce garden was developed in the yard around the house and much time and energy went into gently tending and watering it. Inside was a desk, a phone and a changing array of notices. Some informal signs painted on exterior walls suggested the localised nature of authority (see Fig. 6.3).

What these two CDEP offices established, in Pmara Jutunta and Nturiya, was a physical infrastructure of daily work and localised authority. They provided a place for CDEP participants to turn up four mornings per week and have their attendance noted by supervisors and managers. They also provided a place for storage and access to equipment associated with CDEP activities, like gardening, landscape maintenance and art. This emulated the existing arrangements at Engawala and Laramba, which both had community offices and equipment/activity spaces where CDEP participants would turn up four mornings per week.

159

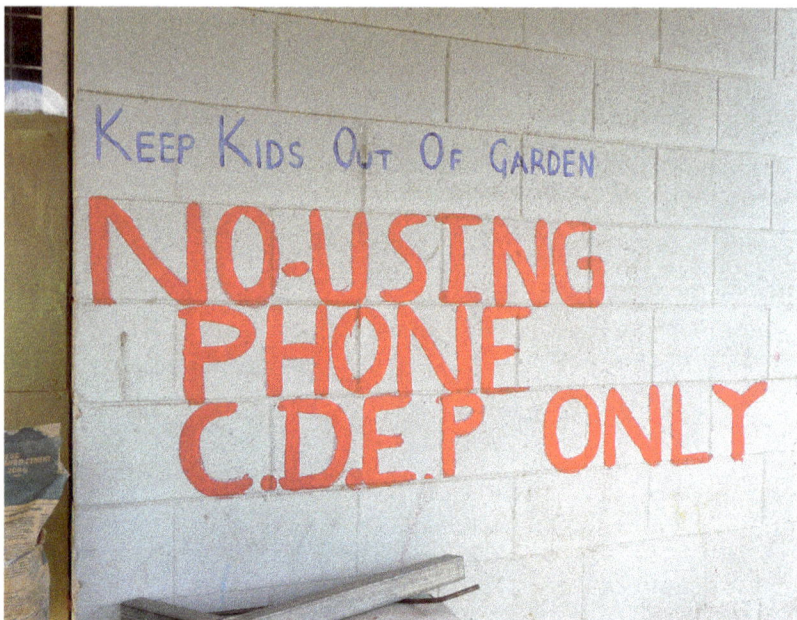

Fig. 6.3 Nturiya CDEP Office signs
Source: Photograph taken by author.

Horticulture and a men's shed: Activities at Pmara Jutunta and elsewhere

During 2007, CDEP activities at Pmara Jutunta were substantial. An area of grape farms to the southwest of Pmara Jutunta, dating back to the 1960s, provided winter pruning work for CDEP participants and a chance to earn 'top-up'. An adjacent horticultural research station owned by the Northern Territory government also became involved in supervising these CDEP participants and providing them with a certificate course in horticulture. These activities took the Pmara Jutunta CDEP participants out of their community, but the office in the settlement was still the meeting place at which they would assemble four mornings per week and from which they would be transported elsewhere to activities.

Another development during this time was that the male CDEP participants developed the idea of recladding the frame of an old mechanic's shed over the road from the community office in Pmara

Jutunta. There was enough money in the CDEP budget to buy the materials and over a six-month period, with some technical help from the organisation 'Indigenous Community Volunteers', the shed was restored to a reasonable level of safety and workability. This allowed the male CDEP workers to assemble at the shed each morning, rather than at the community office, which became more the women's domain.

By comparison with this level of activity at Pmara Jutunta, Nturiya struggled to keep its CDEP participants occupied. The only link outside the settlement on which they seemed able to draw for activities was a community-owned pastoral operation, which very occasionally called on their labour. Just turning up at the office four mornings per week wore a little thin, as there was only so much watering of the grass and tending to the produce garden that eight to 10 participants could do. At Pmara Jutunta, the infrastructure of localised authority and daily work habits was operating well, whereas at Nturiya it was more minimal. Though I visited Laramba and Engawala less during 2007–08, I heard reports that daily work routines and activities were working well in the former, but more minimal and variable in the latter.

The CDEP at Wilora in the north of Anmatjere presented another model again. It had not become part of ACGC's CDEP in 2006, but had continued to be run as a southern outpost of a Barkly regional CDEP further to the north. With no office in the settlement, Wilora CDEP struggled to maintain a work routine of turning up four mornings per week for activities. But CDEP in Wilora did appear to be a useful mechanism for organising bursts of community effort on particular projects. Alyuen ran as an outpost of Pmara Jutunta, also experiencing bursts of activity around projects.

Job Network and continuing CDEP under Central Desert Shire

Another development during 2007 was that a Job Network provider, the Tangentyere Job Shop, established an office in Ti Tree. CDEP participants were now being encouraged to register with a Job Network provider and, if they did, there were funds available to support their activities, including in CDEP. My interactions with Tangentyere Job Shop suggested that, in comparison with elsewhere, ACGC did not greatly draw on their resources. This was probably because ACGC was having trouble filling its 150 CDEP places and had plenty of funds to spend on CDEP participants from internal resources. Tangentyere Job Shop dealt with the jobseekers in the Anmatjere region largely independently of ACGC and its CDEP, which led to a slight sense of competition and tension between the two organisations rather than close cooperation.

Two larger significant developments that were occurring during 2007 and 2008 were the closures of some nearby CDEPs, as a result of the Australian Government's emergency Intervention into Northern Territory Aboriginal communities, and the shires reform within Territory local government. In central Australia, closures of CDEPs from September 2007 started south of Alice Springs and had not reached Anmatjere by the time they were abandoned on the election of the Rudd Labor Government in November (see Chapter 2). ACGC was thus spared the trauma of closing its CDEPs and then being given the opportunity to reopen them some months later, as occurred further south (see Kennedy 2013: Chapter 3). But ACGC's CDEPs did still have to negotiate the transition to Central Desert Shire in mid-2008.

With the emergence of Central Desert Shire, the Anmatjere CDEPs were merged with one at Atitjere in the east and four in Warlpiri country to the west. The new Shire had over 300 CDEP participants operating out of all nine of its service centres across four wards (see Fig. 6.4). The Shire's main administrative office was established in Alice Springs, 100 km south of its southern boundary. For Engawala and Laramba, this felt like they had been given back a more independent settlement status as they no longer had to answer to an office in Ti Tree. Around Ti Tree, the coming of the Shire led to less consciousness of the distinction between the Nturiya and Pmara Jutunta CDEPs. These became seen as part of one CDEP around the Shire's Ti Tree service centre, as too did Wilora when in 2009 it was transferred from the Barkly CDEP to Central Desert Shire. The new Shire developed a central CDEP administration in Alice Springs, but understood that the CDEPs around its nine service centres could sometimes look quite different, both because of their histories and due to current staff capabilities. Central Desert Shire, like ACGC before it, proved a quite sensitive 'federal' administrator of CDEP and other programs. However, it did not have ACGC's fine-grained geographic sensitivity to differences in CDEPs within the centre of the Anmatjere region around Ti Tree (Sanders 2008a). This can be seen in Fig. 6.5, which shows the Pmara Jutunta CDEP men's shed labelled by Central Desert Shire as part of Ti Tree CDEP.

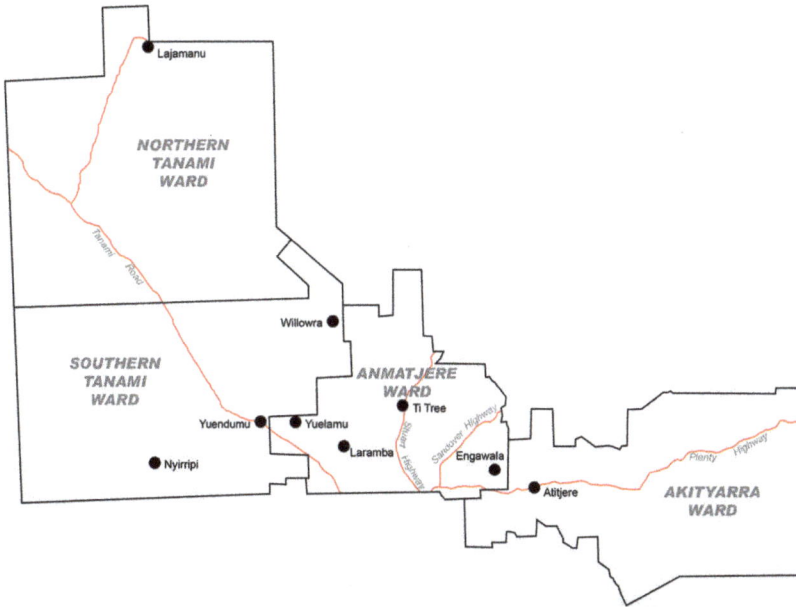

Fig. 6.4 Four wards and nine service centres of Central Desert Shire
Sources: Map supplied by Central Desert Shire and modified by John Hughes, CAEPR ANU.

In 2009, Central Desert Shire was successful in winning a new three-year contract for the provision of CDEP around all nine of its service centres. With the changes in CDEP policy from July 2009 (see Chapter 2), the Shire began acquiring CDEP participants who were social security income support recipients, alongside those remaining on wages as Shire employees. Managing these two different groups of CDEP participants was not always easy and the reaction of Central Desert Shire (unlike some other providers) was to let the number of wages-based CDEP participants lessen over time by natural attrition. By 2011, the Shire had less than 100 wages-based CDEP participants and the number was continuing to decrease. On-cost support resources for CDEP participants were, by contrast, expanding during this period. There was plenty of money available for equipment to support activities and even for more substantial infrastructure, like new activities centres. The range of activities that CDEP participants could undertake was, however, slightly more restricted than in previous years. This partly reflected a new policy of pushing the funding of service-type jobs out of CDEP onto other government departments, like night patrol to the Attorney-General's department and rangers to the Environment department. Restriction also reflected a policy push away from seeing art production as a legitimate CDEP activity, except for skills development without commercial sales.

Fig. 6.5 CDEP men's shed at Pmara Jutunta with Central Desert Shire sign
Source: Photograph taken by author.

On my assessment, Central Desert Shire did quite a good job of navigating the changing policy landscape of CDEP during the years 2009 to 2012. While their number of wages-based CDEP participants decreased dramatically, their total number of CDEP participants remained up over 250 and the Shire was good at bringing in support money for activities. New CDEP activities centres were applied for and built in many of the Shire service centres. These helped provide kitchens and classrooms in which women's CDEP teams, in particular, could undertake activities. Men's CDEP teams seemed to prefer sheds, equipment and outdoor activities, though they could occasionally be found in the classrooms and kitchens. CDEP's basic infrastructure of localised authority and work habits, four mornings per week, was well established and administered by Central Desert Shire across a dispersed array of settlements, as it had been previously by ACGC.

From Job Services Australia and CDEP to RJCP

One of the other developments in the 2009–12 contract triennium was that the Job Network became remodelled as Job Services Australia (JSA). Tangentyere Job Shop was not awarded the new contract in Anmatjere, but the new provider, Jobfind, moved into the same premises in Ti Tree, providing some minimal sense of continuity (see Fig. 6.6). As registration with a JSA became more common among CDEP participants receiving Newstart Allowance and among other unemployed in Anmatjere, it became clear to all these 'jobseekers' that JSAs had a very different mode of operation to CDEPs. JSAs required attendance at a meeting with a case manager about once a month, which focused on the development and maintenance of an individual participation plan. This was very different from the CDEP mode of operation, which had a strong sense of being undertaken in teams four mornings per week. The two modes of operation could coexist, if JSA meetings for CDEP participants were scheduled for the afternoon or if participants were given leave from CDEP activities to attend JSA meetings. Some of this did begin to occur during the 2009–12 contract triennium. But the parallel operation of CDEP and JSA also opened up questions about the relationships between these two very different processes. Did they constitute an unnecessary duplication of employment services or were they usefully complementary? Was one mode of operation seen as more valuable than the other or were they equally valued? As Figs 6.6 and 6.7 suggest, both programs in Anmatjere saw things as possible, but one focused on 'anything' and the other on 'everything'! CDEP's informal sign also suggested more localised authority.

Fig. 6.6 Jobfind office in Ti Tree 2009–13

Source: Photograph taken by author.

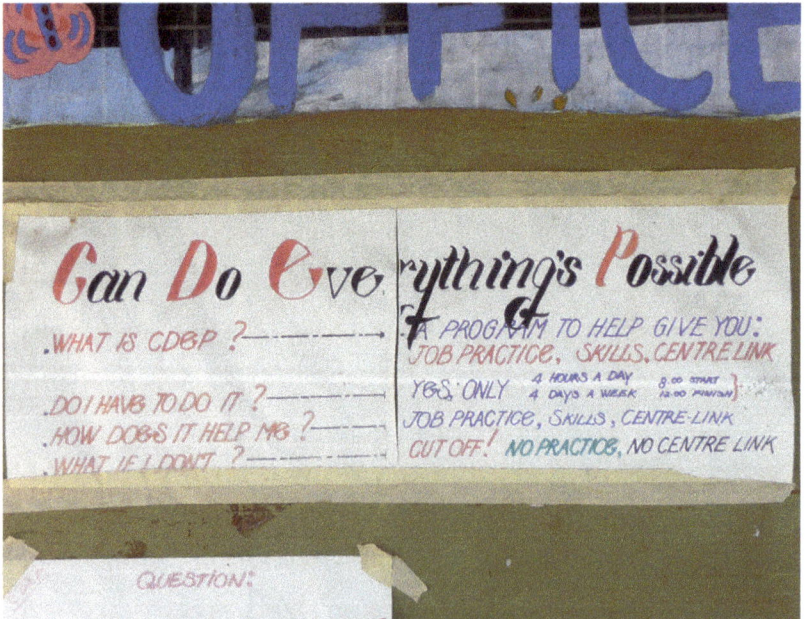

Fig. 6.7 Informal CDEP sign 2013

Source: Photograph taken by author.

The Gillard Labor Government's review of 'remote participation and employment servicing' in late 2011 tended towards a negative view of the program 'arrangements' that already existed. The combination of JSA and CDEP, along with the Indigenous Employment Program and Disability Employment Services, was variously described as 'fragmented', 'confusing', 'inflexible and unresponsive' (Arbib et al. 2011: 7). The proposed new model of 'a single provider' in each region, subsuming all four previous programs, was promoted as 'simpler, more integrated and more flexible', as well as more 'tailored' to the 'diverse' communities of remote areas (Arbib et al. 2011: 8). This negative framing of the old was reinforced in May 2012, when it was anticipated that the new RJCP would be 'more integrated and flexible' and that the single provider would have a 'permanent presence' in the region, enabling it to provide more 'personalised support for job seekers' (Macklin et al. 2012a).

What was not said in this official analysis, but was clearly inevitable, was that there would be competition and rationalisation of CDEP and JSA providers in the year leading up to the commencement of RJCP in July 2013. The call for 'expressions of interest' in being an RJCP provider in October 2012 noted that 'interested organisations' could apply as 'individual providers or in partnership with other organisations'. It also noted that there was $15 million available 'to help build the capacity of potential providers' and that the government wanted 'as many local Indigenous organisations delivering the new program as possible' (Macklin et al. 2012b).

Central Desert Shire was interested in becoming an RJCP provider largely because it foresaw that the new single provider program would have major implications for its constituents. As well as having experience running CDEP around all nine of its service centres, the Shire also had some limited experience running JSA, in conjunction with Job Futures, around its eastern service centre at Atitjere (see Fig. 6.4). The Shire thus had experience in both major preceding programs and would be a credible RJCP applicant, but there were also a couple of problems. One was that the Shire boundaries did not correspond with those of RJCP regions. RJCP region 25 fell in the centre of the Shire in its Anmatjere and Southern Tanami wards. However, around its edges the Shire was part of three more RJCP regions (see Figs 6.4 and 6.8). This related to a second problem, which was that, under its local government legislation, the Shire could not act outside its boundaries and had some restrictions on its ability to enter into partnerships with other organisations.

The Shire became an individual applicant for RJCP in region 25 and part of a partnership application in region 24 overlapping its eastern boundaries. The application was successful in region 25, but not in region 24. The Shire thus became an RJCP provider in 2013 around five of its service centres (Ti Tree, Laramba, Yuelamu, Yuendumu and Willowra), but not the other four (Atitjere, Engawala, Lajamanu and Nyirripi). In these latter areas, the Shire had to negotiate with the successful RJCP applicants for their access to former CDEP infrastructure and resources.

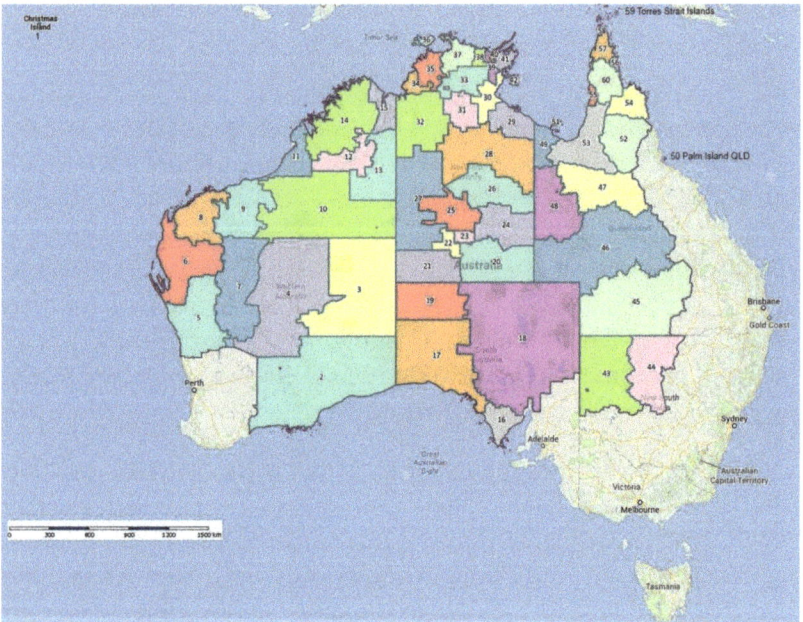

Fig. 6.8 Map of 60 RJCP regions
Source: Department of Employment, Education and Workplace Relations 2013.

The question that most intrigued me, as I observed the emerging transition to RJCP in Anmatjere, was how the two different modes of operation of CDEP and JSA would come together in this new single program? Would there be teams of participants undertaking activities on a daily and weekly basis or would case workers doing monthly interviews with individual jobseekers be the predominant mode of operation? In Anmatjere, it turned out to be the latter and my impression is that this has been the dominant pattern elsewhere as well, although not inevitably and invariably so.[1] What possibly led Central Desert Shire in this direction was some embracing of the rhetoric of past policy and program failure.

While existing CDEP administrators were central to the Shire's bid for RJCP, there was also a sense that RJCP would not be a continuation of CDEP within Central Desert. Even before it was known in May 2013 that one of the Shire's bids for RJCP had been successful, it became apparent that there would be some quite significant changes in personnel and mode of operation. CDEP staff would have to apply for new jobs with new duty statements, which could be quite different from existing ones. CDEP staff started leaving in quite large numbers in early 2013, unsure that they would have a job by mid-year even if the Shire was successful in winning an RJCP provider contract. When I visited Laramba and the communities around Ti Tree in the early days of June 2013, CDEP had effectively already shut. Resignations and absences over the previous couple of months had reduced CDEP supervisory staff to one person in Laramba and one based in Ti Tree covering both the Pmara Jutunta and Nturiya offices. The women's CDEP teams in these places had ceased to operate a month or more before and the men's teams were reduced to a few individuals hanging around the shed. The two remaining supervisory staff were 'outdoor' workers who could not see themselves being applicants for the RJCP case manager 'office' jobs that were being advertised at the time of my visit. So they too were uncertain about their future employment.

In many ways, the senior management at Central Desert Shire had little choice but to employ new people to get RJCP up and running in mid-2013. The contract was based on an Employment department model of registering individual jobseekers, meeting with them monthly and developing individual participation plans in return for the provider organisation receiving a basic service fee. While there were aspirations to have activities for jobseekers, and resources that could be drawn on for this purpose, the more basic task was the office job of

---

1   This impression comes from working with PhD student Lisa Fowkes on an Australian Research Council Linkage Project (LP130100226) with Jobs Australia as contributing Industry Partner, entitled *Implementing the Remote Jobs and Communities Program: How is policy working in Indigenous communities?*

getting individuals entered in the computer system and meeting basic requirements so that the service fees to the provider could start flowing. This was more the style of expertise that came from JSA operations than from CDEP. While Central Desert Shire had some experience with JSA, this was probably not enough. The Shire needed new staff who could do this computer-based case management work. The expertise of CDEP staff was more collaborative and activity-based, which would be good in the longer term, but was not the immediate priority. But Central Desert Shire also, to some extent, accepted the predominant rhetoric that CDEP had been a failure and needed to be left behind.

During the latter months of 2013, as RJCP was transferred administratively into the Department of the Prime Minister and Cabinet (see Chapter 2), I observed Central Desert Shire and its constituents continuing to struggle with RJCP. Former CDEP participants were perplexed by the monthly meetings, intended to develop individualised participation plans but without much activity in between. Compared to their former four mornings per week work habit in localised teams, this monthly individual check-in regime seemed empty, as if something had been taken from them, as indeed it had. Around Ti Tree, there was the added complication that RJCP was not physically reaching out to the outlying communities of Pmara Jutunta and Nturiya. The new activity centre and RJCP office, built in the last year of CDEP but never used, was in Ti Tree town (see Fig. 6.9). This required transport in from the communities where most people lived. On occasions I saw quite angry exchanges between RJCP case managers and former CDEP participants who came to their monthly meetings from very different perspectives and past experiences.

During 2014, Central Desert's administration of RJCP did begin to include activities, as well as case management. The September 2014 edition of *Central Desert News* included two stories about RJCP, one about an arts activity in the 'old Op Shop' at Yuelamu, which had produced a large painting being 'donated to the new council building', and the other about a team of RJCP men who had helped lay 18 km of pipe to 'deliver drinking water to Alyuen'. When I visited Ti Tree in October 2014, there were two activities supervisors working alongside the case manager focused on office work. When they said they were having trouble getting RJCP participants to come into town for activities, I suggested reopening the men's shed at Pmara Jutunta. The reaction was immediate. At 8am the next day, when the supervisors opened the gates of the yard around the Pmara Jutunta shed, no less than 8 to 10 men walked up from their houses ready for activities. Over 18 months since the shed last operated, the daily work habits of CDEP participants were easily reinvigorated.

Fig. 6.9 New CDEP/RJCP Activity Centre and Office in Ti Tree 2013
Source: Photograph taken by author.

I did not visit Anmatjere in 2015, so I cannot say with any authority how RJCP is progressing. I suspect that monthly meetings and individual case management are still predominating and possibly always will due to the structure of the employment services contract. However, I am also conscious that, under the Department of the Prime Minister and Cabinet and the Abbott Coalition Government, the funding agreements and compliance frameworks for RJCP were significantly reworked to emphasise activities. I will leave analysis of these changes to future observation and writing. But in conclusion I wish to turn more explicitly to an argument about practice and its relationship to policy and program review.

Maintaining good practice: A first rule of policy and program review

Public policy is by nature aspirational. It constructs existing social and economic circumstances as in some way deficient and problematic and then tries to improve them. As the great American social scientist Charles Lindblom (1990) put it in the subtitle of his book *Inquiry and Change*, this 'attempt to understand and shape society' is often 'troubled', achieving less than is hoped. When policies and programs are seen as not achieving high hopes, it is understandable that they become analysed as failures, and new policies and programs are suggested to replace them. However, there is a downside to this well-intentioned dynamic, which may indeed have been what predominated when the Gillard Labor Government reviewed 'remote participation and employment servicing' in 2011 and decided that CDEP and JSA were 'fragmented'. Another more positive analysis, hinted at above, might have pointed to the two very different modes of operation of these programs and suggested that they were usefully complementary. But this was not to be. The negative analysis of what already existed prevailed easily and, before we knew it, existing good practice was being thrown out in the process of introducing a single new program to replace the existing four.

To some extent, Central Desert Shire embraced the idea of past policy and program failure and tried to build something new in RJCP. The unexpected outcome was that the Shire lost what it already had in CDEP and, two years on, was still trying to rebuild. I am aware of a handful of RJCP providers across the 60 regions who did not accept this 'failure and change' style of analysis. These providers deliberately tried to maintain through RJCP good practice already established under CDEP (and to lesser extent JSA).[2] This required some strategic alliance building between the skill sets of JSA and CDEP, as the RJCP contract clearly required JSA-type skills. However, maintenance of existing good practice also required some self-conscious holding of a line against the reframing of CDEP as a 'failure' and 'passive welfare' (see Chapter 2). Organisations that had long and deep involvement in wages-based CDEP knew that it was 'better than welfare' in a number of significant ways that were worth

---

2   See footnote 1.

preserving, even against the prevailing rhetoric and analysis of the change to RJCP. Having only administered CDEP since 2008, alongside its local government functions, Central Desert Shire did not have a deep enough understanding of how it could and would have to hold this line against reframing in order to maintain good existing practice.

Previously I have written about how the 'failure and change' style of analysis became dominant in Australian Indigenous affairs during the fourth term of the Howard Coalition Government from 2004 to 2007, producing a 'generational revolution' of policy and institutional redesign (Sanders 2008b). While ostensibly pushing back against this style (with the apology to the stolen generations and stopping the immediate abolition of CDEP in the Northern Territory), on balance the Rudd Labor Government continued the generational policy revolution in Australian Indigenous affairs (Hunt & Sanders 2010). The Gillard Government's review of 'remote participation and employment servicing' and its combining of CDEP and JSA into RJCP can also be seen as a continuation of this style of analysis leading to major institutional change. Once a 'failure and change' discourse is established as dominant, it can itself be hard to change. Maintaining good existing practice, like the work habits and localised authority of CDEP, can become very hard amidst the constant policy and program reviews of a long-running generational revolution. But if we are analytically self-aware of the downside of policy and program review, we may at least have some prospect of maintaining good practice. The good practice work habits of the CDEP men at Pmara Jutunta were able to be reinvigorated after 18 months of shut gates at their shed. So existing good practice can survive the aspirations of policy review and the downsides of program change, but only if maintaining good practice becomes a self-conscious rule of policy review. This is the precautionary principle of 'first do no harm' in another guise.

References

Arbib M, Macklin J & Ellis K (2011). *The future of remote participation and employment servicing arrangements: discussion paper,* Minister for Indigenous Employment and Economic Development, Minister for Families, Housing Community Services and Indigenous Affairs, Minister for Employment Participation and Childcare, Australian Government, Canberra.

Hunt J & Sanders W (2010). Sorry, but the Indigenous affairs revolution continues. In Aulich C & Evans M (eds), *The Rudd Government: Australian Commonwealth administration 2007–2010,* ANU E Press, Canberra.

Kennedy A (2013). Values, voice and choice: Western Arrernte outstation engagement in the Northern Territory intervention, PhD thesis, Southern Cross University, Lismore, New South Wales.

Lindblom C (1990). *Inquiry and change: the troubled attempt to understand and shape society,* Yale University Press, New Haven.

Macklin J, Shorten B & Collins J (2012a). *Remote Jobs and Communities Program: jobs and stronger communities for people in remote Australia,* Minister for Families, Community Services and Indigenous Affairs, Minister for Employment and Workplace Relations, Minister for Indigenous Employment and Economic Development, Australian Government, Canberra.

Macklin J, Shorten B & Collins J (2012b). *Call for providers to deliver new $1.5b remote jobs program,* media release, Minister for Families, Community Services and Indigenous Affairs, Minister for Employment and Workplace Relations, Minister for Indigenous Employment and Economic Development, Australian Government, 2 October 2012, Canberra.

Sanders W (2008a). Regionalism that respects localism: the Anmatjere Community Government Council and beyond. In Hunt J, Smith D, Garling S & Sanders W (eds), *Contested governance: culture, power and institutions in Indigenous Australia,* CAEPR Research Monograph No. 29, ANU E Press, Canberra, 283–309.

Sanders W (2008b). In the name of failure: A generational revolution in Indigenous affairs. In Aulich C & Wettenhall R (eds), *Howard's fourth government: Australian Commonwealth Administration 2004–2007,* UNSW Press, Sydney: 187–206.

7

Bawinanga and CDEP: The vibrant life, and near death, of a major Aboriginal corporation in Arnhem Land

Jon Altman

Introduction

In this chapter, I examine the Bawinanga Aboriginal Corporation (also referred to as Bawinanga or BAC) located at Maningrida in Arnhem Land. Bawinanga is an Aboriginal corporation and for over 20 years it was also a Community Development Employment Projects (CDEP) organisation. It was established in 1979 and, during the first decade of the 21st century, it became one of the largest and most financially successful Indigenous corporations in Australia. For a number of years between 2004–05 and 2010–11, Bawinanga was ranked as the second-largest Indigenous corporation in Australia by the Office of the Registrar of Indigenous Corporations.

Bawinanga succeeded in remote and difficult circumstances largely devoid of market opportunity where others, including the Australian colonial state from 1957, have failed. Its only serious competitor in the Maningrida region is the Maningrida Progress Association, a community-owned organisation that focuses on retail trade in the township of Maningrida. Much of Bawinanga's success can be linked historically to its productive deployment and reconfiguring of CDEP funding support from the Australian government.

I focus here on the relationship between CDEP and Bawinanga, as their life cycles are closely related; Bawinanga was established as a small community-based outstation resource agency in 1979 two years after CDEP began. Both were new and innovative institutions of what Tim Rowse (2002) has termed 'the Indigenous sector'.

Despite an early application for CDEP funding in 1980, it was not until 1989 that access to CDEP was provided to Bawinanga to be delivered initially to 'unemployed' (in a formal Western labour market sense) residents of the outstations in its 10,000-square-kilometre-sphere of geographic influence.

From then, Bawinanga gradually changed into a successful regional development corporation. Its growth, highly contingent on the entrepreneurial zeal and political acumen of its senior management, was largely underwritten by access to CDEP.

From 1989 to 2009 Bawinanga grew quickly. This period can be roughly divided by the period between 1989 and 1996, when CDEP was incrementally integrated into Bawinanga's operations, and the time after 1996 when the corporation became increasingly involved in small business development and the delivery of diverse services with associated normalisation and developmental undercurrents.

From 2009 the corporation's fortunes declined, reflecting in some measure significant changes to CDEP. These changes had been signalled for some time, at least since the transfer of the program on 1 July 2004 from the Aboriginal and Torres Strait Islander Commission (ATSIC) to the Department of Employment and Workplace Relations (DEWR) when the former was effectively abolished. Much of this policy history has been told in early chapters of this monograph (see also Sanders 2012; and Appendix 1, this volume). A key element of this administrative change saw CDEP shift from operating as a grant-in-aid program to being defined as a contracted service. This change reflected the new public management or managerialism infusing Indigenous policy at the time (Sullivan 2011: 67–83).

From 2005 CDEP was slowly dismantled as the effective means to underwrite community development, and abolished a decade later. This 'reform' coincided with a rapid decline in Bawinanga's fortunes that was also greatly influenced by changes in its management and operating style and enhanced instability in political relations with the Australian Government.

In October 2012 Bawinanga went into special administration, what I term 'near death', owing to short-term insolvency, a situation from which it has recovered from July 2014, much reduced and deeply indebted. During the period of special administration, CDEP was replaced by the Remote Jobs and Communities Program (RJCP) and Bawinanga was selected as the regional provider despite its financial troubles.

In this chapter, I provide an account of the consequences of the demise of CDEP for Bawinanga, its members and the regional population more generally. My focus is on the multiple somewhat contradictory roles of Bawinanga as an economic development agency (Altman & Johnson 2000) as well as a political institution (Rowse 2001a) and community development institution (Martin 2001). This is counter to an increasingly dominant narrative that irrationally emphasises CDEP as a labour market program only and hence measures success or failure in terms of 'real' jobs—a euphemism for forms of regular employment that are very limited in number in the Maningrida region. This shift is linked to a wider discourse that seeks to blame the policy of self-determination and ATSIC for disappointing outcomes in Indigenous affairs generally. This same discourse proposes to Close the Gap through mainstreaming or normalisation, even in remote Arnhem Land.

The CDEP reform agenda has been deeply influenced by a discourse brought to national prominence by Noel Pearson around 'welfare poison', the need for Aboriginal engagement in 'real' jobs in the 'real' economy, and the overarching need for Aboriginal individuals to be 'responsibilised' (Kowal 2012). The use of the term 'real' is a trope that not only requires imagination in the unreal circumstances of remote Indigenous Australia, but is also contingent on a certain settler belief and value system. In this increasingly dominant narrative, CDEP has been depicted as a form of welfare and as a form of exceptionalism that has operated as a barrier to the engagement of Aboriginal people with the labour market.

In this chapter, I begin by outlining my entanglements as a policy anthropologist with Bawinanga. This is mainly because I use a particular voice in this chapter; not the voice of the dispassionate, analytic and detached academic, but rather, the voice of someone who has worked closely with this organisation for much of my academic life: I have had an entanglement with Bawinanga for a long time and I lament its decline.

Next I describe the shifting nature of Bawinanga according to a selection of the many texts produced by the corporation itself. Then I say something about what Bawinanga did, focusing my attention on a decade-long period of relative growth and stability when it had a 'vibrant life' to 2009 when it went into decline. I explore and look to critically theorise the reasons for Bawinanga's success according to both internal and external at arms-length assessments, including my own.

In this analysis, I highlight one short period 2005–06 when, after CDEP administration was transferred from ATSIC to DEWR, Bawinanga and DEWR engaged in a bitter political struggle that I refer to metaphorically as 'the CDEP wars'. Bawinanga struggled to gain acceptance for its approach to running CDEP, something that it had been doing with growing efficiency and confidence for 16 years before what I have termed 'metropolitan managerialism' (Altman 2005) bore down on the organisation from distant Canberra, as far away bureaucrats sought to impose a particular interpretation of the imagined failings of CDEP on Bawinanga. Evidence of this dispute is on the parliamentary record that I visit to ask: Why it is that expert and local knowledge have been disqualified or discarded as legitimate forms of knowing about CDEP?

I then provide a brief account of the rapid decline of Bawinanga from 2009 until 2012 when it went into special administration. I end by assessing what has been lost and by speculating whether the belated attempts to revive CDEP from late 2015 as the Community Development Program (CDP), linguistic similarities aside, might revive the fortunes of Bawinanga.

Entanglements: Bawinanga and me

Over the years I have written a great deal about Bawinanga. I have also worked for Bawinanga as a consultant and advocated hard for Bawinanga including by assisting the corporation as the joint plaintiff in a High Court case Wurridjal v Commonwealth over the compulsory leasing of Aboriginal land during the Northern Territory (NT) Intervention and in submissions to and as an expert witness in parliamentary inquiries.

I have repeatedly visited the Maningrida region since 1979. My research has been heavily divided between working with a regional community of Kuninjku-speaking people first and foremost (many of whom are also members of Bawinanga) and working with Bawinanga.

The history of my intellectual and formal engagement with Bawinanga over the past 37 years is lengthy and complex. Suffice to say, I have personally known every chair of Bawinanga since 1979, most board members and most members of the senior management team, some of whom are friends with whom I have co-resided on many occasions when visiting. Over the years, I have also got to know many Indigenous and non-Indigenous residents of the region, which currently has a population of over 3,000.

I relate this to be quite transparent and disclose my abiding interests. I am sure there are some who view my close allegiances to Bawinanga with suspicion and as a weakness because it might foreclose openness to alternate viewpoints from other actors in the region. This may well be a valid criticism; I note though that I have worked with other organisations and have enjoyed cordial relations with their Aboriginal boards and staff despite shifting institutional rivalries and alliances typical of small-town politics and clearly evident over time in Maningrida.[1] All these associations with Bawinanga have not stopped me from being a critical—sometimes highly critical—friend of Bawinanga and the operations of some of its business units, and being unpopular at times with board and management for providing frank advice.

---

1   I have worked in a voluntary capacity for the Maningrida Progress Association whose board I have also advised; and with the Maningrida Council until absorbed into the West Arnhem Shire in 2008.

I highlight these entanglements for two reasons. I want to write this chapter in a slightly different register, delving into a considerable archive of transcripts of Bawinanga's achievements, challenges and problems, especially focusing here on issues related to CDEP without replicating earlier writing on this subject (Altman & Johnson 2000). I do this in particular by focusing on material contained in Bawinanga's narrative annual reports published 1999 to 2011 and its financial records. I am keen to bring material from this grey literature, Bawinanga's and my own archives, into the public domain highly conscious that there is a great deal more that can be said about Bawinanga's life cycle and circumstances. This particular contribution is very much intended as an economic history of Bawinanga's dialectical engagement with the CDEP scheme, how at once CDEP contributed to the making of Bawinanga and, conversely, how Bawinanga has demonstrated what could be done with CDEP and how paradoxically CDEP was instrumental in what I term here Bawinanga's 'near death' experience when it went into special administration.

On the final page of the postscript to a volume, *The Indigenous Welfare Economy and the CDEP Scheme*,[2] that reported the proceedings of a large and mixed academic, bureaucratic and Indigenous community conference on CDEP, Rowse (2001b: 233) noted that there was urgent need for the articulation of an independent community-based conception of what CDEP is all about. This was especially important, he suggested, as a counter to the government's dominant representation, as I have noted already, of CDEP as an employment scheme only. Rowse urged academics to play a role in formulating political and cultural rationales that CDEP managers could present to government. There has been considerable representation by Bawinanga and myself both before and after the 2001 volume, although its lack of influence is telling. Rowse also suggested in his postscript that CAEPR has a close proximity to the central agencies of government—perhaps geographically as both are based in Canberra, but not, as this chapter will demonstrate, in terms of ameliorating the destructive reform of CDEP.

---

2   To which the Bawinanga accountant Rupert Manners (2001) contributed a chapter on catering for mobility and diversity.

Bawinanga's objects and vision

In his book *Indigenous futures: Choice and development for Aboriginal and Islander Australia*, which summarised and critically analysed CAEPR research 1990–2000, Rowse (2002) devotes a chapter to Indigenous institutions and the labour market. Rowse (2002: 67) highlights the many difficulties in defining the objects of CDEP because of its multiple rationales. At the time of his writing there were 270 CDEP organisations with over 30,000 participants nationally (Sanders 2004: 4).

A similar observation can be made of Bawinanga as a CDEP institution. Over its life, and in the words of its annual reports and constitution (now Rule Book), there have been changes over time. In its first narrative annual report for 1999–2000, an attempt is made to provide a brief overview of the corporation's history over the preceding 20 years (Johnson 2000: 1): 'initially Bawinanga was incorporated under the federal *Aboriginal Councils and Associations Act 1976* as an outstation resource centre incorporating an earlier manifestation set up in 1974 as a branch of the Maningrida community council.' Johnson notes how in the 20 years since 1979 the corporation had expanded and diversified, not just providing support for up to 800 people residing at 32 outstations in the hinterland, but also administering CDEP with 512 participants and shifting to operate as a regional development agency establishing small commercial enterprises to promote economic development options for outstation residents and members. Johnson (2000: 1) further notes that the central tenet of all decisions made by the corporation is the maintenance of land, language and culture.

This statement of organisational philosophy was clearly stated after Bawinanga developed its first strategic plan 2004–06, a process facilitated by Dan Gillespie of Tallegalla Consultants (2003) with parts published in the corporation's annual report for 2003–04 (Johnson 2004: 6) in the following terms:

Our Mission Statement

Bawinanga Aboriginal Corporation's mission is derived from its constitution and is twofold:

- At the regional level we act as a force for the political integration and representation of the interests of over 100 regional land owning groups of our members

- As a service delivery agency BAC provides cultural and natural resource management programs, essential municipal and social services and labour market and economic development opportunities to its members in Maningrida and surrounding outstation communities.

The maintenance of language and traditions and the management of and sustainable use of customary lands and resources underpin our work.

Our Vision

Our vision is to be:

- A successful agency for the representation and mediation of the interests of our members to other regional stakeholders, private enterprise and Government; and
- A leading Indigenous service delivery and business organisation managed by Aboriginal people for Aboriginal people and renowned for our innovation and best practice.

More recently, in the current Rule Book[3] the objectives of the corporation are defined in the following terms:

The objectives of the corporation are to provide services [to] the communities and lands set out in the map in Schedule 4:

a. to promote the maintenance of language, culture and traditional practice;

b. to promote the sustainable use of traditional lands;

c. to promote community development;

d. to promote the welfare of residents;

e. to provide or assist in the provision and maintenance of education, employment, housing, health, communications and other services;

f. to foster business opportunities and to promote economic independence;

g. to operate and maintain a gift fund to be known as — The Bawinanga Aboriginal Corporation Gift Fund in accordance with the requirements of the Income Tax Assessment Act 1997; and

h. to promote, in all its endeavours, the common good and mutual benefit of its members through fair, equitable and representative action and enterprise.

---

3 Available like much documentation about Bawinanga back to 2006 when the *Aboriginal Councils and Associations Act 1976* was replaced by the *Corporations (Aboriginal and Torres Strait Islanders) Act 2006* at register.oric.gov.au/document.aspx?concernID=100029, accessed 21 September 2015.

The map referred to is a version of the following Fig. 7.1.

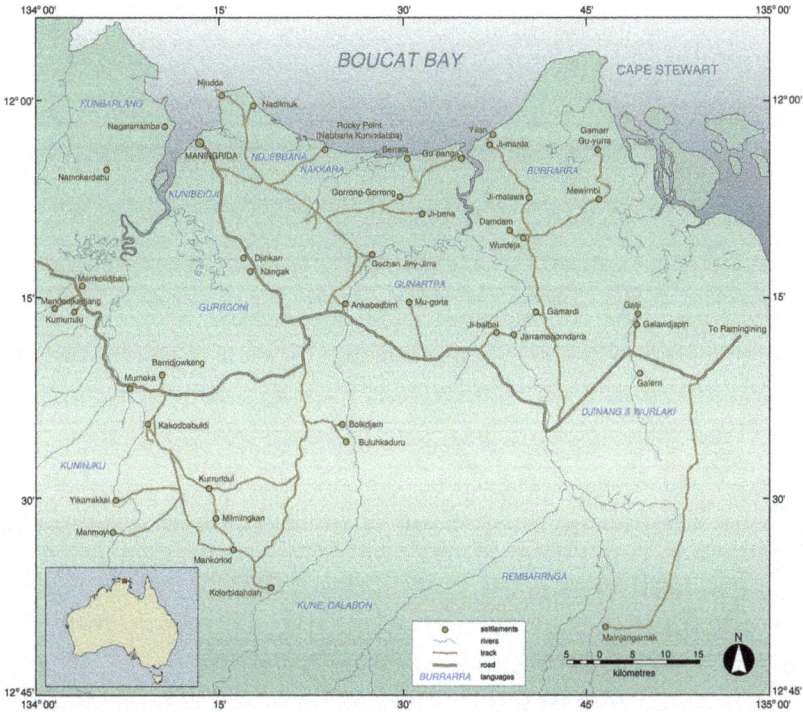

Fig. 7.1 A version of the map in Schedule 4 of BACs 'rule book'
Source: Map drawn for author with material provided by Bawinanga Aboriginal Corporation.

Such fine aspirational statements are not unusual, but in Bawinanga's case they have some important implications. First, given that the region of about 10,000 sq km is all Aboriginal-owned land,[4] the corporation clearly has a major political role to play in mediating land owner interests, although in formal and legal terms this is the statutory responsibility of the Northern Land Council. Second, the objectives of Bawinanga extend beyond its membership (which numbers about 200 registered adults aged over 18 years) to include other non-member residents of the region. This reflects how Bawinanga has increasingly operated.

---

4   Barring a few special purpose leases and public lands in Maningrida that predated passage of the *Aboriginal Land Rights (Northern Territory) Act 1976.*

Bawinanga 1999–2010

In 2000, I undertook a detailed review with Victoria Johnson of the Bawinanga CDEP as part of a wide-ranging study that included the above-mentioned conference, 'The Indigenous Welfare Economy and the Community Development Employment Projects (CDEP) Scheme: Autonomy, Dependence, Self Determination and Mutual Obligation' with proceedings subsequently published (Morphy & Sanders 2001). Johnson had been employed by Bawinanga between 1998 and 2000 and the corporation was a financial and in-kind contributor to the review that ended with a set of recommendations, including that there is need for quarantined resourcing for more effective outcomes monitoring (Altman & Johnson 2000: xi, 33).

On completion of the review, senior management at Bawinanga engaged Johnson to produce the corporation's first narrative annual report. Subsequently, as shown in Table 7.1, 11 further reports were prepared with 10 published. The 2000–01 annual report included the recommendations from the CDEP review. From 2003–04, after early resistance from senior management, the annual report included some summary financial statements from the corporation's audited accounts. From 2005–06 the annual reports became more political as transcripts with a Chairman's message and CEO's report that engaged with current policy settings and challenges.

Table 7.1 Bawinanga annual reporting 1999–2011

BAC annual report	Author/compiler	Published	Pages
1999–2000	V Johnson	2000	28
2000–2001	V Johnson	2001	18
2001–2002	A McCall	Incomplete	23
2002–2003	V Johnson	2003	28
2003–2004	V Johnson	2004	28
2004–2005	C McAuliffe	2005	32
2005–2006	W Manners	2006	34
2006–2007	W Manners	2007	32
2007–2008	W Manners	2008	32
2008–2009	W Manners	2009	32
2009–2010	C Summers	2010	57
2010–2011	C Summers	2011	65

Source: Prepared by the author.

All the authors of annual reports had worked for Bawinanga and so were able to compile information provided by the heads of business units. I was recently informed by Ian Munro, the Bawinanga instigator of such annual reporting, that in general 500 copies of the report were printed with a copy sent to every federal and Northern Territory politician.[5]

It is hard to know how to capture the wide range of activities reported in nearly 400 pages over this 12-year period, including vividly descriptive colour photographs that illustrate the degree of local people's pride in the corporation.[6] Furthermore, these annual reports, as valuable a record as they are, only represent a series of snapshots of what ended up being a decade-long cumulative and incremental growth of the corporation and its social, physical and developmental capitals.[7]

In an attempt to capture the complexity of Bawinanga, I have prepared a synoptic table of its range of activities that fall into three categories: activities that have ended; activities that have begun at some point during the period; and those that are core activities that continued throughout the period. To some extent, this approach has introduced some room for error as some activities are not reported even though undertaken. And it has also resulted in under-reporting because some smaller, but still important, activities are not separately reported.

An example of such a small but symbolically important activity is the mud-brick factory that is an iconic CDEP enterprise that began in 1989. In a comprehensive feasibility study report, Dan Gillespie of Tallegalla Consultants (2009: 1, 9) notes that the enterprise has provided employment continuously for up to 15 Indigenous people for almost 20 years. To date, over 130 buildings have been constructed from mud-brick, including a range of housing types and other

---

5   Ian Munro pers. comm. June 2015. Munro also related to me how on one occasion a staff member spotted Claire Martin, then Chief Minister of the NT, reading a Bawinanga annual report on a flight from Alice Springs to Darwin.

6   Obviously the annual reports were largely produced for external audiences and reflect what might be thought of as 'whitefella' accountability. But there has also been a degree of pride expressed especially by members of the Bawinanga board about the reports.

7   A spreadsheet assets register prepared in 2008 as part of the Wurridjal v Commonwealth case that I have lists all Bawinanga's fixed and non-fixed assets, which totalled nearly 600 items and were valued at over $24 million—the main fixed assets include 100 outstation buildings and numerous houses and business premises in Maningrida.

facilities at outstations, housing for Bawinanga and other agency staff, commercial and office buildings for Bawinanga and the Maningrida Progress Association, and major buildings such as the Maningrida Motel and Aged Care facility operated by the Malabam Health Board.

Furthermore, a lot of activity has been subsumed in one category. For example, under financial and related services, the 2006–07 annual report shows that Bawinanga assisted members and staff with online banking, internet banking, truck accounts (of which there were 200, or one-third of the CDEP payroll saving for vehicles), bill saving authorised deductions from CDEP, ceremonial support, again via payroll deductions, assistance to borrow money and assistance to access services (Manners 2007; Fogarty & Paterson 2007).

The message from this table is that over the decade covered, community services and businesses were established that provided CDEP participants with meaningful activity destinations and the means to earn additional income. While during these years there were some variations, on average Bawinanga had 600 participants who fell into four categories: those employed by Bawinanga (about 200); those hosted by other Maningrida agencies and organisations like the school and health board (about 50); about 300 getting income support at outstations (who generally supplemented their CDEP payments with art sales to Maningrida Arts and Culture); and the balance of about 50 who received basic income support while on CDEP.

Rupert Manners (2001: 211–13) explains how this worked, although there have been many adaptive variations over the years approved by the board, particularly of the 'no work no pay' rule that was a critical element of attempts to manage labour. In general, there were three pay rates: one for participants who were supervisors; one for those who were working or training; and another for those at outstations. And then there were variations in hours: those at the highest two award plus pay rates could work for up to 4.6 hours a day for three days on CDEP and then get additional top up, including for extra days of work; those at outstations but also at funerals, ceremonies, sick, on maternity leave or working as a medical escort were paid for 3.6 hours a day; and, those referred to as on 'sit down' would get only 2 hours a day and would only be eligible for such payments under CDEP for a short time before being redirected to Centrelink for welfare.

Table 7.2 Range of BAC activities by headings reported in narrative annual reports 1999–2000 to 2010–11

Service/business activities	'99–'00	'00–'01	'02–'03	'03–'04	'04–'05	'05–'06	'06–'07	'07–'08	'08–'09	'09–'10	'10–'11
Housing and essential services	x	x	x	x	x	x	x	x	x	x	x
BAC constructions							x	x			
Education outstation	x	x									
Health outstations	x	x									
Road party	x	x	x	x	x	x	x	x	x	x	x
BAC workshop	x	x	x	x	x	x	x	x	x	x	x
BAC fuel	x	x	x	x	x	x	x	#			
Tucker run/bush deliveries	x	x	x	x	x	x	x	x	x	x	x
Balmarrk Supermarket						x	x	x	x	x	x
Good Food Kitchen					x	x	x	x	x	x	x
Environmental work (Maningrida)	x										
BAC nursery	x	x	x		x	x	x	x		x	
Babbarra Women's Centre	x	x	x	x	x	x	x	x	x	x	
Maningrida Arts and Culture	x	x	x	x	x	x	x	x	x	x	x
MAC Darwin							x	x	x	x	x
Djelk rangers	x	x	x	x	x	x	x	x	x	x	x
Djelk women rangers			x	x	x	x	x	x	x	x	x
Djelk sea rangers				x	x	x	x	x	x	x	x
Wildlife centre					x	x	x	x	x	x	x
Crab harvesting					x	x	##				
Maningrida municipal (Ye'Ya)	x	x	x	x	x	x	##	x	x		

Service/business activities	'99–'00	'00–'01	'02–'03	'03–'04	'04–'05	'05–'06	'06–'07	'07–'08	'08–'09	'09–'10	'10–'11
Safari hunting		x									
Human services			x	x	x	x	x				
Doctors####			x	x							
Aged care			x	x	x	x	x	x	x	x	x
Disability support			x	x	x						
Substance misuse					x	x					
Child safety					x		x	x	x	x	x
Youth development						x					
BAC tourism###			x	x	x	x	x	x	x	x	x
BAC training				x	x	x			x	x	x
BAC Outdoor supplies						x	x	x	x	x	x
BAC Freight services								x	x		
Financial services							x	x	x	x	
Expanded money management service									x	x	x
Maningrida Employment Services										x	x
Maningrida Crèche										x	x
BAC Air Services											x

\#   amalgamated with Balmarrk supermarket
\##   amalgamated with Djelk Wildlife Centre
\###   Arnhem Land Eco-cultural tours
\####   transferred to Malabam Health Board Aboriginal Corporation
Source: Prepared by the author from Bawinanga Aboriginal Corporation annual reports.

Managing the tension between the corporation's rules around CDEP payments and the diverse aspirations of its members should not be understated. There was continual negotiation between the board, management and membership over the years and some minor changes, but as a general rule some version of the three-tiered arrangement was maintained.

These guidelines were discussed by supervisors and management and approved by the board. In the mid-2000s, Bawinanga businesses were paying CDEP participants extra wages of $1–2 million per annum, while by 2007–08 Maningrida Arts and Culture was purchasing art from several hundred artists for well over $1 million per annum, although not all were on CDEP.

Under the Bawinanga umbrella were some of remote Indigenous Australia's most successful cultural and land management entities, each developed and underwritten by CDEP. Some of these entities produced their own discrete annual reports for a number of years as a marker of institutional maturity. These include Maningrida Arts and Culture, which provided arts market brokerage to hundreds of artists from Maningrida and the region (e.g. see Kohen 2007; Kohen & Summers 2008), and the Djelk Rangers. The Djelk Rangers were sustained by CDEP for over 10 years before they were moved onto Working on Country program wages in 2007; they began managing the Djelk Indigenous Protected Area when declared in 2009 (see Pascal & Ansell 2009; May, Ansell & Koenig 2010).

The complexity of Bawinanga is also reflected in financial transcripts—its annual audited financial statements. In 2005–06 and 2006–07, these audits were undertaken by Chartered Accountant Frank Redpath, with information provided by Bawinanga's accounting and bookkeeping team. I use these two years as an illustrative example because audits were prepared in a particularly comprehensive and detailed manner at the time, covering over 100 pages that gave a sense of both the scale and financial complexity of the corporation. In 2006–07, Bawinanga was managing 56 grants and contracts, the most significant by far being CDEP wages at $6.7 million (for 600 participants) and CDEP operational at $2.5 million.[8] It also had 21 trading accounts, 17 that were profit-making and three that were loss-making.

The four big profit-makers that year were the supermarket ($750,000 profit), Maningrida Arts and Culture ($487,000), road contracting ($467,000) and the fuel store ($138,000). The loss-makers were small, only bush deliveries ($82,000), BAC tourism ($27,000) and MAC Darwin ($21,000) stand out. Clearly the profits outweighed the losses that year and, indeed, for most years (see Table 7.3).

There are two crucially important features of Table 7.3. In almost every year Bawinanga's trading and other income exceeded its grants income, quite a remarkable achievement in the context of remote Indigenous Australia. This meant that at the very least it was able to capture a significant proportion of the funding coming into the region and generate profit for regional benefit. While exact figures are not readily available for all financial years, during most years CDEP funding accounted for almost 80 per cent of non-trading income—this was the big, core funding fundamental to Bawinanga's success, mainly made up of notional equivalents of welfare and its administration.[9]

And during most of what I term 'the period of vibrancy', Bawinanga increased its turnover in both real and monetary terms and until 2011–12 generally ran small profits after accounting for depreciation. Tallegalla Consultants (2009: 4) notes that the corporation's turnover exceeded $30 million for the first time in 2007–08. It has been noted that the corporation's turnover was more than half of the revenue of the Darwin City Council and 50 per cent more than the revenue of the Alice Springs Town Council (ACIL Tasman 2007: 12).

---

8   As noted earlier, once CDEP was transferred from ATSIC it was not a grant per se, but rather a contract awarded after competitive tender.

9   Ian Munro (pers. comm. 11 July 2015) notes that while CDEP income was a big number, from the mid-2000s BAC actually had to use discretionary resources to cover some administration of the program as government formula-based funding was inadequate. CDEP in and of itself was not inherently 'profitable'.

Table 7.3 BAC grants, trading and other income, and total income
2000–01 to 2013–14

Year	Grants ($ million)	%	Trading and other income ($ million)	%	Total income ($ million)##	Surplus (deficit) ($ million)###
2000–01	8.2	48	7.9	52	17.1	n/a
2001–02	9.6	56	7.4	44	17.0	(0.19)
2002–03	9.2	47	10.6	53	19.7	0.12
2003–04	10.5	46	12.1	54	22.6	(0.11)
2004–05	11.6	44	14.7	56	26.3	0.95
2005–06	11.7	45	14.5	55	26.2	(0.3)
2006–07	12.2	45	15.1	55	27.3	1.1
2007–08	13.6	44	17.0	56	30.6	0.2
2008–09	15.8	47	18.0	53	33.8	0.5
2009–10	14.2	39	21.6	51	36.6	1.4
2010–11	18.1	47	19.9	53	38.6	2.7
2011–12	15.2	43	20.1	57	35.3	(4.0)
2012–13	15.6	51	14.5	49	30.3	(7.6)
2013–14#	10.3	32	21.5	68	31.8	0.5

\#   Inclusive of $3.5 million loan from MPA and grant balance write-off and audit reversal
      of $6 million.

\##   The consumer price index increased between June 2001 and June 2014 by
      42 per cent, see www.abs.gov.au/websitedbs/d3310114.nsf/home/Consumer+
      Price+Index+Inflation+Calculator, so 2000–01 turnover of $17.1 million was worth
      $24.2 million in June 2014.

\###   Net of depreciation.

Source: Prepared by the author from Bawinanga Aboriginal Corporation annual reports.

The Bawinanga approach to CDEP success

In 1985, the Miller Review of Aboriginal Employment and Training
Programs (Miller 1985) was commissioned to undertake the first
comprehensive review of the labour market situation of Aboriginal
people Australia-wide. As noted in Chapter 4, Miller recommendations
laid the foundations for the Aboriginal Employment Development
Policy and the late 1980s expansion of CDEP. It was conducted
during the self-determination era and during the progressive Hawke
Government years and was sympathetic to the fundamentally different
needs of remote-living Aboriginal people.

The Miller Review made numerous recommendations that I summarise as follows. First, it differentiated settled from remote Australia. Second, it was sympathetic to the aspirations of Aboriginal people to live on the land that they owned and to pursue diverse strategies for livelihood, including in the non-market sector. Third, it saw the issue of work in remote Australia holistically, understanding that the economic base needed to be built slowly and employment generation integrated with community development, especially in situations where there were no mainstream labour markets and limited commercial opportunity. Along with the Blanchard Report, *Return to Country*, some two years later, which examined the homelands movement in Australia (Blanchard 1987), these two national inquiries greatly influenced the developmental approach taken by Bawinanga.

Twenty years later, in 2005, the House of Representatives Standing Committee for Aboriginal and Torres Strait Islander Affairs (HRSCATSIA) was asked to inquire into positive factors and examples among Indigenous individuals and communities that improved employment outcomes (HRSCATSIA 2007: xiii). This inquiry began just after the abolition of ATSIC and ended some two years later just before the Northern Territory National Emergency Response Intervention (the NT Intervention). I will return to this inquiry later, I bring it up here because Ian Munro, then General Manager of BAC, made a submission (no. 20) in April 2005 and subsequently members of the inquiry committee visited Maningrida to take verbal evidence in July 2006 from board members and Munro, who was by then CEO.[10]

In seven pages of submission (Munro & Manners 2005) and evidence delivered to the committee in Maningrida on 17 July 2006,[11] elements of the Bawinanga CDEP model were outlined. To briefly paraphrase, the evidence tendered highlighted how Bawinanga had achieved employment outcomes by creating a job market where one did not formerly exist. A short document prepared for DEWR by Munro

---

10   To be transparent I also made a submission (no. 88) to the committee in May 2005 (some 20 years after I had made a submission to the Miller Inquiry) and gave verbal evidence in Canberra on 13 February 2006. My written submission focused on official statistics demonstrating the success of CDEP generally, my oral evidence was more specific and used much material about Bawinanga—see www.aph.gov.au/Parliamentary_Business/Committees/ House_of_Representatives_committees?url=atsia/indigenousemployment/hearings.htm.

11   Available at www.aph.gov.au/Parliamentary_Business/Committees/House_of_Representatives _committees?url=atsia/indigenousemployment/hearings.htm, accessed 21 August 2015.

and Rupert Manners—BAC's financial controller—emphasised that the development of commercial enterprises is a cornerstone of the Bawinanga model. Munro and Manners (2005) note:

> [o]ur operations provide training and employment opportunities, deliver efficient services to the community, address consumer demand, and generate profits which can be reinvested in local economic growth. Managers are required to demonstrate a commitment to economic growth constrained only by cultural considerations, the shortage of development capital, and the need to avoid disproportionate levels of non-Aboriginal employment.

Later they note:

> [c]ultivation of the regional economy is somewhat challenging, requiring a degree of anthropological knowledge, an intimacy with the funding matrix and a willingness to speculate scarce capital on untested ventures remote from markets. We have had our share of business failure. It will always be so.

At the heart of the model were three components: responsiveness to local aspirations and realism about cultural priorities of its members; the skilful deployment of CDEP labour; and the prudent investment of corporation profits in commercial and social enterprises.

In 2009, as he was planning to move on, CEO Ian Munro approached the NT Government's Department of Housing, Local Government and Regional Services, suggesting that a consultant be commissioned to document Bawinanga's success and transportability to other communities. Peter Anderson Consulting Pty Ltd was commissioned and provided a report with the Jonathan Swift-like title,[12] *Bawinanga Aboriginal Corporation Achievements Review in order to identify practices which might productively be pursued elsewhere in remote areas of the Northern Territory*, dated May 2010 (Anderson 2010).

Peter Anderson was an interesting choice of consultant. He had lived in Maningrida as a child, had undertaken a number of business planning assignments in Maningrida for BAC and other agencies and was an

---

12   *A Modest Proposal for Preventing the Children of Poor People From Being a Burthen to Their Parents or Country, and for Making Them Beneficial to the Publick* (1729).

associate of ACIL Tasman, who had undertaken a report *Business Opportunities in the Maningrida Area* commissioned by Bawinanga in 2007.[13]

Anderson's report is not widely available but provides an arms-length perspective based on a critical engagement with a selection of the literature about Bawinanga and interviews with a diverse range of Indigenous and non-Indigenous stakeholders, including me.

Focusing on employment, Anderson notes that there are three ways to increase this, excluding outmigration that is not a local preference: the replacement of *balanda* (non-Indigenous) employees, but this will be slow at best due to a local skills deficit; increased subvention by government, something that happened during the Intervention but at insufficient levels; and/or through the creation and operation of sustainable enterprises. Anderson notes that in 2010 there were 600 CDEP participants and 200 non-CDEP Maningrida jobs, further noting that the conversion rate does not add up (Anderson 2010: 19). In 2010, when CDEP was already in rapid decline, Anderson notes that Bawinanga was highly vulnerable because of its high dependence on the scheme. This observation was hardly insightful as the corporation had already experienced this vulnerability some five years earlier.

The CDEP wars: Metropolitan rationalism versus remote realism

> The greatest challenge in the coming year will undoubtedly be the need to maintain the trajectory of our CDEP success. The demise of ATSIC has seen CDEP move to the Department of Employment and Workplace Relations. Regrettably, DEWR's inexperience and lack of understanding of Aboriginal people and communities threatens to destabilise the successes of our CDEP. We need to work with DEWR and other Government departments to ensure that continued support results in outcomes which are realistic, achievable and appropriate. (Otto Campion, Chairman's message prefacing the BAC annual report 2004–05 in McAuliffe 2005: 2)

---

13   Peter Anderson had also worked for me as a sub-consultant when I undertook the MAC Business Development Plan in 1999 and was the CEO appointed by KordaMentha for a short time between July and October 2013 when Bawinanga was still in special administration. He is also a friend of David Bond who had been CEO for 24 years from late 1980 to 2005.

There has been major conflict between BAC and the Department of Employment and Workplace Relations (DEWR) over the operations of the CDEP program, resulting in their decision in June this year to discontinue our CDEP funding. Following strong representations by BAC, funding has been reinstated but tensions continue. The gulf between us relates principally to the question of 'real jobs'. It is the stated objective of BAC to attain unsubsidised employment for all CDEP participants. The means by which this can be achieved forms the basis of the entrenched dispute with DEWR. (Ian Munro, CEO Report, BAC Annual report 2005–06 in Manners 2006: 8–9)

Much of the employment policy debate in the post-ATSIC era has focused on whether CDEP jobs are 'real' jobs; and whether such jobs result in government agencies and others reneging on their obligations to Indigenous Australians as citizens by utilising CDEP labour paid for with notional welfare equivalents (for a discussion of the former issue see Chapter 5).

In a review of research on CDEP undertaken by researchers at CAEPR, Rowse (2002: 65–78) argues that a policy focus on 'the individual' and individual welfare has obscured the non-labour market outcomes of the CDEP scheme. I concur. The material provided in this chapter demonstrates the range of these non-labour market outcomes in relation to Bawinanga, including social externalities, community development and social and cultural outcomes. Rowse suggests that a CDEP scheme is a form of Indigenous authority: as CDEP organisations mediate between government and participants, they exercise authority over workers and become players in the regional political field. In short, they are a form of local or regional political authority whose relationship with government is open to negotiation. That is the way it was in 2002, although I would add that CDEP organisations, like Bawinanga in their regional development manifestation, are also political economy institutions.

In his postscript to the Indigenous Welfare Economy volume already mentioned, Rowse (2001b) made three points that seem especially pertinent now with the benefit of hindsight observing developments over the following 15 years.

Even back then, Rowse noted the emerging use of what he termed the jargon of the 'real' economy as employed by Noel Pearson (2000). Rowse warned that this jargon needed to be critically challenged lest a view emerged that CDEP work was less 'real' than other forms of employment. This warning, as I will show, was prescient because the language of the 'real' economy and 'real' jobs has become ubiquitous, even naturalised, in Indigenous policy over the last decade and a half—in Canberra it is hard to come across a politician or bureaucrat who does not use the term. As Rowse notes, and again I concur, there is nothing necessarily 'second-best' about CDEP work.

A related point that Rowse (2001a, 2001b, 2002) highlights is that the CDEP scheme was never just about employment and must be recognised as having multiple objectives. Yet the scheme has always struggled for recognition of this difference, not just because it does not fit neatly into bureaucratic boxes as Sanders (2001) suggests, but also because it challenges the new 'normalisation' direction of Indigenous policy (Altman 2014).

Finally, Rowse (2001b) notes that CDEP was in a strong position because if government decided to abolish the scheme (which it has now done) then what would replace it? Rowse suggested that CDEP was doing so many necessary jobs in so many different ways in so many places that it was quite entrenched in the Australian system of government. It may not have been getting the recognition it deserved but it was going to be hard to get rid of. But get rid of it government did.

The process of abolition began in earnest on 1 July 2004, but took over a decade to complete. Sanders (2004) noted the danger of these new administrative arrangements and predicted that CDEP would sit uncomfortably in the employment portfolio, warning that because DEWR had a strong employment and labour market focus it would lose patience and interest in the community development and income support aspects of CDEP.

In my view, Sanders' analysis was a little too benign because he interpreted the prospects for CDEP within DEWR in terms of bureaucratic politics only, somewhat detached from the broader political context and the new managerialism identified by Sullivan (2011).

This became very clear to me late in 2004 when, in my one and only formal meeting with then secretary of DEWR Peter Boxall (and Bob Harvey, his lieutenant charged with CDEP reform), he defended his economic rationalist view that CDEP participants could be forced by market signals into mainstream employment either in community or through labour migration.[14] This reflected the emerging domination that Rowse (2001b) had identified, a shift in policy thinking for remote Australia from a focus on community-building to a focus on the individual, as if the two are somehow separable. But this heightened focus on the individual and agency has increasingly ignored the politico-structural circumstances in remote Indigenous Australia, as well as in parts of more settled Australia (as argued in Chapter 4). Those advocating for engagement in the 'real' economy have been careful to never precisely define what this constitutes in its actually existing form, choosing to ignore the views of local experts about local economic realities. Here was a clear triumph of ideology.

Just how this attempted reform played out in remote Australia can be demonstrated with reference to a bitter and complex political conflict that emerged in 2005 and 2006 between DEWR and Bawinanga. As Otto Campion noted in his Chairman's message at the start of this section, this conflict not only had the potential to destabilise growth and success to date but also to erode relations of trust and cooperation with key funding agencies. Locally, this conflict was referred to as 'the CDEP wars' (Altman 2005, 2008). While Rowse (2001a: 232) had previously noted a plea from CDEP organisations for respectful engagement from government agencies, there was nothing respectful in this exercise of raw fiscal and political power over a relatively small and successful Indigenous organisation.

At the heart of this dispute were conflicting views on how CDEP should be delivered in the Maningrida region. In correspondence to the Commonwealth Ombudsman dated 8 July 2006, Ian Munro, then CEO, noted that:

> BAC feel that they have been dealt with unfairly by DEWR and we can cite instances of decisions apparently being influenced by malice within the ranks of DEWR staff. We believe that this stems from two things. First BAC has promoted our model of CDEP quite forcefully and DEWR resents the challenge to their policy. Secondly, the BAC model is inconsistent with the DEWR doctrine, and our obvious success diminishes the credibility of the DEWR preferred model (Munro 2006).

---

14   University of Chicago–trained Boxall has described himself as 'an unabashed rationalist' (Boxall 2012). Bob Harvey received a Public Service Medal 'for outstanding public service in implementing reforms to the Community Development Employment Projects program for Indigenous Australians www.gg.gov.au/sites/default/files/files/honours/ad/ad2007/medianotesPSM.pdf.

I cannot dwell in too much detail on this complex conflict. At its heart were divergent views about what constituted 'real jobs' and how many of its 600 CDEP workers Bawinanga should be exiting to unsubsidised and sustained mainstream work in Maningrida. The dispute flared on two occasions as Performance Funding Agreements had to be negotiated for the 2005–06 and 2006–07 financial years, and DEWR refused to approve these unless Bawinanga guaranteed to exit 30 and then 60 CDEP participants into mainstream employment. This was something that the board and senior management were unwilling to do with their knowledge of the severely limited Maningrida labour market and the aspirations of their CDEP participants and members. It was a clear case of realistic local knowledge about remote circumstances versus disconnected 'metropolitan managerialism' that looked to apply crude percentage formulas to funding agreements without proper assessment of local circumstances. This is a fundamental structural failing of the dominant economic system that cannot deliver despite the rhetoric of politicians and officials. And so the dominant then reconstrue this systemic failing as the personal shortcoming of the people who are the policy targets.

I use the term 'metropolitan' here because there was clearly a disconnect not just between DEWR and Bawinanga, but also between the Canberra headquarters and Darwin regional office of DEWR, and between DEWR and the highly unstable series of Commonwealth agencies in the immediate post-ATSIC era purportedly representing the interests of remote-living Indigenous people.

The low point in this dispute occurred in April 2006 around the time that Cyclone Monica, the most intense tropical cyclone on record to impact Australia, crossed the coastline near Maningrida. At this time, while Bawinanga was deploying CDEP labour to assist in the clean-up of a severely damaged Maningrida, DEWR was negotiating with the CEO of the Maningrida Council about the possible transfer of a proportion of CDEP participants from Bawinanga to the council, counter to the directions of elected councillors.

In correspondence dated 16 June 2006, the Maningrida Council wrote to Peter Boxall and made it quite clear that they did not support the unauthorised action of their CEO in his endeavours to see the council win back CDEP allocations that it had lost a decade earlier. DEWR was delving into community politics as a means to break the resistance of Bawinanga to its demands.

A political highpoint of sorts occurred when Bawinanga Board members and senior management were afforded democratic opportunity to explain their successful approach and to place the dispute with DEWR on the public record as evidence to a parliamentary inquiry on Indigenous employment. Thirty pages of evidence provide rare insights, from a community perspective, on how local success can be jeopardised as part of a broader national agenda of imagined improvement.[15]

The visit to Maningrida clearly had an impact on one member of this parliamentary inquiry, Danna Vale, Liberal Party MP for the electorate of Hughes in New South Wales. In a second reading speech on the Corporations (Aboriginal and Torres Strait Islander) Bill 2006 on 11 October 2006, she referred in some detail to Bawinanga and made the following summary comment:

> The Bawinanga Aboriginal Corporation at Maningrida is an excellent example of a well-organised and well-managed Indigenous corporation that provides essential services to its people and initiates activities that create economic development, training and job creation. Its work is invaluable to the people of the Maningrida community. Reading through its recent annual report [2004–05], one sees that this corporation deals with income in the tens of millions of dollars, almost half of which is in the form of government grants. In his message, the chairman states that the success of these projects will rely on our commitment, vision and effort, supported by increased levels of government support.[16]

Unfortunately, these observations were not reflected in the final report *Indigenous Australians at Work* (HRSCATSIA 2007), where the considerable input of Bawinanga was given no attention and the issue of CDEP was largely overlooked. However, in a minority report by four members of the Australian Labor Party, Bawinanga was mentioned directly in relation to the importance of CDEP to its developmental work:

---

15   Available at www.aph.gov.au/binaries/hansard/reps/commttee/r9499.pdf, accessed 21 September 2015.
16   See parlinfo.aph.gov.au/parlInfo/download/chamber/hansardr/2006-10-11/toc_pdf/5017-3.pdf;fileType=application%2Fpdf#search=%22chamber/hansardr/2006-10-11/0016%22, accessed 2 July 2015.

> CDEP plays a critical role in this process [regional development]
> because it has had 'the flexibility necessary for the difficult tasks of
> growing the regional economy' in an area where there is no mining,
> manufacturing or agricultural activity and where the challenge of
> 'accommodating a willing workforce in relevant and productive
> employment requires creative and clever solutions.' The corporation,
> frustrated in finding other sources of funding, have used profits from
> their successful trading enterprises set up under CDEP to provide
> seed capital for business development and to top up wages. This may
> well represent a legitimate future direction for CDEP in communities
> with limited opportunities for conventional employment (HRSCATSIA
> 2007: 216–7).

These competing discourses raise a lot of questions not just about the
turbulence of the Indigenous policy cycle, but also about the ability
of politicians and bureaucrats to 'disqualify' (Foucault 1980) local and
expert knowledge. The views expressed in the minority report did
not, unfortunately, translate into policy change when the ALP was
elected to government five months later, a reflection of the growing
consensus in the neoliberal governmentality of remote Indigenous
communities (Altman 2014).

The Great Crash: Bawinanga's 'near death' experience

> There have been too many policy changes over the last few years,
> first as part of the Intervention and now with the reformed CDEP. We
> are overwhelmed, and find it difficult to keep up with the detail and
> understand how the policies will be implemented. Our members are
> unsettled and worry about the future. How will the reformed CDEP
> affect them and their families? What will happen after the program is
> phased out in 2011? (Jimmy Pascoe, Chairman's message prefacing the
> BAC annual report 2008–09 in Manners 2009: 3)

After 'the CDEP wars' policy changes occurred rapidly (as outlined
in Chapter 2 and the annotated timeline in this volume). Three weeks
after the parliamentary report was completed, the NT Intervention was
announced and Bawinanga entered into other political battles with the
Australian Government particularly in its organisational opposition to
the Intervention. In July 2007, as an additional Intervention measure,
Minister Brough announced that CDEP was to be abolished after he

discovered that participants on wages could not be income managed. But then in November 2007 CDEP got some temporary reprieve with a change of federal government that then embarked on a reform agenda of its own, which saw CDEP fundamentally altered from July 2009 and then abolished from 1 July 2013 with the establishment of RJCP.[17]

In June 2009, Ian Munro, the manager who had overseen Bawinanga's rapid growth over the previous decade, left Maningrida worn down by 'the CDEP wars' and overseeing organisational opposition to the Intervention and in need of a break after 18 years at Maningrida. Unfortunately, he left without an appointed or suitably inducted successor and so for 12 months Bawinanga had a series of acting CEOs before Luke Morrish was appointed in mid-2010.

Munro's departure coincided with implementation of a new version of CDEP introduced by Jenny Macklin that signalled, in my view, the beginning of the end of Bawinanga's earlier success because it could not accommodate the flexibility it required.

This new approach divided participants into two streams—those engaged in community development and those engaged in job search. This division was imposed by the Rudd Government and so drastically reduced the autonomy of CDEP organisations to make their own decisions.

And, more significantly, two categories of CDEP participants within these two streams were created with a stroke of policy unilateralism. Those already on CDEP were 'grandfathered' as employed and as wage earners, while new CDEP entrants were limited to receive Newstart from Centrelink, classified as unemployed and not afforded the option to earn additional income without the disincentive of the social security taper—deprived of a significant benefit of CDEP participation locally referred to as 'top up'.[18]

---

17   As Thomas Michel reminded me in reviewing this chapter, in the midst of all this CDEP reform upheaval, the NT Government also introduced reform of local government with the amalgamation of 53 councils with predominantly Indigenous populations into eight regional shires with its own set of intended and unintended consequences (see Michel & Taylor 2014).
18   See www.dss.gov.au/sites/default/files/documents/05_2012/cdep_program_guide.pdf.

These changes not only affected the well-being of the many individuals who could no longer earn top up without losing some income support but also undermined their incentive to work. This resulted in Bawinanga struggling to recruit CDEP participants to its enterprises as they could not earn income above Newstart.

The modus operandi of Bawinanga shifted quite dramatically even though a number of CDEP participants, particularly those associated with outstations were grandfathered. Being grandfathered had a small added bonus as these participants were categorised as wage earners, and were thus not subject to compulsory income management, one of the purported reasons CDEP was to be abolished in July 2007 as an Intervention measure.

All the dire warnings that Bawinanga would become a fundamentally different organisation without CDEP came to fruition—the organisation went into fiscal decline. This decline can be explained by a combination of factors including the recruitment of a revolving door of new staff, some of whom did not live in community but commuted from Darwin; financial pressure on some of Bawinanga's iconic businesses, especially MAC, which after the Global Financial Crisis went from being a surplus-generating entity into a loss-making liability (as analysed by Munro 2010); and the adoption of a fundamentally new approach by management to enterprise development that included establishing enterprises without rigorous business planning or a realistic assessment of risk.

The last factor represented a critical change in management approach from one based on organisational expansion and business development based on a stated vision, cultural understanding, client focus, sound risk assessment and risk management techniques— good business practice—to poor business practice that lacked the personal commitment of management (except self-interest) or interest in the aspirations of the membership. It was, at its heart, based on either a genuine or cosmetic adherence to the neoliberal logic of the Intervention.

The most obvious departures from sound past practice were twofold. First, government funds allocated to specific purposes, especially CDEP wages, were carried over and allocated to non-CDEP purposes. These carryovers were reported in audited financial reports, but they did not trigger timely intervention either by the funding body—the Department of Families, Housing, Community Services and Indigenous Affairs—or by the regulator—the Office of the Registrar of Indigenous Corporations—with whom reports were lodged.

Second, even as businesses like Maningrida Arts and Culture were failing (Munro 2010), new ventures including BAC Air Services and the expansion of outstations services provision, first to the Ramingining region to the east and then to the Oenpelli region to the west, were established. Not only was such expansion over-ambitious, it was debt financed rather than being prudentially financed as in the past from organisational surpluses.

This new direction was signalled in BAC's last two published annual reports for 2009–10 and 2010–11, which indicated that Bawinanga was embarking on a new expansionary phase (see Sommers 2010, 2011). Arguably this new, somewhat reckless approach was forced on the corporation owing to external policy changes. Information in Table 7.3 shows financial details of Bawinanga's financial decline. In 2011–12 and 2012–13, the corporation was in unprecedented debt and in October 2012 it went into special administration because its cash flow situation had deteriorated to such an extent that it could not pay its staff, including CDEP workers. Not long before then, in July 2012, the board had terminated the contract of CEO Luke Morrish after only two years, during which time he had turned the corporation from one making profit to one that was deeply indebted.

I cannot analyse what has happened at Bawinanga since it went into special administration in October 2012 here in any detail, in part because these issues still (in August 2016) remain sensitive and inaccessible. Suffice to say that for a period Bawinanga became an organisation marred by opaque processes, deep uncertainty, high staff turnover, struggling businesses and an inability to effectively meet its diverse objectives. There have also been periodic tensions between the board—which, since 2014 has included two non-member directors appointed by the Registrar of Indigenous Corporations—senior management, staff and the members themselves over the direction the corporation should take and its key priorities.

Under such circumstances it is perhaps unsurprising that there have been no annual reports published since 2010–11, a historical series that began in 1999–2000 and ended abruptly. Peter Anderson, when CEO in September 2013, told me Bawinanga had no resources to expend on such glossy documents.[19]

In the short term, Bawinanga has been rescued from winding up by the Australian Government 'shelving' a debt of over $6 million and its main local 'competitor', the Maningrida Progress Association, providing a loan of $3.5 million over five years to pay off private creditors.

Much information on Bawinanga's period of special administration (October 2012 to July 2014) is available at the website of the Office of the Registrar of Indigenous Corporations so this detail will not be recited here.[20] The most recent audited financial statement for 2014–15, also on the Office of the Registrar of Indigenous Corporations website, shows that Bawinanga might be slowly recovering. To what extent it was changes in CDEP, as distinct from changes in Indigenous policy more generally, that had been responsible for Bawinanga's rapid decline is what I now turn to in conclusion.

Challenging 'Regimes of Truth': Where to now for Bawinanga?

When MPA time, we left Maningrida and went home to the bush. Then BAC came and all that time it was good with BAC. We worked with BAC but then the government rules changed and BAC started to change too. Then the government came and they made BAC do what the government wanted and then they didn't want to work with us anymore. They got tired of us Bininj [Aboriginal people]. They weren't interested in us anymore. That was after Ian Munro time. BAC used to make roads for us and so on, but the government policies changed, BAC's policies changed and they didn't want to support us anymore. (Bulanj Nakardbam, February 2015 quoted in Altman 2015)

---

19   Bawinanga management had initially resisted my recommendation that a narrative annual report be produced, but subsequently Ian Munro (pers. comm. 31 July 2015) informed me that he estimated that a $10,000 investment in the report annually probably generated $250,000 per annum for the corporation in additional grant support.
20   See register.oric.gov.au/document.aspx?concernID=100029, accessed 3 July 2015.

Now that CDEP has been abolished, it is useful to reflect on what this program was and did, how this abolition was justified, why expert local knowledge about the local labour market was ignored, what has been lost following the reform process and how might any loss be recovered? While Bawinanga provides just one case study, the wealth of historical information about it provides a sound basis for such reflections.

CDEP was a program with multiple objectives that was established in recognition of the reality that there are limited mainstream employment opportunities in remote Australia and an escalating problem of surplus labour. And so the program empowered communities participating in the scheme to find creative ways to generate activity, pay wages and engage in community and enterprise development. While CDEP was an institution of the self-determination era, it nevertheless became increasingly governmental. This transition was a consequence of the Australian Government delegating authority to Aboriginal organisations to decide on the methods for the payment of income in accord with the rules governing boards of these organisations set. This is one aspect of CDEP that stands out most today: while it was always an Indigenous-specific program and never welfare, the cost of the program was largely offset by welfare—the notional entitlements of participants to income support and the cost of its delivery that government has to bear in remote places.

In the case of Bawinanga, as this chapter shows, a great deal was achieved with CDEP in a number of areas. Initially, CDEP provided an appropriate form of income support to outstations and generated operational funds to allow better service delivery to over 30 outstations scattered over a large remote region. Then, as CDEP expanded, it allowed for enterprise development, expanded community services and the provision of employment and training opportunity for up to 600 participants. It is interesting in this regard that while CDEP has been criticised for allowing cost shifting from government onto a government-funded community organisation in a situation of labour surplus, such service delivery work was an important avenue for job creation in aged care support, night patrol and other services more usually associated with government.

While all these different elements of CDEP developed incrementally over time, they operated symbiotically and constituted a virtuous cycle: CDEP labour could be deployed in community services provision and enterprise development and the financial surpluses generated— especially when supported by complementary government grants— could be rolled back into job creation and associated income generation for individuals, households and the community. While Bawinanga's initial focus was on outstations, its expanded role as a regional organisation from 1989 saw its activities increasingly focused on the township of Maningrida where a growing proportion of its membership lived.

Using the lenses of formal performance evaluation and outcomes monitoring, it is difficult to fault Bawinanga as a CDEP organisation; indeed it was often lauded, including as a case study of governance success in a report, *The top 500 Aboriginal and Torres Strait Islander corporations 2009–2010* (Office of the Registrar of Indigenous Corporations 2011: 9–10). With access to CDEP, Bawinanga became one of the largest and most robust Indigenous corporations in Australia, regularly ranking between second- and fourth-largest of several thousand in the first decade of the 21st century.

While Bawinanga was a successful CDEP performer there were many other CDEP organisations that, in their own ways, achieved a great deal in very difficult circumstances. So how was the Australian Government able to mount a plausible case to reform this program to extinction?

It is worth recalling here a growing policy debate about and mounting discursive assault on CDEP that began some 20 years ago and escalated rapidly during the post-ATSIC era. In rapid succession, a review of the scheme by the Human Rights and Equal Opportunity Commission (1997) questioned whether it was delivering income support equitably, the Spicer Review (1997) challenged the efficacy of the scheme as an employment program, and a combination of Pearson (2000) and McClure (2000) questioned whether CDEP jobs were 'real' and how CDEP fitted into a 'mutual obligation' framework (Altman 2001). Sanders (2001) captured these emerging challenges by noting that CDEP was being reshaped in two directions at once: a greater focus on integration into the social security system for unemployed participants and a greater focus on mainstream employment for those seeking exit.

Rowse (2001a) noted astutely at that time that CDEP was practically strong but ideologically weak as it struggled to escape the government's negative representations of CDEP. Rowse believed that while CDEP was not getting all the recognition it deserved for all the things that it did, it was still going to be hard to get rid of. But the government did get rid of CDEP, the scheme being eliminated by a pincer combination of the new managerialism and an increasingly shrill narrative of negativity.

In her recently completed doctoral research, Juliet Checketts (2016) analysed the federal parliamentary record to show how four dominant discourses combined to create what Foucault termed 'A Regime of Truth' (Foucault 1980) in the Australian Indigenous policy cycle. Regimes of Truth are established forms of knowledge and speech acts that frame social problems in a particular way, imagine government-directed interventions and envision the characteristics of desirable citizens that such interventions will create. The discourses Checketts identified were: highlighting of past failure, focused especially on ATSIC and the self-determination era; an ongoing concern with statistical gaps; a focus on Aboriginal culture and community as a barrier to progress; and a proposed solution to deliver the 'good life' enjoyed by mainstream settler Australians based on altering Indigenous subjectivities in remote Australia to embrace dominant norms and values. I cannot go into detail here analysing policy statements that encapsulated this emerging Regime of Truth, but two that stand out for me were Amanda Vanstone's (2007) speech on 'conspicuous compassion'[21] and Malcolm Brough's (2006) speech, 'Blueprint for action on Indigenous affairs'. Both were powerful narratives of sameness and individualism for Indigenous Australia dressed up as tolerance of community and cultural difference.

These broader shifts in the Indigenous policy cycle can be transposed onto what was supposedly happening with CDEP according to the dominant narrative: the program was ATSIC's largest, and so could

---

21   A term probably borrowed, without acknowledgement, from West's book *Conspicuous Compassion: Why Sometimes it Really is Cruel to be Kind* (2004).

be linked to ATSIC's perceived failure; redefined as an employment program it could be held responsible in part for the government's inability to close the employment gap;[22] CDEP's emphasis on flexibility, including to accommodate cultural prerogatives like ceremony, explained participants' lack of regimentation for mainstream work; and the only way to enjoy the good life was through mainstream so-called 'real' jobs.

This Regime of Truth became so 'naturalised' that it was difficult to challenge. Have the supposed millions, sometimes billions, spent delivered acceptable outcomes? Can rich Australia tolerate such employment gaps? Can Australia really condone custom that precludes regular work or work readiness? And surely everyone deserves a decent livelihood based on full-time employment? Indigenous Australians should not be expected to tolerate second-class forms of employment and second-rate employment and training services. This is despite capitalism's core structural problem of low employment creation around its peripheries, especially where there are no markets to create.

In its attempts to counter such a dominant narrative in 'the CDEP Wars' and through evidence of its performance to parliamentary inquiries, Bawinanga, powerful as it was in regional political terms, could not counter this groundswell of critique. It was fighting a local battle for CDEP based on evidence of performance in a national ideological war in Australian Indigenous affairs in which inevitably Bawinanga ended up as the loser—its community-based developmental approach, even if successful, was out of broader policy fashion. Here was a classic case of social injustice, to invert Nancy Fraser's (2009) scales of justice framework to the negative: Bawinanga's efforts were poorly recognised, the organisation and its membership were poorly represented, and the redistribution of resources for Bawinanga was always inadequate to allow it to break its high dependence on the state and associated vulnerability.

---

22 Rowse (2001a: 232) highlighted the dominant message from Peter Shergold, then head of the powerful Employment portfolio, at the Indigenous Welfare Economy and CDEP conference: that CDEP is all about employment and as an employment program it is failing. But Shergold, of course, failed to specify what would work better.

In their submission to the parliamentary inquiry into Indigenous employment, Munro and Manners (2005) ask: What would a post-CDEP environment look like for Bawinanga, its members and the Maningrida region?

First and foremost, they predicted a depopulation of outstations in the region because of lack of services support and a means to make a livelihood through CDEP and top up in cash from art, or in-kind from hunting and fishing. This prediction has come to fruition and is reflected in the statement above from Bulanj Nakardbam in an interview conducted in February 2015 in Maningrida (Altman 2015).

Next, they noted the importance of CDEP for regional natural resource management and the associated maintenance of Indigenous environmental knowledge.[23]

They then suggested that without CDEP individuals will be deprived of self-esteem, there will be heightened social dysfunction and associated health and incarceration costs for the state. They also predicted that the service delivery undertaken by Bawinanga, including in delivering income support entitlements, will fall on a less locally attuned state apparatus. This prediction has seen rapid escalation of breaching by Centrelink for non-compliance since the establishment of RJCP (recently renamed CDP).

And finally they predicted that the quest for 'real jobs' will see Aboriginal people move from CDEP work to welfare while non-Indigenous people from outside Maningrida will increasingly take on the real or salaried jobs owing to superior qualifications and higher labour productivity in a market sense. Analysis comparing 2006 and 2011 census information supports this view, with non-Indigenous local employment increasing significantly during this period.[24]

The rhetoric of recent Australian governments highlights the need to empower communities and close the gap and to focus the policy effort of its Indigenous Advancement Strategy on remote Australia.

---

23   Some of this loss might have been offset by the introduction of the Working on Country program in 2007, but such 'working on country' without people living on country will prove far less effective.

24   From 126 in 2006 to 178 in 2011, according to ABS community profiles with median individual incomes for non-Indigenous employees nearly five times higher than for Indigenous people. Since 2011 this level of outsider employment has increased further.

But the Bawinanga case indicates quite clearly that these goals are only considered if on the government's terms, irrespective of organisational performance. To some extent, Bawinanga has become too preoccupied with its own corporate survival and now risks meeting none of its objectives properly—in the support of outstations, in delivering community services, in developing viable small businesses and in providing locally realistic and flexible forms of training and work. When it successfully tendered for the role of regional RJCP provider as a financial survival strategy in 2013, the organisation acquiesced in large measure to the government's vision for the region rather than its own.

Bawinanga's symbiotic engagement with CDEP, carefully configured and nurtured over many years, is now broken. Without CDEP there is little incentive for individuals to work, as top up is not payable, and the organisation itself faces constrained incentive to perform as operating surpluses need to be earmarked for debt repayment rather than innovative enterprise development. Having created this terrible mess, the Australian Government is now belatedly looking for a semantic solution—renaming RJCP as the Community Development Programme—to a deeply entrenched structural problem that CDEP once empowered Bawinanga to address in a relatively successful way.

In the essay 'What is Living and What is Dead', historian Tony Judt (2015: 336) reminds us, as does Tim Rowse (2001a: 233), that social democrats need to speak more assertively of past gains. According to Judt it is those from the Right, those that espouse neoliberal ideology, that look to destroy and innovate in the name of a universal project of sameness. But this grand project would certainly not accord with the aspirations of many remote-living Indigenous Australians. CDEP may have been far from perfect and its contributions to ameliorate development challenges partial. But, as Judt (2015: 336) suggests in a broader global context that has strong resonances with the Maningrida local, 'Imperfect improvements upon unsatisfactory circumstances are the best that we can hope for, and probably all we should seek'.

Unfortunately, circumstances today are more unsatisfactory than at any time during the era of CDEP administered by Bawinanga: people are moving from outstations, more are engaging in unproductive make work under CDP just earning the Newstart Allowances, and livelihoods are more precarious (Altman 2015).

This chapter does not seek to provide an uncritical idealisation of the past under CDEP, even though there is little question in the Maningrida region that those participating in the scheme were better off than those on welfare, with the overall numbers of adults pretty evenly divided between the two categories of CDEP participation and welfare. It is difficult to argue that a return to some halcyon period when CDEP was operating strongly is 'the' development solution; the regional challenges are too great to be solved by one organisation and one program. But there is no doubt that with CDEP Bawinanga delivered a great deal to its members and to the region, something that one would hope to see replicated in the future.

It is for this reason that in my view the current 'Regimes of Truth' about CDEP need to be sternly challenged with a counter-narrative built around three facts.

First, CDEP was never welfare; it was an innovative program with a notional financial nexus to welfare entitlements that empowered Aboriginal organisations like Bawinanga.

Second, Bawinanga did some very productive things with CDEP resources that are proving extremely difficult to emulate today without CDEP.

And finally, whatever its shortcomings, CDEP as administered by Bawinanga was better than welfare, for individuals, the Maningrida community and its network of outstations, for the region, and ultimately for the Australian nation.

Acknowledgements and a disclosure of interest

Over many years since 1979, too many people to name individually have assisted me with research in the Maningrida region. I would like to specifically thank Dan Gillespie and Ian Munro for checking the factual basis of my recollections and providing commentary on this chapter; and Kirrily Jordan, Melinda Hinkson, Bree Blakeman and especially Thomas Michel, as well as anonymous reviewers, for expert critical commentary on an earlier version.

When I write about Bawinanga Aboriginal Corporation it is proper that I disclose that I am a foundation director of Karrkad-Kanjdji Ltd, a company that has been established to assist the Djelk Rangers (and adjoining Warddeken Rangers) in their land and resource management activities in Western Arnhem Land. Directors of Karrkad-Kanjdji Ltd are trustees for the Karrkad-Kanjdji Trust, established with deductible gift recipient status to financially assist the Djelk Rangers. The Djelk Rangers are in turn one of the most significant business units of BAC. The views that are expressed in this chapter are mine as an academic researcher and do not reflect the views of anyone else including other directors of Karrkad-Kanjdji Ltd.

References

ACIL Tasman (2007). *Business opportunities in the Maningrida area: scoping report on business opportunities, infrastructure and capacity*, Prepared for Bawinanga Aboriginal Corporation, ACIL Tasman Pty Ltd, Perth.

Altman JC (2001). 'Mutual obligation', the CDEP scheme, and development: prospects in remote Australia. In Morphy F & Sanders W (eds), *The Indigenous welfare economy and the CDEP scheme*, CAEPR Research Monograph No. 20, ANU E Press, Canberra.

Altman JC (2005). *The governance of outstations in the Maningrida region, north-central Arnhem Land, and the challenges posed by the new arrangements*, ICGP Occasional Paper No. 11, Indigenous Community Governance project, CAEPR, The Australian National University, Canberra.

Altman JC (2008). Different governance for difference: the Bawinanga Aboriginal Corporation, In Hunt J, Smith DE, Garling S & Sanders W (eds), *Contested governance: culture, power and institutions in Indigenous Australia*, ANU E Press, Canberra, 177–203.

Altman JC (2014). Indigenous policy: Canberra consensus on a neoliberal project of improvement. In Miller C & Orchard L (eds), *Australian public policy: progressive ideas in the neoliberal ascendancy*, Policy Press, Bristol, 117–134.

Altman JC (2015). Living the good life in precarious times. *Inside Story*, 2 June 2015, insidestory.org.au/living-the-good-life-in-precarious-times.

Altman JC & Johnson V (2000). *CDEP in town and country Arnhem Land: Bawinanga Aboriginal Corporation*, CAEPR Discussion Paper No. 209, CAEPR, The Australian National University, Canberra.

Anderson P (2010). *Bawinanga Aboriginal Corporation achievements review in order to identify practices which might productively be pursued elsewhere in remote areas of the Northern Territory*, Peter Anderson Consulting Pty Ltd, Darwin.

Australian Government (1987). *The Aboriginal Employment Development policy*, Policy Paper No. 3, Community-based Employment, Enterprise and Development Strategies, Australian Government Publishing Service, Canberra.

Blanchard A (chairman) (1987). *Return to Country: the Aboriginal Homelands movement in Australia,* Australian Government Publishing Service, Canberra.

Boxall P (2012). Reflections of an 'unabashed rationalist.' In Wanna J, Vincent S & Podger A (eds), *With the benefit of hindsight: valedictory reflections from departmental secretaries, 2004–2011*, ANU E Press, Canberra.

Brough M (2006). *Blueprint for action in Indigenous affairs*, Speech delivered at the National Institute of Governance, University of Canberra, Canberra, 6 December 2006, www.formerministers.dss.gov.au/2917/blueprint-for-action-in-indigenous-affairs/.

Checketts JC (2016). The pulse of policy: mapping movement in the Australian Indigenous policy world, unpublished PhD thesis, The Australian National University, Canberra.

Fogarty B & Paterson M (2007). *Constructive engagement: impacts, limitations and possibilities during a national emergency intervention*, Report for BAC, PIA Consultants, August 2007, www.aph.gov.au/Parliamentary_Business/Committees/Senate/Legal_and_Constitutional_Affairs/Completed_inquiries/2004-07/nt_emergency/submissions/sublist.

Foucault M (1980). Truth and power, *Power/knowledge: selected interviews and other writings 1972–1977*, C Gordon (ed.), Pantheon Books, New York.

Fraser N (2009). *Scales of justice: reimagining political space in a globalizing world*, Columbia University Press, New York.

HRSCATSIA (House of Representatives Standing Committee on Aboriginal and Torres Strait Islander Affairs) (2007). *Indigenous Australians at work: successful initiatives in Indigenous employment.* Commonwealth of Australia, Canberra.

Human Rights and Equal Opportunity Commission (1997). *The CDEP scheme and racial discrimination: a report by the Race Discrimination Commissioner*, Commonwealth of Australia, Canberra.

Johnson V (2000). *Bawinanga Aboriginal Corporation annual report 1999/2000*, Bawinanga Aboriginal Corporation, Maningrida.

Johnson V (2004). *Bawinanga Aboriginal Corporation annual report 2003/2004*, Bawinanga Aboriginal Corporation, Maningrida.

Judt T (2015). *When the facts change: essays 1995–2010*, J Homans (ed.), Penguin Press, New York.

Kohen A (2007). *Maningrida Arts & Culture, annual report, 2006–2007*, Maningrida Arts and Culture, Maningrida.

Kohen A & Sommers C (2008). *Maningrida Arts & Culture, annual report, 2007–2008*, Maningrida Arts and Culture, Maningrida.

Kowal E (2012). Responsibility, Noel Pearson and Indigenous disadvantage in Australia. In Hage G & Eckersley R (eds), *Responsibility*, Melbourne University Press, Melbourne.

Manners R (2001). Catering for mobility and diversity: Bawinanga Aboriginal Corporation CDEP, Northern Territory. In Morphy F, & Sanders, W (eds), *The Indigenous welfare economy and the CDEP scheme*, ANU E Press, Canberra.

Manners W (2006). *Bawinanga Aboriginal Corporation annual report 2005/2006*, Bawinanga Aboriginal Corporation, Maningrida.

Manners W (2007). *Bawinanga Aboriginal Corporation annual report 2006/2007*, Bawinanga Aboriginal Corporation, Maningrida.

Manners W (2009). *Bawinanga Aboriginal Corporation annual report 2008/2009*, Bawinanga Aboriginal Corporation, Maningrida.

Martin D (2001). Community development in the context of welfare dependence. In Morphy F & Sanders W (eds), *The Indigenous welfare economy and the CDEP scheme*, ANU E Press, Canberra.

May K, Ansell S & Koenig J. (2010). *Djelk Rangers annual report 2009/2010*, Djelk Rangers, Bawinanga Aboriginal Corporation, Maningrida.

McAuliffe C (2005). *Bawinanga Aboriginal Corporation annual report 2004/2005*, Bawinanga Aboriginal Corporation, Maningrida.

McLure P (chair) (2000). *Participation support for a more equitable society: final report of the Reference Group on Welfare Reform*, July 2000, Department of Families and Community Services, Canberra.

Michel T & Taylor A (2014). Death by a thousand grants? The challenge of grants funding reliance for local government councils in the Northern Territory of Australia. *Local Government Studies*, 38 (4): 485–500.

Miller M (chairman) (1985). *Report of the Committee of Review of Aboriginal Employment and Training Programs*, Australian Government Publishing Service, Canberra.

Morphy F & Sanders W (eds) (2001). *The Indigenous welfare economy and the CDEP scheme*, CAEPR Research Monograph No. 20, ANU E Press, Canberra.

Munro I (2006). Correspondence to the Commonwealth Ombudsman, dated July 8 2006.

Munro I (2010). *Organisational review of Maningrida Arts and Culture*, June 2010, Ian Munro Consulting.

Munro I & Manners R (2005). *Submission (no. 20) to the House of Representatives Standing Committee on Aboriginal and Torres Strait Islander Affairs Inquiry Indigenous Australians at Work on behalf of the Bawinanga Aboriginal Corporation,* available at www.aph.gov.au/parliamentary_Business/Committees/House_of_ Representatives_Committees?url=atsia/indigenousemployment/ subs.htm.

Office of the Registrar of Indigenous Corporations (2011). *The top 500 Aboriginal and Torres Strait Islander corporations 2009–2010,* Office of the Registrar of Indigenous Corporations, Canberra.

Pascal H & Ansell S (2009). *Djelk Rangers annual report, 2008–2009,* Bawinanga Aboriginal Corporation, Maningrida.

Pearson N (2000). *Our right to take responsibility,* Noel Pearson and Associates, Cairns.

Rowse T (2001a). The political dimensions of community development. In Morphy F & Sanders W (eds), *The Indigenous welfare economy and the CDEP scheme,* CAEPR Research Monograph No. 20, ANU E Press, Canberra.

Rowse T (2001b). Postscript. In Morphy F & Sanders W (eds), *The Indigenous welfare economy and the CDEP scheme,* CAEPR Research Monograph No. 20, ANU E Press, Canberra.

Rowse T (2002). *Indigenous futures: choice and development for Aboriginal and Islander Australia,* UNSW Press, Sydney.

Sanders W (2001). Adjusting balances: reshaping the CDEP scheme after 20 good years. In Morphy F & Sanders W (eds), *The Indigenous welfare economy and the CDEP scheme,* CAEPR Research Monograph No. 20, ANU E Press, Canberra.

Sanders W (2004). Indigenous centres in the policy margins: the CDEP scheme over 30 years, *CAEPR Topical Issue 12/2004,* caepr.anu.edu.au/sites/default/files/Publications/topical/ CDEP%20Sanders2004.pdf.

Sanders W (2012). Coombs' bastard child: the troubled life of CDEP. *Australian Journal of Public Administration,* 71 (4): 371–91.

Sommers C (2010). *Bawinanga Aboriginal Corporation annual report 2009/2010*, Bawinanga Aboriginal Corporation, Maningrida.

Sommers C (2011). *Bawinanga Aboriginal Corporation annual report 2010/2011*, Bawinanga Aboriginal Corporation, Maningrida.

Spicer I (1997). *Independent review of the Community Development Employment Projects (CDEP) scheme*, Aboriginal and Torres Strait Islander Commission, Canberra.

Sullivan P (2011). *Belonging together: dealing with the politics of disenchantment in Australian Indigenous policy*, Aboriginal Studies Press, Canberra.

Tallegalla Consultants Pty Ltd (2003). *Bawinanga Aboriginal Corporation, strategic plan 2004–2006*, Unpublished report, Tallegalla Consultants Pty Ltd, Noosaville, Queensland.

Tallegalla Consultants Pty Ltd (2009). *Bawinanga Aboriginal Corporation Maningrida NT, Ye Ya mud brick factory—feasibility study report*, Tallegalla Consultants Pty Ltd, Brisbane.

Vanstone A (2007). Beyond conspicuous compassion: Indigenous Australians deserve more than good intentions. In Wanna J (ed.), *A passion for policy: essays in public sector reform*, ANU E Press, Canberra.

West P (2004). *Conspicuous compassion: why sometimes it really is cruel to be kind*, Civitas: Institute for the Study of Civil Society, London.

Appendix 1:
Annotated timeline of key developments

Bree Blakeman

1976

Then ministers for Aboriginal Affairs, Social Security, Employment and Industrial Affairs meet to discuss difficulties arising because of Indigenous peoples' access to social security benefits. Concern is expressed that a large proportion of Indigenous people of workforce age in remote areas could end up on unemployment benefits, so an alternative is sought.[1] An Interdepartmental Working Party on Aboriginal Employment is established.

1977

On 26 May 1977, the Minister for Aboriginal Affairs, Ian Viner, announces the creation of the Community Development Employment Projects (CDEP) as part of a package of measures designed to deal with the employment problems noted in the Working Party's report. CDEP is seen as having particular value for communities that do not have access to a mainstream (waged) labour market.[2] CDEP starts as a pilot scheme in Wugularr (Bamyili) community in the Northern Territory.

At its inception, CDEP has the following characteristics:

- it is set up administratively with no legislative basis;
- it is designed to reduce the high level of Aboriginal unemployment;

---

1   Sanders W (2007: 1).
2   Altman JC, Gray MC & Levitus R (2005: 28).

- a secondary concern is the social effect on Indigenous communities of direct cash payments received as a result of unemployment benefits;
- the program is administered by the Department of Aboriginal Affairs (DAA);
- DAA provides block grants to Indigenous community councils or incorporated organisations to employ CDEP participants in community development projects (additional grants are made for on-costs like administration and capital expenditures);
- payments are notionally linked to unemployment benefits. That is, money is paid indirectly to CDEP participants as a basic wage approximating the unemployment benefits they would otherwise receive.

By August, a number of South and Western Australian Pitjantjatjara communities join CDEP on a pilot basis.[3] There are now four communities participating in the program. This expands to approximately 10 by 1978.

1980

A review of the CDEP Pilot scheme is carried out.[4] CDEP continues to expand under the Fraser Government. By 1981 there are approximately 1,300 participants across 18 communities. Expenditure has almost doubled to $6.9 million.[5]

1983

The Hawke Government furthers the expansion of CDEP into remote communities. Funding increases to meet the growing level of demand for CDEP.

1985

The *Report of the Committee of Review of Aboriginal Employment and Training Programs* (the Miller Report) is released. The Miller Report recommends that CDEP be expanded on account of its potential

---

3   Johns M (2008: 10).
4   Department of Finance and Deregulation, Office of Evaluation and Audit (Indigenous Programs) (2009: 81).
5   Johns op. cit., p.10.

to provide employment, commercial and other entrepreneurial opportunity in remote communities.[6] CDEP continues to expand and by 1986 takes in 38 remote communities and about 4,000 participants.

1987

Acting on recommendations of the Miller Report, the Hawke Government develops the Aboriginal Employment Development Policy (AEDP). The AEDP recommends an expansion of CDEP into 'wider target groups' in areas where Aboriginal people have poor employment prospects, opening the way for the introduction of CDEP into non-remote areas.[7] CDEP becomes the largest single program in the federal Aboriginal affairs budget. By 1986–87, there are 63 projects involving 6,000 participants and costing almost $40 million.[8]

* * *

The House of Representatives Standing Committee on Aboriginal Affairs releases *The Return to Country: The Aboriginal Homelands Movement in Australia* report (the Blanchard Report). The Blanchard Report recommends that CDEP be expanded to all homeland centres wishing to participate in the scheme.

* * *

The *Economic Viability of Aboriginal Outstations and Homelands* report is prepared for the Australian Council for Employment and Training. The report recommends 'careful consideration' with regard to expanding CDEP to homeland centres and outstations, as the economic impact of CDEP on outstations has not yet been adequately reviewed. The report observes that CDEP is often used at outstations for income support rather than for developing programs for the community.[9]

1988–90

CDEP begins to expand into southern regional and urban areas. The first non-remote CDEPs are established in New South Wales and Victoria in 1988–89. By early 1990, there are 2,900 participants in

---

6   Johns op. cit., p.10–11.
7   Department of Finance and Deregulation op. cit., p.78.
8   Altman, Gray & Levitus op. cit., p.29.
9   Altman JC & Taylor L (1989: 51).

13 newly participating Aboriginal communities in more settled areas of Australia along the eastern seaboard of Queensland, in New South Wales, Victoria and southern South Australia.[10]

1989

The Australian National Audit Office (ANAO) raises a concern that DAA cannot, in every instance, verify that CDEP payments are being made to entitled recipients.[11]

1990

The DAA initiates a review into CDEP funding and administration. The review recommends that expansion of CDEP be slowed in order to allow for administrative and policy issues to be resolved.[12] The Hawke Government responds by indicating that no new communities will be included in the CDEP scheme in the 1990–91 budget year.[13]

* * *

The Aboriginal and Torres Strait Islander Commission (ATSIC) is established and takes over the running of CDEP. By this time CDEP is a major nationwide program.

* * *

In November the *Report of the Auditor-General No. 12, 1990–91, Aboriginal and Torres Strait Islander Commission – Community Development Employment Projects* is released. It focuses on planning and implementation issues to ensure the efficiency and effectiveness of the scheme, and is referred to the House of Representatives Standing Committee on Aboriginal Affairs for review.[14]

1991

The budget for CDEP in 1990–91 is over $180 million and the program now includes 188 organisations and 18,000 participants.[15]

---

10 Altman JC & Sanders W (1991a: 13).
11 Altman JC & Sanders W (1991b: 3).
12 CDEP Working Party (1990).
13 Altman & Sanders 1991b op. cit., p.3.
14 House of Representatives Standing Committee on Aboriginal Affairs (1991).
15 Ibid., p.2.

* * *

The House of Representatives Standing Committee on Aboriginal Affairs releases its *Review of Auditor-General's Report No. 12*. It finds that 'CDEP is proving to be a sound and effective scheme that has much to offer', but owing to the rapid rate of its expansion the efficiency of its implementation could be considerably improved.[16] This is particularly so in areas such as coordination, monitoring and appropriate training for CDEP administrators in communities.

* * *

ATSIC releases the report of an interdepartmental review of the administration of CDEP. The report—*Community Development Employment Projects: Review of Funding and Administration*—notes concerns about the possibility of so-called 'double dipping', in that CDEP participants can theoretically access partial unemployment benefits if their CDEP income is below a certain threshold (as can normal waged workers). It recommends the government prevents this either by increasing CDEP wages or legislating to prevent CDEP participants from receiving unemployment benefits.[17]

* * *

The *Social Security Act* is amended to make CDEP participants ineligible for unemployment benefits because they are deemed to be already receiving another form of Commonwealth Government income support.[18]

* * *

The *Royal Commission into Aboriginal Deaths in Custody* makes a number of recommendations with regard to the CDEP scheme. These recommendations include the following:

203: Recommends that the highest priority be accorded to facilitating social, economic and cultural development plans by Aboriginal communities and regions as a basis for future planning for CDEP schemes. In particular, it notes that the preparation of CDEP work

---

16   Ibid., p.1.
17   Race Discrimination Commissioner (1997: 9–10).
18   Department of Finance and Deregulation op. cit., p.78.

plans (community development plans) should be a participative process involving all members of the community, and should draw on the knowledge and expertise of a wide range of professionals as well the views and aspirations of Aboriginal people in the local area. It states that the processes by which plans are developed must be culturally sensitive, unhurried and holistic in approach, and that adequate information on the following matters must be made available to participants:

- The range of Aboriginal needs and aspirations
- The opportunities created by government policies or programs
- The opportunities and constraints in the local economy
- The political opportunities to influence the local arena.

317: Recommends that further extension of CDEP (or some similar program) to rural towns with large Aboriginal populations and limited mainstream employment opportunities for Aboriginal people be considered.

318: Recommends that in view of the considerable demands placed on staff of ATSIC by the expansion of CDEP, consideration be given to devolving responsibility for some aspects of CDEP administrative support to appropriate consenting Aboriginal organisations, in particular resource agencies.[19]

1991-92

The moratorium on CDEP's expansion in the 1990–91 budget is lifted in the budget for 1991–92.[20] A total of 185 CDEP projects are now funded, involving 20,100 participants and costing $205 million. The scheme accounts for around one-third of Aboriginal affairs portfolio expenditure.[21]

1992

Auditor-General's Report No. 44, Entitlement checks in localities with CDEP is released.

19   Royal Commission into Aboriginal Deaths in Custody (1991).
20   Altman & Sanders 1991b op. cit., p.3.
21   Altman, Gray & Levitus op. cit., p.29.

* * *

The House of Representatives Standing Committee on Aboriginal and Torres Strait Islander Affairs releases *Mainly Urban: Report of the Inquiry into the needs of urban dwelling Aboriginal and Torres Strait Island people*. It finds that CDEP is 'proving of great value in rural towns' where there is intractable and structural Aboriginal unemployment. It recommends the further expansion of CDEP into urban areas, but suggests introducing a 'sunset clause' for phasing out CDEP after a certain period where there are other jobs available.[22]

1993

No Reverse Gear, A National Review of the Community Development Employment Projects Scheme is prepared for ATSIC by Deloitte Touche Tohmatsu.[23] The review recommends that CDEP's expansion be slowed due to lack of clear objectives or goals. It further recommends an increase in the capital component of CDEP to support increased investment in community development.

1994

Responsibility for CDEP is devolved to ATSIC regional councils.[24]

1995

By 1995 there are 252 CDEP organisations with approximately 27,000 participants.

* * *

An Interdepartmental Committee of Review of CDEP finds that CDEP participants are unable to access a range of tax and social security benefits available to the unemployed. ATSIC releases a report stating that 'this situation can no longer be tolerated'.[25]

* * *

---

22   House of Representatives Standing Committee on Aboriginal and Torres Strait Islander Affairs (1992: 114).
23   McCullagh G (1993).
24   Department of Finance and Deregulation op. cit., p.78.
25   ATSIC (1995: 92).

The ANAO releases an audit of the CDEP scheme. Phase one examines the operations of one central, one state and one regional office, finding examples of good practice with room for improvement in administrative matters. Phase two of the audit is to be completed in 1997.[26]

1996

The newly elected Howard Government stops the allocation of new CDEP places and cuts funding by 12 per cent for communities with less than 150 participants.[27]

1997

The *Independent Review of CDEP* by Ian Spicer (the Spicer Review) is released. It is generally positive about CDEP, stating that its importance 'cannot be overstated ... Without it, some remote communities would simply not exist.' It lists benefits including skills enhancement, improved quality of life, social and cultural outcomes, pride, enterprise development and economic growth. It also notes concerns that up to one-third of participants do not work (some therefore receiving very little income under 'no work no pay' rules). The review recommends moving these participants onto unemployment benefits where they will be financially better off and refocusing the scheme's objectives to provide work 'as defined by the community'. The report also emphasises that the principle challenge is ensuring that, where possible, CDEP acts as a conduit to unsubsidised employment options.[28]

* * *

Phase two of the ANAO audit is completed. It focuses on the operational and planning aspects of CDEP. The audit recommends focusing on setting priorities, resource allocation and performance information over and above the operational plan of CDEP.[29]

* * *

26   Johns op. cit., p.12.
27   Department of Finance and Deregulation op. cit., p.78.
28   Spicer I (1997: 1–4).
29   Johns op. cit., p.12.

The Race Discrimination Commissioner releases *The CDEP Scheme and Racial Discrimination*, which deals in part with allegations that lack of access of CDEP participants to social security entitlements is discriminatory. It finds that there is no 'significant issue of racial discrimination'. However, it notes that different government departments treat CDEP participants differently; for example, the tax office treats them as wage earners for the purposes of calculating income tax payable, but the Department of Social Security (DSS) treats them as participants in a publicly funded employment program and as such precludes them from becoming DSS customers. This prevents CDEP participants from accessing a range of social security payments available to ordinary wage earners. The review urges the government to consistently treat CDEP participants as ordinary wage earners.[30]

* * *

The ATSIC Office of Evaluation and Audit (OEA) completes a report into the employment outcomes of urban CDEP schemes and the financial and non-labour market outcomes and benefits of the scheme for both urban and non-urban CDEPs.[31] The report finds that CDEP schemes generally produce positive outcomes for participants in urban areas when compared to urban unemployed Indigenous people. The report also finds that CDEP provides significant training opportunities for participants, while training opportunities are more limited in rural and remote areas.

* * *

By June, CDEP covers 268 participating communities and 30,133 participants, comprising 20,501 participants in remote localities and 9,630 in non-remote areas. For many Indigenous people in remote locations, the local CDEP scheme provides the only alternative to unemployment.

1999

The Howard Government introduces the Indigenous Employment Policy (IEP), recommending that CDEP be considered a pathway to unsubsidised employment. A CDEP placement incentive is paid

30 Race Discrimination Commissioner (1997).
31 Johns op. cit., p.12.

to CDEP organisations when participants exit the scheme for other paid work. Key functions within the IEP are delivered through the Department of Employment and Workplace Relations (DEWR).

* * *

Amendments to the Social Security Act[32] introduce a 'CDEP Scheme Participant Supplement' of $20 per fortnight. This gives CDEP participants an equivalent payment to that received by Newstart and Youth Allowance recipients involved in Work for the Dole activities. It also means CDEP participants become Centrelink (formerly DSS) customers for the first time, such that they can access a range of other government payments previously inaccessible to them.

2001

The ANAO draws attention to the fact that a range of government services in Indigenous communities are being funded through the CDEP program.[33] This 'substitution funding' (in which CDEP participants are paid to do municipal services type jobs, shifting costs onto the CDEP program and away from government agencies that would otherwise be responsible) has long been recognised, but has not always been interpreted as a problem.[34]

* * *

ATSIC releases *Outcomes Report on the Relevant, Responsive Remote CDEPs Workshop,* which seeks to evaluate CDEP schemes in order to rethink policy directions for CDEP in rural and remote areas.

2002

From February, the Howard Government introduces Indigenous Employment Centres (IECs) in cities and regional centres. These are designed to assist up to 10,000 CDEP participants move from 'work experience' into unsubsidised employment or other employment assistance. CDEP organisations are encouraged to take on the role of IECs.[35]

---

32   *Further 1998 Budget Measures Legislation Amendment (Social Security) Act 1999.*
33   Department of Finance and Deregulation op. cit., p.78.
34   Altman & Sanders 1991b op. cit., p.9.
35   Champion M (2002: 29).

* * *

COAG agrees to trial working together with Indigenous communities in up to 10 regions to provide more flexible programs and services based on priorities agreed with the communities. A number of the trial sites include CDEP provider services.[36]

2003

At 30 June, ATSIC counted 272 CDEP projects with just over 35,000 participants, operating on total grants of $484 million, three-quarters of which ($365 million) is offset against welfare entitlements.[37]

* * *

Budget 2003–04 announces the addition of 1,000 extra CDEP places each year for the following four years (where previously an approximate increase of 550 places were funded per annum). The places are allocated to remote communities to support projects that seek to prevent and address family violence and substance misuse.[38]

* * *

The Howard Government releases Stage One of its report on the IEP. It recommends moving CDEP participants into more 'open employment'. Stage Two, focusing on the effectiveness of the components of IEP, is to be completed by 2004.

* * *

ATSIC convenes a workshop on proposed reforms to CDEP, which recommends streaming CDEP into two directions: community development on the one hand, and enterprise and employment programs on the other.

---

36   Department of Finance and Deregulation op. cit., p.78.
37   Altman, Gray & Levitus op. cit., p.29.
38   Department of Finance and Deregulation, op. cit., p.78.

2004

ATSIC is disbanded amid controversy. Responsibility for CDEP is transferred to DEWR. Under DEWR's administration, the formal aims of CDEP shift further towards moving CDEP participants into unsubsidised employment.[39]

2005

DEWR commences a reform process, which leads to significant changes to CDEP. According to DEWR there are around 37,000 CDEP participants in 2005.[40] This number includes non-Indigenous CDEP participants, who make up an estimated 10 per cent of the total (usually spouses or de facto partners of Indigenous participants).

* * *

The Remote Area Exemptions (RAE) for activity testing for unemployment benefits are progressively removed from 2005 (and phased out entirely by 2009). When an income support recipient has their RAE removed they are assessed by Centrelink; if they have sufficient work capacity they are required to enter into an activity agreement. This will include participation in CDEP, Job Network or a structured training course.[41]

* * *

In April, DEWR releases the discussion paper *Building on Success CDEP – Future Directions*, suggesting that CDEP 'has become a destination rather than a stepping stone towards jobs' in many communities.[42] It argues for a 'stronger focus on results' in three areas of employment, community activities and business development, better links between CDEP and the mainstream Job Network, and an expansion of IECs.

2006

Performance Audit of CDEP Performance Information is released by the Office of Evaluation and Audit (Indigenous Programs).

* * *

---

39   Sanders W (2007).
40   Department of Employment and Workplace Relations (2005).
41   Department of Finance and Deregulation op. cit., p.79.
42   Department of Employment and Workplace Relations op. cit., p.3.

The *Indigenous Potential meets Economic Opportunity* discussion paper is released by DEWR in March. It proposes major changes including ceasing CDEP in urban and regional areas.[43] Kevin Andrews, Minister for Employment and Workplace Relations, suggests that around 7,000 participant places in 40 CDEP organisations will be removed from the scheme from June 2007, out of a national total of 35,000 participants. These proposed closures are in areas with what are described by the government as 'strong labour markets'. Affected participants and organisations will instead be offered opportunities to participate in general DEWR programs and an expansion of the Indigenous-specific Structured Training and Employment Projects (STEP) 'brokerage service'. STEP provides funding and assistance for employers to take on Indigenous staff. IECs are to cease and all CDEP and IEC organisations are required to compete for contracts if they wish to become STEP providers.[44] CDEP participants in non-remote areas are required to register with a Job Network member, and new participants are limited to 12 months' participation in the scheme.[45] In remote areas, a lower youth rate is introduced for new CDEP participants aged 20 years and under, and income limits are changed in an attempt to encourage CDEP participants into non-CDEP work.[46]

2007

Minister for Workplace Relations Joe Hockey states that the objective of CDEP is to move people off welfare and into 'real employment'. He characterises CDEP as a form of social welfare that prevents participants from gaining 'real' employment.[47]

* * *

From 1 July, around 60 urban and regional CDEPs are closed in areas deemed to have strong labour markets with unemployment rates of below 7 per cent. Around 6,000 people are exited from the program.[48]

* * *

---

43   Johns op. cit., p.15.
44   Department of Employment and Workplace Relations (2006).
45   Sanders W (2007).
46   Department of Finance and Deregulation op. cit., p.79.
47   Johns op. cit.
48   Altman JC (2007).

In July, Minister for Indigenous Affairs Mal Brough and Joe Hockey announce plans to abolish CDEP in the Northern Territory as part of the Northern Territory Emergency Response (NTER). This will make former participants subject to income management, another element of the NTER. Members of the Australian Labor Party (ALP) raise concerns about the proposed closure of CDEP in the Northern Territory. Jenny Macklin, Shadow Minister for Indigenous Affairs, argues that removing CDEP will 'make communities, parents and children more vulnerable' and commits to retaining it if the ALP wins office at the next election. Warren Snowdon, Shadow Parliamentary Secretary for Northern Australia and Indigenous Affairs, argues closing CDEP will move people onto 'sit down money' and 'spell the death knell' of many positive initiatives in Indigenous communities.[49]

* * *

From September, CDEP programs in the Northern Territory begin to be closed on a community-by-community basis. With the election of the Rudd Government in late November a moratorium is placed on further dismantling CDEP in the Northern Territory. By this time CDEP has closed in around 30 communities, representing 16 CDEP organisations and more than 2,000 CDEP participants.[50]

* * *

CDEP administration is moved from the Employment portfolio to the Department of Families, Housing, Community Services and Indigenous Affairs (FaHCSIA).

* * *

In December, funding is committed to convert 1,600 CDEP positions supporting Australian Government-funded services into 'real jobs'. The Australian Government is also matching dollar for dollar up to $10 million to create a further 2,000 Northern Territory Government and local government jobs from the conversion of CDEP positions where these were providing municipal type services.[51]

---

49   Jordan K (2011: 15).
50   Altman JC & Johns M (2008: 10).
51   Department of Finance and Deregulation op. cit., p.79.

2008

The Rudd Government releases *Increasing Indigenous Economic Opportunity – A discussion paper on the future of the CDEP and the Indigenous Employment Program*. This report foreshadows further major reform of CDEP from July 2009.

* * *

From July, the Australian Government begins to reinstate a modified version of CDEP in Northern Territory remote communities where it was closed under the NTER. This is for an initial period of 12 months. However, not all of the CDEP positions that had been 'dissolved' under the NTER are reinstated.[52]

* * *

Also in July, the Northern Territory Government announces the creation of 'super-shires', including the amalgamation of local Aboriginal community councils. Control of some CDEP schemes in the Northern Territory is handed to shires. Only a small number of the original CDEP organisations in the Northern Territory remain.

* * *

In December, Minister for Indigenous Affairs Jenny Macklin outlines key elements of the Rudd Government's new Indigenous employment strategy that centres on significant changes to CDEP and reform of the IEP. The proposed changes will see CDEP cease to operate in all remaining non-remote areas as of 1 July 2009. In remote areas, new entrants to the scheme from 1 July 2009 will receive income support instead of CDEP wages.

* * *

Additional funding is announced to convert a further 2,000 CDEP jobs in municipal services delivery into fully funded Australian Government jobs.[53]

---

52   Jordan op. cit., p.15.
53   Department of Finance and Deregulation op. cit., p.66.

2009

From 1 July, CDEP closes in all non-remote areas. This sees it removed from an additional 30 locations, with just under 2,000 participants exiting the scheme. CDEP is now delivered only in areas deemed to be 'remote'. New participants in remote areas are to receive social security payments instead of CDEP wages. 'Grandfathered participants' are told they will be eligible to continue receiving CDEP wages and 'top up' until 30 September 2011.[54] All participants are also required to sign up to mainstream employment services with Job Services Australia (JSA). JSA and CDEP providers are asked to work together to assist their joint clients find mainstream jobs.

* * *

The net effect of changes to CDEP under the Howard and Rudd governments means that by October 2009 total participant numbers have declined dramatically to around 14,500 people.[55]

2010

The date for cessation of CDEP wages for grandfathered participants is extended until April 2012. In announcing this change, Jenny Macklin suggests this will 'provide stability to the program while ongoing discussions about the way services are delivered are held with local communities to ensure they reflect local needs'. She reiterates that the changes to CDEP 'aim to see people transition out of CDEP into work with proper wages and conditions including superannuation and leave entitlements'.[56]

2011

CDEP participant numbers continue to decline, to just under 10,500 in February 2011.[57]

* * *

54   Jordan op. cit., p.15–16.
55   Jordan op. cit., p.15.
56   Macklin J, Plibersek T & Arbib M (2010).
57   Jordan op. cit., p.15–16.

In June, the Gillard Government announces a major review of remote employment services, with the aim of developing a new scheme to be in place by 1 July 2013. The review will seek advice from a new 'Remote Participation and Employment Services Engagement Panel' and from consultation sessions in 20 remote communities in August and September.[58]

* * *

A discussion paper is released to frame the review into remote employment services. Titled *The Future of Remote Participation and Employment Service Arrangements*, it suggests that existing services under CDEP, JSA, IEP and Disability Employment Services (DES) are 'fragmented' and 'their goals ... not always aligned'. It says these arrangements are 'inflexible and unresponsive to community needs and aspirations' and 'confusing for the communities and the people living in them' as a result of being 'delivered by several different providers'. The 'current market driven employment services', it says, are 'suited to urban and regional Australia' and do 'not adequately address the issues specific to remote Australia'.[59]

2012

In April, the Gillard Government announces the creation of the Remote Jobs and Communities Program (RJCP), which brings together and replaces the CDEP, JSA, DES and IEP in remote areas, creating one single integrated service.[60] RJCP is to commence on 1 July 2013. All participants will be required to engage in Work for the Dole activities for 15–20 hours per week for social security payments, although grandfathering arrangements for those still on CDEP wages are extended until 2017. (In other parts of the country, this 'mutual obligation' activity requirement applies only to those unemployed for more than six months, and then only six months in each year.)[61] The changes are ostensibly designed to provide better support to help participants get jobs and participate in activities that improve their communities.[62]

* * *

58   Arbib M, Macklin J & Ellis K (2011).
59   Sanders W & Fowkes L (2015: 1).
60   Macklin J, Shorten B & Collins J (2012).
61   Sanders & Fowkes op. cit., p.2.
62   Macklin, Shorten & Collins op. cit.

The 2012–13 Budget states that extending the payment of CDEP wages to grandfathered participants to 30 June 2017 will 'support Indigenous people in remote communities with work and training opportunities ... [and] provide stability to CDEP wage participants as they move to the new Remote Jobs and Communities Program'.[63]

2013

From 1 July, CDEP is replaced by RJCP. The new service is delivered in 60 remote regions, by organisations selected on the basis of competitive tender. These include some Indigenous organisations with a history of delivering CDEP as well as shires, for-profit and not-for-profit providers. RJCP retains features of both CDEP and JSA, including CDEP's focus on delivering activities and training, and JSA's focus on mandatory client assessment and minimum monthly appointments to monitor progress on agreed commitments.[64] There are around 500 former CDEP participants who fall outside these designated RJCP regions; these participants are moved over onto JSA.[65] RJCP is not an Indigenous-specific program, but the large majority of participants are Indigenous.

* * *

In August, Opposition Leader Tony Abbott announces that, if the Coalition wins office at the next federal election, Indigenous employment and training programs will be the subject of a review headed by mining magnate Andrew Forrest.[66]

* * *

After the election of the Abbott Government in September, the new Minister for Indigenous Affairs Nigel Scullion is reported as describing RJCP as 'a complete disaster' because participants had become disengaged and meaningful activities were not being delivered. He is reported as saying that the old system of CDEP, which both ALP and Coalition governments had dismantled, was a better alternative.[67]

---

63 Commonwealth of Australia (2012).
64 Sanders & Fowkes op. cit., p.1.
65 Macklin J, Shorten B & Collins J (2012).
66 Cullen S (2013).
67 Karvelas P (2013).

2014

Some 3,000 CDEP participants are still employed on wages within RJCP and can remain so until 2017.[68]

* * *

Creating Parity, the report of the Forrest Review, is released on 1 August. It says that CDEP participants were better off financially than the unemployed on Newstart but recommends bringing forward the cessation of CDEP wages for grandfathered participants from 2017 to 2015 in the name of 'equity'.[69]

* * *

On 6 December, Nigel Scullion announces that RJCP will be reformed with the expressed aim of delivering 'better opportunities for remote job seekers' and fostering 'stronger economic and social outcomes in remote Australia'.[70] He suggests that the RJCP has failed because 'it wasn't geared to the unique social and labour market conditions of remote Australia'.[71] Scullion also announces that, based on the recommendation of the Forrest Review, grandfathered CDEP wages will cease on 30 June 2015. The changes to RJCP will ostensibly ensure jobseekers are active and contributing to their communities.

2015

Nigel Scullion announces on 3 June that from 1 July RJCP will be renamed the Community Development Programme (CDP). CDP participants will be required to participate in Work for the Dole activities for up to 25 hours per week for 12 months of the year (with some provisions for identified leave). At the commencement of CDP there are over 35,000 participants, with around 30,000 required to undertake Work for the Dole activities.[72]

* * *

---

68   Sanders & Fowkes op. cit., p.2.
69   Forrest A (chair) (2014: 134).
70   Moran M, Porter D & Curth-Bibb J (2014).
71   Scullion N (2014).
72   Scullion N (2015).

In December, Nigel Scullion tables new legislation in parliament seeking to remove income support recipients in remote regions from the standard social security legislation.[73] Instead, he proposes that remote income support recipients will be subject to different administrative and compliance arrangements under a separate legislative instrument. Broad-ranging powers would allow the Minister for Indigenous Affairs (presently Scullion) to determine how the social security system would function in remote areas, including the obligations of social security recipients and penalties for non-compliance, although there would be a requirement for 'consultation'. Scullion indicates these changes are in response to Aboriginal peoples' concerns about the closure of CDEP. They appear to attempt to resurrect some features of that scheme, but without a return to CDEP wages. The Bill is referred to the Senate Finance and Public Administration Legislation Committee for inquiry in January 2016. The majority report of the Senate committee recommends the changes be approved by parliament. Two dissenting reports—from the Australian Labor Party and Australian Greens—recommend the legislation be withdrawn.

References

Altman JC (2007). Neo-paternalism and the destruction of CDEP, *Topical Issue No. 14*, Centre for Aboriginal Economic Policy Research, The Australian National University, Canberra.

Altman JC, Gray MC & Levitus R (2005). *Policy issues for the Community Development Employment Projects scheme in rural and remote Australia*. Discussion Paper No. 271, Centre for Aboriginal Economic Policy Research, The Australian National University, Canberra.

Altman JC & Johns M (2008). *Indigenous welfare reform in the Northern Territory and Cape York: a comparative analysis*. Working Paper 44, Centre for Aboriginal Economic Policy Research, The Australian National University, Canberra.

---

73 Social Security Legislation Amendment (Community Development Program) Bill 2015.

Altman JC & Sanders W (1991a). *From exclusion to dependence: Aborigines and the welfare state in Australia*, Discussion Paper 1, Centre for Aboriginal Economic Policy Research, The Australian National University, Canberra.

Altman JC & Sanders W (1991b). *The CDEP scheme: administrative and policy issues*, Discussion Paper 5, Centre for Aboriginal Economic Policy Research, The Australian National University, Canberra.

Altman JC & Taylor L (1989). *The economic viability of Aboriginal outstations and homelands, a report to the Australian Council for Employment and Training*, Australian Government Publishing Service, Canberra.

Arbib M, Macklin J & Ellis K (2011). *Government reviews remote employment services*, media release, 29 June.

ATSIC (Aboriginal and Torres Strait Islander Commission) (1995). *Recognition rights and reform: a report to Government on Native Title social justice measures*, Aboriginal and Torres Strait Islander Commission, Canberra.

CDEP Working Party (1990). *Community Development Employment Projects: review of funding and administration*, unpublished report, Department of Aboriginal Affairs, Canberra.

Champion M (2002). *Urban CDEPs as Indigenous employment centres: policy and community implications*, Discussion Paper 228, Centre for Aboriginal Economic Policy Research, The Australian National University, Canberra.

Commonwealth of Australia (2012). *Budget Paper No. 2: budget measures 2012-13*, Commonwealth of Australia, Canberra.

Cullen S (2013). Election 2013: Tony Abbott promises $45 million for Indigenous training, employment scheme. *ABC News online*, www. abc.net.au/news/2013-08-17/abbott-pledges-$45m-for-indigenous-job-scheme/4894172.

Department of Employment and Workplace Relations (2005). *Building on success CDEP-future directions*, Discussion Paper, Department of Employment and Workplace Relations, Canberra.

Department of Employment and Workplace Relations (2006). *Indigenous potential meets economic opportunity*, CDEP Discussion paper, November, Department of Employment and Workplace Relations, Canberra.

Department of Finance and Deregulation, Office of Evaluation and Audit (Indigenous Programs) (2009). *Evaluation of the Community Development Employment Projects (CDEP) program, evaluation report*, Department of Finance and Deregulation, Canberra.

Forrest, A (chair) (2014). *The Forrest review: creating parity*, Australian Government, Canberra.

House of Representatives Standing Committee on Aboriginal Affairs (1991). *Review of Auditor-General's Report No. 12, 1990-91*, Aboriginal and Torres Strait Islander Commission, Community Development Employment Projects, Australian Government Publishing Service, Canberra.

House of Representatives Standing Committee on Aboriginal and Torres Strait Islander Affairs (1992). *Mainly urban: report of the inquiry into the needs of urban dwelling Aboriginal and Torres Strait Islander people*, Australian Government Publishing Service, Canberra.

Johns M (2008). Annotated chronology of the Community Development Employment Projects (CDEP) program, 1977–2008. In Altman J, Submission to the Australian Government's Increasing Indigenous Employment Opportunity Discussion Paper, *Topical Issue 16*, Centre for Aboriginal Economic Policy Research, The Australian National University, Canberra.

Jordan K (2011). *Work, welfare and CDEP on the Aṉangu Pitjantjatjara Yankunytjatjara Lands: first stage assessment*, Working Paper No. 78, Centre for Aboriginal Economic Policy Research, The Australian National University, Canberra.

Karvelas P (2013). Aboriginal jobs program a complete disaster, says Nigel Scullion, *The Australian*, 18 October.

Macklin J, Plibersek T & Arbib M (2010). *Increasing employment and participation in remote Indigenous communities*, media release, 9 December.

Macklin J, Shorten B & Collins J (2012). *Jobs and sustainable communities for people in remote Australia*, media release, 26 April.

McCullagh, G (1993) *No reverse gear: a national review of the Community Development Employment Projects Scheme*, Deloitte Touche Tohmatsu, Sydney.

Moran M, Porter D & Curth-Bibb J (2014). *Funding Indigenous organisations: improving governance performance through innovations in public finance management in remote Australia*. Issues paper no 11. Produced for the Closing the Gap Clearinghouse. Canberra: Australian Institute of Health and Welfare & Melbourne: Australian Institute of Family Studies.

Race Discrimination Commissioner (1997). *The CDEP scheme and racial discrimination*. Report by the Race Discrimination Commissioner, Human Rights and Equal Opportunities Commission, December 1997.

Royal Commission into Aboriginal Deaths in Custody (1991). *Royal Commission into Aboriginal deaths in custody: National reports* [Vol 1–5], and regional reports, Australian Government Publishing Service, Canberra.

Sanders W (2007). Changes to CDEP under DEWR: Policy substance and the new contractualism. *Quarterly of the Australian Council of Social Services*, March 2017.

Sanders W & Fowkes L (2015). *A survey of Remote Jobs and Communities Programme providers: one year in*, Working Paper No. 97, Centre for Aboriginal Economic Policy Research, The Australian National University, Canberra.

Scullion N (2014). *More opportunities for job seekers in remote communities*, media release, 6 December.

Scullion N (2015). *Remote employment programme to improve communities*, media release, 3 June.

Spicer I (1997). *Independent review of the Community Development Employment Projects (CDEP) scheme*, Aboriginal and Torres Strait Islander Commission, Canberra.

Appendix 2:
Annotated bibliography of author publications on CDEP 2005–15

Compiled by Bree Blakeman

Altman JC (2005). CDEP 2005—A new home and new objectives for a very old program? *Topical Issue No. 07/2005*, Centre for Aboriginal Economic Policy Research, The Australian National University, Canberra.

The Community Development Employment Projects (CDEP) scheme has existed since 1977; it is arguably the oldest Indigenous-specific program still in existence, relatively unchanged. From 1 July 2004, with the division of Aboriginal and Torres Strait Islander Services (ATSIS) Indigenous-specific programs between Australian mainline departments, it has been located in the Australian Government Department of Employment and Workplace Relations (DEWR). At face value, its new administrative home suggests that this innovative and highly flexible program might have a stronger, or even singular, labour market focus. This paper provides a perspective on CDEP based on analysis of National Aboriginal and Torres Strait Islander Social Survey (NATSISS) 2002 data and explores the various impacts of the scheme on Indigenous participants, especially in rural and remote Australia. Using this evidence base, the paper questions if there is any need for fundamental change in this program, and if so, what?

Altman JC & Gray MC (2005). The CDEP scheme: A flexible and innovative employment and community development program for Indigenous Australians. In Considine M, Howe B & Rosewarne L (eds), *Transitions and risk: New directions in social policy*, International Social Policy Conference, Centre for Public Policy, University of Melbourne, Melbourne, 1–9.

The CDEP scheme is an unusual program for Indigenous people, primarily underwritten by welfare entitlements. Currently there are 39,000 CDEP places and around 60,000 Indigenous people participate in the scheme each year. This paper discusses the roles that the scheme plays. First, the scheme provides flexible employment opportunities, often in remote contexts where there are no, or minute, labour markets. Second, it provides income security and the opportunity to earn additional income from employment and enterprise. Third, it provides opportunity for education and training. Fourth, and most innovatively, it acts as an instrument for economic and community development. This is especially so in remote and very remote Australia where people reside on the Indigenous estate and operate within an unorthodox 'hybrid economy' where customary (non-market) activity looms relatively large. The customary sector has considerable economic value, both for Indigenous people directly and in spillover benefits to other Australians. The links between the CDEP scheme and the operations of the hybrid economy are explored.

Altman JC & Gray MC (2005). The economic and social impacts of the CDEP scheme in remote Australia. *Australian Journal of Social Issues*, 40 (2): 399–410.

Despite the significance of the CDEP scheme, in recent times, relatively little attention has been given to the potential for the scheme to be used as an instrument for economic and social development in remote areas of Australia. This paper presents new evidence on the impact of the CDEP scheme on economic and social outcomes for Indigenous people in remote areas of Australia. It concludes that the scheme has been successful in generating positive economic and community development outcomes at minimal cost to the Australian taxpayer.

Altman JC, Gray MC & Levitus R (2005). *Policy issues for the Community Development Employment Projects scheme in rural and remote Australia*. Discussion Paper No. 271, Centre for Aboriginal Economic Policy Research, The Australian National University, Canberra.

The CDEP scheme is one of the most important programs for Indigenous community and economic development. CDEP employs around 35,000 Indigenous Australians and accounts for over one-quarter of total Indigenous employment. This paper reviews the evidence on the social and economic impacts of the scheme. The available evidence demonstrates that the scheme does have positive economic and community development impacts and that it is cost-effective in achieving these outcomes. The paper argues that the CDEP program should continue to be supported and resourced and outlines options for future policy directions in regard to Indigenous economic development and the role of the CDEP scheme.

Altman JC, Gray MC & Levitus R (2005). *Skilling Indigenous Australia: Policy issues for the Community Development Employment Projects scheme in rural and remote Australia*, Chifley Research Centre, Canberra.

This paper reviews the evidence on the social and economic impacts of the scheme and canvasses options for future policy directions in regard to Indigenous economic development and the role of the CDEP scheme. While the main focus of the paper is on the operation of the scheme in regional and remote areas of Australia in which the majority (73 per cent) of CDEP participants live, there is some discussion of the role and future of the scheme in major cities.

Hunter BH (2005). The role of discrimination and the exclusion of Indigenous people from the labour market. In Austin-Broos D & Macdonald G (eds), *Culture, economy and governance in Aboriginal Australia*, University of Sydney Press, Sydney, 79–94.

This paper presents a statistical analysis of the five census counts between 1981 and 2000. It explores the extent to which discrimination against Indigenous people operates in the labour market, especially in regard to employment. The CDEP scheme is identified as a positive reform that enhanced employment prospects of Indigenous people in the mainstream labour market. The introduction of the CDEP scheme in 1977 was instrumental in creating 'employment' in areas where there are no or few jobs available. Under the CDEP scheme, Indigenous community organisations get an allocation of a similar magnitude to their collective unemployment benefit entitlement to undertake community-defined 'work'. In the course of this paper, Hunter notes that a Human Rights and Equal Opportunity Commission review (1997) found that the CDEP scheme did not appear to raise any significant issue of racial discrimination, although it had some specific concerns with the administration of the scheme. While the CDEP scheme is race-based and applies only to Aboriginal and Torres Strait Islander peoples, it is designed to deal with the disadvantage experienced by Indigenous communities in their access to social security and mainstream labour market programs and opportunities. Moreover, it seeks to do so in ways that enhance the economic, social and cultural rights of Indigenous peoples. The CDEP scheme is also not racially discriminatory insofar as it does not disadvantage non-Indigenous people. The social security service delivery agency, Centrelink, is now part of the CDEP scheme's administration and the Australian Government Department of Family and Community Services (DFACS), which oversees the social security system, also has a background policy presence. The recent reshaping of the CDEP scheme has brought it, and its participants, considerably closer to the social security system than ever before.

Sanders W (2005). CDEP under DEWR: The flexibility challenge. *Impact: News Quarterly of the Australian Council of Social Service*, Summer 05(7).

The CDEP scheme funds Indigenous organisations to employ community members part-time, as an alternative to their receiving unemployment payments. The scheme has been in existence since 1977, overseen by the Commonwealth Department of Aboriginal Affairs until 1990, and then by the Aboriginal and Torres Strait Islander Commission (ATSIC). In July 2004, anticipating the abolition of ATSIC, the CDEP scheme was transferred to DEWR. What will this mean for the CDEP scheme and for DEWR? In this paper, Sanders argues that the challenge for DEWR will be to keep CDEP flexible.

Sanders W (2005). CDEP and ATSIC as bold experiments in governing differently—but where to now? In Austin-Broos D & Macdonald G (eds), *Culture, economy and governance in Aboriginal Australia*, University of Sydney Press, Sydney.

Both ATSIC in the late 1980s and CDEP in the mid-1970s were bold experiments in governing with an emphasis on difference. They strove to achieve better public policy by ensuring that people in dissimilar circumstances were treated, or governed, differently. This paper begins with the CDEP scheme, which the author has previously analysed in relation to ideas of equality, difference and appropriateness. The paper then asks 'where to now' with the enactment of difference in Australian Indigenous affairs—now that ATSIC has been abolished and CDEP has transferred to DEWR.

Sanders W (2005). Indigenous centres in the policy margins: The CDEP scheme over 30 years. *Australian Council of Social Service Congress 2005*, Strawberry Hills, NSW, 75–82.

Thirty years ago, the CDEP scheme grew out of some rather marginal policy concerns within the Australian social security system about the inclusion of Aboriginal people in unemployment payments. Those concerns were, at the time, unable to be fully accommodated within the social security system and so the CDEP scheme was established within the Aboriginal or Indigenous Affairs portfolio. While CDEP began as a somewhat marginal concern within the Indigenous affairs portfolio, over time it became the largest single program in that portfolio and a policy centre in its own right. Recently, with the demise of ATSIC and the 'mainstreaming' of its programs, the CDEP scheme has been transferred to the Employment and Workplace Relations portfolio within the Australian Government. In this paper, the author asks, will this new program location lead to a new marginalisation of the CDEP scheme? The answer to that question is: possibly, but not inevitably. The paper concludes with a challenge for the Employment and Workplace Relations portfolio; to allow the CDEP scheme to continue as a policy centre in its own right.

Sanders W (2006). Indigenous affairs after the Howard decade: Administrative reform and practical reconciliation or defying decolonisation? *Journal of Australian Indigenous Issues*, 9(2-3): 43–53.

How will the Indigenous affairs policies of the first decade of the Howard Government be remembered in years to come? One history, which the author predicts, is that the worldwide movement towards decolonisation continues apace during the first half of the 21st century and that Australian governments after Howard's return to ideas of self-determination and Indigenous group recognition in Australian Indigenous affairs policy. If this is the more convincing history, then the Howard Government will be seen as perhaps having presided over an administrative revolution in Indigenous affairs with the abolition of ATSIC, but at the same time, as having defied for a brief period the historical trend towards decolonising values in Australian Indigenous affairs policy.

Altman JC (2007). Neo-paternalism and the destruction of CDEP. *Arena Magazine*, August–September 90: 33–35.

This article examines the role of the CDEP in Indigenous communities in the Northern Territory and the consequences of its sudden abolition.

Altman JC (2007). Scrapping CDEP is just plain dumb. *Topical Issue No. 11/2007*, Centre for Aboriginal Economic Policy Research, The Australian National University, Canberra.

Ministers Joe Hockey and Mal Brough's decision to abolish CDEP in remote Indigenous communities in the Northern Territory will have marked impacts on the arts industry, the management of Indigenous Protected Areas, and community-based Caring for Country ranger projects. This article argues that it is not just these success stories that will suffer; it is likely that there will be wider local, regional and national costs from this myopic, ill-considered policy shift. (First published in *Crikey*, 24 July 2007.)

Hunter BH (2007). Arguing over [the] remote control: Why Indigenous policy needs to be based on evidence and not hyperbole. *Economic Papers*, 26(1): 44–63.

Recent public debate on Indigenous issues has focused on the extent to which policies have been effective in improving the living conditions of Indigenous Australians since the era of self-determination commenced. Unfortunately, the quality of historical data is questionable, and hence we need an appreciation of the reliability of estimates. The empirical analysis in this paper begins with a description of national trends in Indigenous employment, because of the instrumental difficulties in disaggregating administrative data on the CDEP scheme, and then outlines some sub-national trends in private sector and public sector employment. The CDEP scheme is found to be a substantial and growing element in Indigenous employment in Australia that cannot be ignored when analysing trends in Indigenous labour force status.

Hunter BH (2007). Conspicuous compassion and wicked problems: The Howard Government's National Emergency in Indigenous Affairs, *Agenda*, 14(3): 35–54.

A 'wicked problem' is a term used in the planning literature to characterise a complex multidimensional problem. The article argues that Indigenous child abuse is one such problem. Whatever the merits of the recent federal intervention into NT Indigenous communities, it is unlikely to succeed without both long-term bipartisan commitment of substantial resources and a meaningful process of consultation with Indigenous peoples. As part of the intervention, for example, Mal Brough also announced that all CDEP employment in the NT will be replaced by 'real jobs'. While some commentators question how meaningful the term 'real job' is, the major unresolved issue is where these new jobs might come from and who might finance such positions. Several NT schemes have already closed, with a concomitant loss of governance capacity for administering community-level initiatives. Brough had previously indicated that he wants the state to deliver development directly to Indigenous families and individuals, thus bypassing mediating institutions and representative structures. While these policy thrusts are not intrinsically inconsistent, the federal government is likely to have difficulty in developing the organisational capacity to deal directly with Indigenous people and their families—especially given the problems recently experienced in hiring and retaining Indigenous employees. If we are to learn from what policies worked (and what did not work), Hunter argues, then it is particularly important that a transparent evaluation framework be established before undertaking policy initiatives.

Sanders W (2007). CDEP under DEWR: Policy changes and the new contractualism. *Impact: News Quarterly of the Australian Council of Social Services*, March 2007 (Autumn): 6–7.

The CDEP scheme is an Indigenous 'workfare' program that has existed since 1977. In 2004, with the abolition of ATSIC, CDEP became a responsibility of DEWR. Since early 2005, DEWR has been engaged in a reform process that has led to some significant changes to CDEP. This article looks at those changes under two headings: policy substance and the new contractualism.

Altman JC (2008). Submission to the Australian Government's Increasing employment opportunity discussion paper. *Topical Issue No. 16/2008*, Centre for Aboriginal Economic Policy Research, The Australian National University, Canberra.

This submission briefly revisits the history of the CDEP scheme, its growth, problems associated with its success, its key shortcomings, the likely impacts of proposed reforms and a few recommendations for more constructive rather than destructive reforms of the program. Many of these issues have been raised in Altman's public seminar 'Closing the Employment Gap, proposed changes to CDEP and the nature of Indigenous affairs policy making today' presented at the Australian Institute of Aboriginal and Torres Strait Islander Studies, Canberra, on 20 October 2008.

Altman JC (2008). Submission to increasing Indigenous economic opportunity—A discussion paper on the future of the CDEP and Indigenous Employment Programs. *Topical Issue No. 14/2008*, Centre for Aboriginal Economic Policy Research, The Australian National University, Canberra.

The Rudd Government has repeatedly claimed that it is only interested in evidence-based policymaking. The attachment to this submission provides statistical evidence about what is good about CDEP, what are the evident problems, the first order problems to address, and some proposed solutions (with numerous references to completed research). In putting forward this statistical evidence it is hoped that this submission assists the Government's CDEP policy reform process.

Altman JC (2008). Killing CDEP softly? Reforming workfare in remote Australia. *Crikey*, 9 October.

This article addresses reforms to the CDEP program proposed as part of the Rudd Government's employment creation strategy. These reforms are couched broadly under the umbrella of the revamped and complicated Universal Employment Services and the less complicated discussion paper 'Increasing Indigenous Economic Opportunity'. Altman argues that successful CDEP organisations with track records over many years should be replicated and supported, not jeopardised by radical reform with uncertain intended and unintended consequences.

Altman JC & Jordan K (2008). *Submission to the House of Representatives Standing Committee on Aboriginal and Torres Strait Islander Affairs Inquiry into developing Indigenous enterprises*, July.

This submission highlights the emerging opportunities for Indigenous enterprise in natural resource management, including in the response to climate change, and the need to identify and support these activities. In doing so, it examines whether current government, industry and community programs offering specific enterprise support programs and services to Indigenous enterprises are effective, particularly in building sustainable relationships with the broader business sector. It suggests that the dominant policy approach to Indigenous economic development has tended to assume that the goal for remote Indigenous communities should be economic independence. For many communities faced with limited opportunities for standard commercial activity, however, this goal may be unrealistic. A more appropriate goal may be economic interdependence, where ongoing state support (such as through CDEP) allows a range of options, including self-employment and enterprise development. Many successful Indigenous enterprises have historically been underwritten by CDEP. This is not an indication of commercial failure. Rather, the CDEP scheme can assist in the development of microbusinesses that generate additional income as well as sociocultural objectives. For example, CDEP allows the development of viable businesses while providing a living wage based on CDEP (as a wage subsidy) plus 'top up' for workers who take on extra hours or responsibilities.

Altman JC & Jordan K (2008). *Submission to the Senate Community Affairs Committee Inquiry into government expenditure on Indigenous affairs and social services in the Northern Territory*, October.

This submission outlines a number of key and apparently intractable issues from the literature that have hampered the funding of Aboriginal communities in the NT on an equitable needs basis. It notes that from 1990 to 2004, ATSIC-funded organisations were often expected to administer the programs of other agencies. This has been a problem in the administering of some CDEP programs, particularly where CDEP organisations have been required to provide infrastructure and services in the absence of any other provider. Since the early 1990s, Altman has been noting this potential pitfall, where CDEP has been seen as a substitution rather than supplementary funding regime, allowing all levels of government to renege on their responsibilities to fund infrastructure and services in Aboriginal communities. This submission also foregrounds the fact that the small size of many Indigenous communities in the NT, along with the mobility of the Indigenous population, creates particular challenges for service delivery. The expenditure of federal and NT moneys needs to better take these concerns into account. For example, as far back as the early 1990s, in a review of the CDEP program, Altman highlighted the different effects of CDEP at different communities, according to size and remoteness region. The submission recommends that in any proposals to reform the CDEP program its suitability for small and dispersed communities is properly considered.

Altman JC & Sanders W (2008). Re-vitalising the Community Development Employment Program in the Northern Territory: Submission prepared in response to the Northern Territory Government's Review of Community Development Employment Program Discussion Paper, *Topical Issue No. 05/2008*, Centre for Aboriginal Economic Policy Research, The Australian National University, Canberra.

This paper addresses perceived shortcomings in the NT Government's discussion paper on CDEP released in March 2008 (Review of Community Development Employment Program). It provides evidence-based research findings that CDEP is an important and beneficial program for NT Aboriginal communities and individuals. Rather than engage issue by issue with the NT Government's CDEP Discussion

Paper, the authors take up the invitation to provide an alternative approach that should be considered, and hopefully adopted. Their alternate visioning is based on a body of evidence-based research that they and their colleagues have undertaken at the Centre for Aboriginal Economic Policy Research (CAEPR) since 1990.

Hunter B (2008). Is policy the problem or the solution for Indigenous people? *Agenda*, 15(3): 95–7.

This paper is a rejoinder to Gary Johns' in the previous issue of *Agenda* (2008), which asked whether the underlying cause of Indigenous disadvantage in the NT is a 'wicked problem' or the result of 'wicked policy' of 'self-determination'. The policy 'take-away' of Johns' paper is a radical change in the set of incentives for mobility facing Indigenous people: the removal of unconditional income support and services provided in such communities by CDEP schemes or other government initiatives. The optimal level of mobility depends on both the individual and the social costs and benefits of moving. Even if one is willing to ignore Indigenous perspectives on culture and interventions made on their behalf, however, it is not entirely clear that mobility will necessarily result in the benefits anticipated by Johns—especially when one takes into account the likelihood that there will be substantial short-run adjustment costs (for example, in social dislocation) and the difficulty that many Indigenous people have in securing employment in complex labour markets. Another factor that is discounted in Johns' analysis is that the ongoing existence of an authentic and living Indigenous culture has a considerable market and non-market value to both Indigenous and non-Indigenous Australians. From a national perspective, CDEP jobs are also important for much of the natural resource management work undertaken in remote Australia. For example, Indigenous Protected Areas are an integral part of the conservation estate, and ensuring that such areas are adequately maintained is in the national interest. One aspect of Johns' argument that Hunter does agree with is that the CDEP scheme supports the existence of remote Indigenous communities that might not continue to exist if all government support were withdrawn. In that sense, the CDEP scheme provides tangible support to Indigenous culture in such areas. Furthermore, mainstream (non-CDEP) jobs provide more protection against entrenched Indigenous disadvantage than CDEP scheme jobs. Consequently, one can argue that there *is*, in a sense, a trade-off between cultural maintenance (which is clearly supported by the CDEP scheme) and other important socioeconomic dimensions of Indigenous social exclusion.

Altman JC (2009). A nation building and jobs plan for Indigenous Australia. *Crikey*, 12 February.

This article is a response to the announced decision to progressively close down regional CDEPs from 1 July 2009 and to end 'grandfathering' arrangements (i.e. abolish CDEP wages) in remote CDEPs from 1 July 2011. The author proposes that the Australian Government suspend the planned abolition of CDEP, and re-fund those CDEP projects with a proven track record that have either recently been de-funded or that are facing closure. He argues that CDEP should never have been abolished, but this is even more the case given the predicted dire downturn in the Australian labour market in 2009 and beyond.

Altman JC & Jordan K (2009). *Submission to Senate Community Affairs Committee inquiry into the Family Assistance and Other Legislation Amendment (2008 Budget and Other Measures) Bill 2008*, 20 April.

During the 2007 federal election campaign, the Australian Labor Party (ALP) committed to a reformed CDEP. Instead, in December 2008, just as the Australian economy was slipping into negative growth, the Minister for Indigenous Affairs Jenny Macklin outlined key elements of the Rudd Government's new Indigenous employment strategy that centred on significant changes to CDEP and reform of the Indigenous Employment Program (IEP). The proposed changes will see CDEP cease to operate in non-remote areas as of 1 July 2009. In remote areas existing CDEP participants will continue receiving CDEP wages until 30 June 2011, while new entrants to the scheme from 1 July 2009 will receive income support instead of CDEP wages. Associated with the changes to CDEP will be a new 'jobs package'. While the 'roll-out' of these jobs is due to be completed by 1 July 2009, as yet we have seen no information on where these jobs will be located or what sort of work will be underwritten. Exactly how these changes will affect the number of Indigenous people in paid work is difficult to tell.

Hunter BH (2009). A half-hearted defence of CDEP scheme. *Family Matters*, 81: 43–5.

CDEP was developed as a response to the perceived social threat of 'sit down money' to Indigenous communities in the 1970s. Ironically, Hunter argues, the scheme is now being criticised as being one of the main factors driving the social effects of prolonged welfare dependence. This paper updates the Office of Evaluation and Audit 1997 report that evaluated the scheme. While this paper shows that the CDEP scheme has a significant effect of reducing social pathologies, vis-á-vis unemployment, the positive effect of the scheme is generally substantially less than the protective effect of having mainstream (non-CDEP) employment. Consequently, it is the lack of mainstream employment options, rather than the presence of the CDEP scheme that drives the social pathologies identified in recent public debate.

Hunter BH (2010). Socio-economic conditions: Reconciling practical reconciliation with Indigenous disadvantage in the Howard years. In Gunstone A (ed.), *Over a decade of despair: Howard Government and Indigenous Affairs*, Australian Scholarly Publishing, North Melbourne.

This paper evaluates the success of the Howard Government in achieving practical reconciliation between Indigenous and non-Indigenous Australians. The focus is on assessing Howard's legacy in sustainably improving Indigenous socioeconomic outcomes relative to the rest of the Australian population. Accordingly, it is necessary to rehearse some of the arguments about the relative importance of practical and symbolic issues. It does this, in part, in the context of a discussion about the 'social limits' to achieving ongoing improvements in Indigenous socioeconomic status, at least as articulated in the public debate about social inclusion of Indigenous Australians. The CDEP scheme, for example, undeniably supports the existence of remote Indigenous communities that would not probably exist if all government support were withdrawn. In that sense, the CDEP scheme provides tangible support to Indigenous culture in such areas. However, it is also true that mainstream (non-CDEP) jobs provide more protection against entrenched Indigenous disadvantage than CDEP scheme jobs. One can argue, in this sense, that there is a trade-off between cultural maintenance (which is clearly supported by the CDEP scheme) and other important socioeconomic dimensions of Indigenous social exclusion. As with politics, Hunter argues, it is not possible to assume that nothing changes in social and economic contexts, and hence his conclusion elaborates on the prospect for achieving sustained improvements in Indigenous socioeconomic status after the Howard Government.

Kerins S & Jordan K (2010). *Submission to FaHCSIA on the Indigenous Economic Development Strategy draft for consultation*, 26 November.

This submission addresses the Australian Government's draft Indigenous Economic Development Strategy (IEDS), with specific lessons learned from working with Aboriginal people to further their economic development in remote areas. The IEDS Action Plan suggests that the changes to CDEP are designed to 'build individual skills and capacity' and 'create positive incentives to work'. In practice, there is growing evidence that the changes are having the opposite effect in at least some instances. Under the old system of CDEP wages, where CDEP has been well administered, participants have been required to fulfil minimum part-time work requirements and many CDEP workers have been paid additional income ('top up') for extra hours worked or granted 'top up' in cash or in-kind outside their formal workplace. Many participants have used CDEP to undertake paid land and sea management work, apprenticeships and traineeships, or worked for 'third party' employers where they have received additional wages. A number have moved off CDEP into mainstream jobs as they have developed appropriate capacities and as jobs have become available. These are all outcomes the government says it wants. There are also many examples of these successes that the government should be aware of. However, the recent changes to CDEP are undermining these successes by creating a disincentive to participate in the scheme. Without the attraction of 'top-up' wages, participants are well aware that they can receive equivalent income if they exit the scheme and register for Newstart Allowance. Once in receipt of this payment, the reality in remote areas in which we have worked is that the mutual obligation requirements are not enforced and Newstart Allowance becomes 'sit down money'. This is increasing the incidence of passive welfare: ostensibly what the government and common sense seek to curtail and indeed what the CDEP scheme itself was designed to minimise.

Altman JC & Aboriginal Peak Organisations of the Northern Territory (2011). From CDEP to CEEDS? *Arena Magazine*, 111: 36–7.

The Australian Government is seeking to fundamentally reform CDEP throughout remote Indigenous Australia as a part of the NT Intervention. This article seeks to inform a broad audience about the current political status of CDEP. The scheme is characterised here as a mutual obligation workfare program that was a vehicle for engaging Aboriginal people in a range of community development, service delivery and enterprise development projects, funded from block grants roughly equivalent to unemployment benefit entitlements.

Howorth P, Jordan K, Munro I & Aboriginal Peak Organisations of the Northern Territory (2011). *Creating and supporting sustainable livelihoods: A proposal for a new Remote Participation, Employment & Enterprise Development Scheme,* Submission to the Australian Government review of remote participation and employment services, October.

Aboriginal Peak Organisations of the Northern Territory's proposed model for a remote participation, employment and enterprise development scheme builds on the positive achievements of CDEP while overcoming limitations of the current arrangements. Aboriginal Peak Organisations of the Northern Territory's model recognises the reality that many Aboriginal people in remote areas have significant educational disadvantage, including very low literacy and numeracy. It identifies the need for long-term transitional pathways to assist individuals and communities to achieve sustainable livelihoods.

Jordan K (2011). Blaming individuals will get Indigenous employment policy nowhere. *The Conversation*, June 29, 2011.

Consistent with its broader approach that sees paid work as a responsibility as well as a right, the central thrust of the Gillard Government's approach to Indigenous affairs is to pathologise Indigenous disengagement from mainstream employment and implement policies designed to alter individual behaviour. This articles suggests that we should be wary of analyses that cast this lack of engagement with mainstream employment as simply 'bad behaviour' or a lack of 'positive social norms'. Such analyses, Jordan argues, conflate serious social problems with highly valued aspects of Indigenous cultures that can also precipitate conflicting attitudes to paid work.

Jordan K (2011). Work and Indigenous wellbeing: Developing a research agenda. *Insights: Melbourne Business and Economics* 9, April 2011, Faculty of Business and Economics, University of Melbourne, Melbourne.

Differing attitudes to paid work give rise to much misunderstanding, if not animosity. The author shows how such misunderstandings manifest, for example, in activities that some Aboriginal people perceive as highly productive—such as prioritising familial needs over employment commitments—but are perceived by non-Indigenous work managers as 'simply lazy'.

Jordan K (2011). *Work, welfare and CDEP on the Aṉangu Pitjantjatjara Yankunytjatjara Lands: First stage assessment.* CAEPR Working Paper No. 78, Centre for Aboriginal Economic Policy Research, The Australian National University, Canberra.

This paper examines the impacts of changes to the CDEP scheme in 2009 on the Aṉangu Pitjantjatjara Yankunytjatjara (APY) Lands. The author draws on qualitative interviews and administrative data to show that most of the changes appear to be counterproductive. She argues there may be a need for additional policy intervention to ensure that further changes to the scheme scheduled for 2012 do not exacerbate, rather than ameliorate, the multiple disadvantages experienced by many Aṉangu on the APY Lands.

Jordan K (2012). Closing the employment gap through work for the dole? Indigenous employment and the CDEP scheme. *Journal of Australian Political Economy*, 69: 29–58.

The CDEP scheme has been a unique feature of the Indigenous employment landscape since the late 1970s. While there is evidence CDEP has improved outcomes for some Indigenous Australians, in recent years it has been strongly criticised as a barrier to Indigenous participation in the mainstream (non- CDEP) labour market. Successive Australian governments have progressively wound back the CDEP scheme, culminating in recent changes that may see it transformed from a community-managed work program paying the rough equivalent of award wages into a 'Work for the Dole' program within the social security system. While the implications of these changes are strongly contested, this paper draws on fieldwork on the Aṉangu Pitjantjatjara Yankunytjatjara (APY) Lands in remote South Australia to suggest that the unintended consequences may be a greater incidence of welfare passivity and reduced support for remote-living Aboriginal people to find non-CDEP work.

Sanders W (2012). Coombs' bastard child: The troubled life of the CDEP Scheme. *Australian Journal of Public Administration*, 71(4): 371–91.

In the mid-1970s, HC Coombs was a major promoter of the idea behind the CDEP scheme. From this simple idea was born one of the most significant and, in time, one of the largest Indigenous-specific programs Australia has seen. The birth of this scheme, Sanders argues, was not easy and neither has been the subsequent life of what he refers to as Coombs' bastard child.

Altman JC (2013). Seeing through the smoke and mirrors of a black job hunt. *Journal of Indigenous Policy*, 15: 127–32.

Policies are instruments of governance; they operate as ideological vehicles and as agents for constructing subjectivities and organising people within existing systems of power and authority. This, Altman argues, is precisely what we see with Abbott's Indigenous employment review. The issues identified to date focus on conventional labour market approaches for unconventional Indigenous circumstances. Powerful like-minded people have been recruited to head the review with little prospect of innovation or acknowledgement of difference—normalisation pays lip service to the importance of difference then presses on remorselessly to promulgate and support imagined future labour market mainstreaming. The hard issues, he argues, have not been explicitly raised to date: has the abolition of programs such as the CDEP done more harm than good in increasing 'passive' welfare? Do outcomes on Cape York under the Cape York Welfare Reform trials or in jobs with AEC employers represent good value for significant public money? Why did the differential between Indigenous and non-Indigenous employment outcomes increase between 2006 and 2011? Evidently, such questions do not matter. In this paper, Altman suggests that the way this review was established lacks sufficient legitimacy, appropriate conceptualisation and sound governance. Whatever the new government's fine intentions, he writes, it is an early disappointment.

Hunter B & Gray M (2013). Continuity and change in the CDEP scheme. *Australian Journal of Social Issues*, 48(1): 35–56.

The CDEP scheme is an example of a program that combines community development and labour market program elements. This paper describes the nature of CDEP employment in 2008 and the extent to which it changed between 1994 and 2008. The paper also compares a selection of economic and social outcomes of CDEP participants with those of persons who are employed outside of CDEP, unemployed, and not-in-the-labour-force (NILF) in 2008, and the extent to which these associations changed between 1994 and 2008. The analysis shows that the nature of the jobs in which CDEP participants work and the experiences it provides to workers has been largely unchanged, despite substantial changes in underlying policy settings.

Gray M, Howlett M & Hunter B (2014). Labour market outcomes for Indigenous Australians. *The Economic and Labour Relations Review*, 25(3): 497–517.

Recent research has identified a substantial increase in Indigenous mainstream employment since the mid-1990s, but there has been relatively little regional analysis of such employment. This article builds on this previous research using the 2006 and 2011 censuses to provide a more disaggregated descriptive analysis of changes in the character of labour market outcomes for Indigenous Australians aged 15–64 years. The key message of this article is that non-CDEP employment has increased substantially since the mid-1990s (at least until 2011). One of the primary drivers of the increase in employment has been the private sector. Between 2006 and 2011, there were increases in Indigenous employment in most industries, although some sectors played a more important role than others. While mining saw substantial and important increases in Indigenous employment, the changes were small relative to the challenge of closing the large ongoing gap in non-CDEP employment rates between Indigenous and non-Indigenous Australians. Similarly, despite recent increases in self-employment, in 2011, it was still a relatively minor portion of overall Indigenous employment.

Altman JC (2015). Basic income a no-brainer for remote Indigenous Australia. *New Matilda*, 17 September.

This article examines the applicability of a basic income scheme to the current landscape of remote Indigenous Australia. By detailing the history of government programs targeted in these areas, Altman argues that a basic income scheme would be an excellent way to help remedy the issues faced in these areas of Australia.

Altman JC (2015). Remote jobs proposals incoherent and inadequate. *Land Rights News*, Northern Land Council, January.

This article addresses the Abbott Government's proposed reform of the Remote Jobs and Communities Program (RJCP) applicable to 30,000 unemployed Indigenous adults living in remote Australia. Altman argues that the proposals to be introduced from 1 July 2015 are the clearest evidence yet that the 'new' government with a 'new' Indigenous Advancement Strategy focused on remote Australia and Prime Minister with aspirations to make an impact in Indigenous affairs have totally lost their way. Policymaking, he suggests, is in a deep muddle.

CAEPR Research
Monograph Series

1. *Aborigines in the economy: a select annotated bibliography of policy relevant research 1985–90*, LM Allen, JC Altman and E Owen (with assistance from WS Arthur), 1991.

2. *Aboriginal employment equity by the year 2000*, JC Altman (ed.), published for the Academy of Social Sciences in Australia, 1991.

3. *A national survey of Indigenous Australians: options and implications*, JC Altman (ed.), 1992.

4. *Indigenous Australians in the economy: abstracts of research, 1991–92*, LM Roach and KA Probst, 1993.

5. *The relative economic status of Indigenous Australians, 1986–91*, J Taylor, 1993.

6. *Regional change in the economic status of Indigenous Australians, 1986–91*, J Taylor, 1993.

7. *Mabo and native title: origins and institutional implications*, W Sanders (ed.), 1994.

8. *The housing need of Indigenous Australians, 1991*, R Jones, 1994.

9. *Indigenous Australians in the economy: abstracts of research, 1993–94*, LM Roach and HJ Bek, 1995.

10. *The native title era: emerging issues for research, policy, and practice*, J Finlayson and DE Smith (eds), 1995.

11. *The 1994 National Aboriginal and Torres Strait Islander Survey: findings and future prospects*, JC Altman and J Taylor (eds), 1996.

12. *Fighting over country: anthropological perspectives*, DE Smith and J Finlayson (eds), 1997.

13. *Connections in native title: genealogies, kinship, and groups*, JD Finlayson, B Rigsby and HJ Bek (eds), 1999.

14. *Land rights at risk? Evaluations of the Reeves Report*, JC Altman, F Morphy and T Rowse (eds), 1999.

15. *Unemployment payments, the activity test, and Indigenous Australians: understanding breach rates*, W Sanders, 1999.

16. *Why only one in three? The complex reasons for low Indigenous school retention*, RG Schwab, 1999.

17. *Indigenous families and the welfare system: two community case studies*, DE Smith (ed.), 2000.

18. *Ngukurr at the millennium: a baseline profile for social impact planning in south-east Arnhem Land*, J Taylor, J Bern and KA Senior, 2000.

19. *Aboriginal nutrition and the Nyirranggulung Health Strategy in Jawoyn country*, J Taylor and N Westbury, 2000.

20. *The Indigenous welfare economy and the CDEP scheme*, F Morphy and W Sanders (eds), 2001.

21. *Health expenditure, income and health status among Indigenous and other Australians*, MC Gray, BH Hunter and J Taylor, 2002.

22. *Making sense of the census: observations of the 2001 enumeration in remote Aboriginal Australia*, DF Martin, F Morphy, WG Sanders and J Taylor, 2002.

23. *Aboriginal population profiles for development planning in the northern East Kimberley*, J Taylor, 2003.

24. *Social indicators for Aboriginal governance: insights from the Thamarrurr region, Northern Territory*, J Taylor, 2004.

25. *Indigenous people and the Pilbara mining boom: a baseline for regional participation*, J Taylor and B Scambary, 2005.

26. *Assessing the evidence on Indigenous socioeconomic outcomes: a focus on the 2002 NATSISS*, BH Hunter (ed.), 2006.

27. *The social effects of native title: recognition, translation, coexistence*, BR Smith and F Morphy (eds), 2007.

28. *Agency, contingency and census process: observations of the 2006 Indigenous Enumeration Strategy in remote Aboriginal Australia*, F Morphy (ed.), 2008.

29. *Contested governance: culture, power and institutions in Indigenous Australia*, J Hunt, D Smith, S Garling and W Sanders (eds), 2008.

30. *Power, culture, economy: Indigenous Australians and mining*, J Altman and D Martin (eds), 2009.

31. *Demographic and socioeconomic outcomes across the Indigenous Australian lifecourse*, N Biddle and M Yap, 2010.

32. *Survey analysis for Indigenous policy in Australia: social science perspectives*, B Hunter and N Biddle (eds), 2012.

33. *My Country, mine country: Indigenous people, mining and development contestation in remote Australia*, B Scambary, 2013.

34. *Indigenous Australians and the National Disability Insurance Scheme*, N Biddle, F Al-Yaman, M Gourley, M Gray, JR Bray, B Brady, LA Pham, E Williams and M Montaigne, 2014.

35. *Engaging Indigenous economy: debating diverse approaches*, W Sanders (ed.), 2016.

Centre for Aboriginal Economic Policy Research,
College of Arts and Social Sciences,
The Australian National University, Canberra, ACT, 2601

Information on CAEPR Discussion Papers, Working Papers and Research Monographs (Nos 1–19) and abstracts and summaries of all CAEPR print publications and those published electronically can be found at the following website: caepr.anu.edu.au.

www.ingramcontent.com/pod-product-compliance
Lightning Source LLC
Chambersburg PA
CBHW040153270326
41928CB00040B/3309